Elite MBA Programs
at Public Universities

Elite MBA Programs at Public Universities

How a Dozen Innovative Schools Are Redefining Business Education

Edited by Mimi Wolverton
and Larry Edward Penley

Westport, Connecticut
London

Library of Congress Cataloging-in-Publication Data

Elite MBA programs at public universities : how a dozen innovative schools
 are redefining business education / edited by Mimi Wolverton and Larry Edward Penley.
     p. cm.
  Includes bibliographical references and index.
  ISBN 0–275–97811–7 (alk. paper)
  1. Business education—United States. 2. Master of business administration degree—
United States. 3. Business schools—United States. I. Wolverton, Mimi. II. Penley, Larry E.
  HF1131.E48 2004
  650'.071'173—dc22   2004017679

British Library Cataloguing in Publication Data is available.

M/L Library of Congress Catalog Card Number: 2004017679
ISBN: 0–275–97811–7

First published in 2004

Praeger Publishers, 88 Post Road West, Westport, CT 06881
An imprint of Greenwood Publishing Group, Inc.
www.praeger.com

Printed in the United States of America

The paper used in this book complies with the
Permanent Paper Standard issued by the National
Information Standards Organization (Z39.48–1984).

10 9 8 7 6 5 4 3 2 1

Contents

Preface

Traditionally, business schools have prepared industry's mid-level management. Some of the best and the brightest individuals who attend highly touted prestigious universities ultimately become our country's next generation of business leaders. As such, business schools play an important part in supporting the country's economic development and long-term prosperity. The mainstay of these endeavors is the master's degree in business administration, or MBA. This acronym is probably one of the most recognizable today. Its cachet lies in the continued success of business schools in executing their charge to prepare managers and leaders for the workplace. We believe that it is important to understand why some business schools consistently contribute to the country's well-being in this manner and do it better than do their counterparts at other universities.

We are a nation of raters. We rank everything—soft drinks, sports teams, students, and business schools. We do so, primarily, because we are competitive and individualistic. Simply put, we want to be number one. Every year, internationally acclaimed journals rank business schools based on the efficacy of their most recognizable program, the MBA. Some look at programs housed at U.S. universities (*U.S. News & World Report* and *Business Week*); others take an international perspective (*The Financial Times*). All fail to discriminate between programs housed at public versus private universities. Each relies on the same primary factor for determining their rankings—money. For instance, most ask: How much do graduates earn? A second set of criteria focuses on customer satisfaction. *Business Week, f*or example, surveys alumni, corporate managers, and human resource executives to discern the degree to which programs prepare their graduates for employment. A third set focuses on a school's reputation among deans or recruiters. *U.S. News & World Report* surveys both groups, who may know a great deal or perhaps only a little about the schools they rate, on a variety of idiosyncratic criteria.

As a nation of raters, we sometimes forget how little we learn from rankings, which often are based, not on criteria that matter most to us as individuals, but on screening criteria that someone else has imposed. The problem with rankings of this type lies in the propensity of the ranker to lump all organizations into one group. In effect, *U.S. News & World Reports* draws its conclusions about which MBA programs and business schools are the best by placing all universities and programs in a large hopper of sorts and sifting them through various-sized screens to see who falls out and who rises to the top. In doing so, they ignore the very essence of programs that sets them apart—differentiating characteristics and institutional strengths (Cole, Barber, and Graubard, 1994).

We contend that great graduate programs depend on more than how much full-time MBA graduates earn or the program's reputation. Indeed, they are more than the full-time MBA; the driving forces behind such programs and the colleges and universities that house them are really rooted in the faculty they employ, the research that gets conducted, the doctoral programs they offer, the way they deal with diversity, their interactions and partnerships with industry, their contributions to their local communities, and the strategic leadership that drives their creativity. Even though *The Financial Times* considers faculty credentials and productivity in its determination of MBA program rank, salary factors carry twice the weight of faculty qualifications in its considerations. For *Business Week*, factors other than faculty research productivity receive nine times the weight. For *U.S. News & World Reports*, reputational factors and applicants' previous records represent 65 percent of the total weight.

In addition, we firmly believe that programs housed at public universities function under certain constraints that do not befall those located at private institutions. Public universities carry a mandated fiduciary and social responsibility specific to the states in which they are located (Tierney, 1998). Private institutions, such as Harvard, Northwestern, and the University of Pennsylvania, may exercise similar charges as a matter of good practice, but not under the same restrictions. For instance, states expect programs at public universities to be affordable for state residents. Often, they cap tuition levels, thus restricting the revenue generated through tuition charges, yet fail to make up the financial shortfall that results. Harvard Business School, the Kellogg School of Management at Northwestern University, and the Wharton School of Business at the University of Pennsylvania suffer much more limited constraints.

This public responsibility continues, despite the growing privatization of large public institutions. Public universities and their programs are still expected to respond to the social and economic needs of the state. Many large public business schools have retained their business research centers with the production of critical research data for the state in the face of reduced state funding. Georgia State's Economic Forecasting Center provides important urban, regional, and national economic data and insights. The business school at the University of Washington uses university resources to assist the development of small businesses in economically distressed communities through its Business and Economic Development Program. Although private institutions also engage in these types of activities, they have the luxury of limiting their exposure to the expenses incurred in such endeavors should they find them too costly. In the end, business schools at public universities must not only provide the best value for the dollar but also contribute to the economic and social vibrancy of the states they serve.

This book is about business schools but not about ranking them; it is about finding out what really makes them tick. And, it is not about all business schools. Rather, it is about that special breed of exceptional business schools that resides at public universities. We used the following guidelines in determining which schools to include. Each participant is an Association to Advance Collegiate Schools of Business (AACSB) International-accredited, public, U.S. school of business with graduate programs that are highly visible. All schools have MBA programs that are ranked in the top fifty programs in the country. And finally, the twelve schools in the study were willing to participate.

Our intent in writing this book is to help the general reader, prospective students and employers, and other business schools better understand the program quality and opportunities offered by public graduate business schools. We will not engage in evaluating individual schools, nor will we engage in critical commentary on the schools. Instead, the twelve case studies present stories of business school graduate education, not simply the limited view that journalists provide in their periodic lists of MBA program rankings. We anticipate that faculty and administrators from other schools will find this book helpful in making their own strategic choices about program and school direction. We believe that prospective students and future employers will gain insights as to what to look for as they choose schools to attend, in the first instance, and recruit employees, in the second. We also believe that alumni and friends of the study institutions will want to read about them.

Chapter 1 provides a general backdrop for the study. Chapter 2 provides various frameworks for analyzing the cases, and Chapter 3 details the common themes that we found across the cases. Chapters 4 through 15 present the individual case studies. Chapter 16 suggests strategies and recommendations for business schools and prospective students and employers.

Acknowledgments

Acknowledgments are often overlooked by the reader; their sincerity is suspect, and their appeal seems to be to the writer rather than the reader. Despite these challenges, we do indeed heartily acknowledge those who made this book possible.

First and foremost are the business schools that participated; their deans and the people at each business school who helped write the unique cases deserve our thanks—and yours. Without their willingness to give of their time in a frank sharing of information and perspective, your and our opportunity to learn from these leaders would not have been possible. Business deans have much to do; the challenges are great, but those who guide others with their insights are our benefactors and our mentors.

A special thanks goes to Ms. Dorothy Galvez, assistant to the dean at the W. P. Carey School of Business. Without her willingness to contact schools and her time given over to organize and plan, this book would never have appeared. Her professional skills, tireless energy, and real humanity have mattered to us and to the many others who have the pleasure of interacting with her daily.

   We thank those around us—family and colleagues—who tolerated frustration and overwork. And we thank you, the reader, for your willingness to consider this book as a resource. We hope you learn from reading it, just as we did from creating it.

Part I

The Strategic Challenge

More Than a Number

Mimi Wolverton and Larry Edward Penley

In the United States, we seem to rate and rank just about everything. We search for the biggest, the brightest, and the best, to the point where we risk being numbed by the prospect of discovering yet another biggest, brightest, or best. Nevertheless, where we stand in comparison to others counts. As Nike tells us, "We want [at a minimum] to be like [if not better than] Mike." Business schools that house MBA programs are no different. Instead of being "like Mike," however, they aspire to be the Harvard, Stanford, Northwestern, or Penn of wherever they happen to be located.

In doing so, they may well limit their perspectives to the most recognizable names in higher education—the elite, graduate-level business schools—all housed at private, well-established, well-endowed institutions. Yet the preponderance of MBA programs and of graduate business students are found at public universities, which may or may not possess long histories and extraordinarily large funding bases. For public business schools bent on improvement, mimicking private college strategies may not reap expected results for any number of reasons, but two primary ones come to mind. One, funding sources and levels are more than likely different from private schools, and this difference continues despite the growing use by public business schools of substantial fees that are charged on top of tuition. And two, the "Harvard" name carries more cachet than does the moniker, "state university." Students are willing to pay closer to full price at Harvard than at a state university, and recruiters suspect that MBAs are better there.

Having said all this, some of the country's most highly rated business schools and programs are housed at public universities. Many have joined the ranks of Harvard and the rest within the last ten to fifteen years. As of yet, most remain unnoticed by the general public and unheralded by other aspiring public institutions as viable models to emulate. To our minds, however, how these schools reached the status of elite seems most relevant to the newer business schools that are striving to be "like Mike."

With this in mind, we set out to discover the stories of a representative group of public university business schools with elite MBA programs. We invited twenty-eight business schools at public universities across the country to participate in the study. Nineteen expressed interest, and twelve could devote the time required to tell their stories. All participant schools offer MBA programs that rank in the top fifty programs at public and private universities within the United States and are highly recognized abroad as well. Our specific selection criteria included: being public, in the United States, highly visible (especially within the last ten years), AACSB accredited, and willing to participate. The case study institutions are geographically diverse, although five of them are located in the southeast. Table 1.1 provides a breakdown by region of participating business schools.

Table 1.1 Participant Schools by Region

Northeast/Mid-Atlantic	Midwest
University of Maryland	Indiana University
University of Pittsburgh	Purdue University
Southeast	*West/Southwest*
Georgia State University	Arizona State University
Georgia Institute of Technology	Texas A&M University
University of Florida	University of Washington
University of Georgia	
University of South Carolina	

THE STUDY

This is an exploratory study, and as such is qualitative in nature. We asked each study institution to tell its story. The end result is a set of twelve case studies, each told in a voice unique to the case institution and distinct from the other cases. We instructed each participant business school to tell us:

- the story of how the school achieved its level of quality graduate business programs over the last decade, and
- where the school's vision and strategic choices will lead it over the next decade.

A knowledgeable individual at each university (in some instances the college or school dean, in others a director of marketing or communication or a long-time faculty member) wrote the case. Engaging on-site participation and perspective compensated for the lack of prolonged engagement by the principal investigators at each site (Richardson and Skinner, 1991). Each case went through at least three iterations to ensure the coverage was as comprehensive as possible.

One of the goals of the study was to develop a conceptual model that captured the experiences of case study schools in an organized manner. To this end, an explanatory case model was developed using a single case (Yin, 1994; Richardson and Skinner, 1991). The model was then tested against each subsequent case and modified to include new information. Such cross-case analysis ensured that all relevant data had been collected at each site and that they were taken into consideration in the analysis (Manning and Cullum-Swan, 1994; Miles and Huberman, 1984).

This is not a comparative study of business schools that seeks to establish differences and degrees of excellence among them. Rather, it is a comparative study designed to find themes and patterns across institutions that remain consistent over time. To ensure that our analysis was accurate and complete, one researcher looked for patterns and themes across the data and the other researcher validated data coding and modified it where necessary. This process provided definitional clarity and contextual agreement on the themes (Miles and Huberman, 1984; Glaser and Strauss, 1967).

This is a book about leading business schools at public universities. And while the study focuses on organizations in the academic arena, and within it on one specific discipline, business, we believe that these stories are stories about innovative organizations. No two took exactly the same path, yet all share common elements that in total provide a profile of effective change.

Each case details a different picture, history, and journey to elite status. The value to the reader is indeed in the reading of these cases, which are tales of capitalizing on the situations at hand by developing, modifying, and changing strategies and action plans. This is a descriptive study, not a prescriptive one. The guides we provide are merely that—signposts to help schools determine whether they are on the right track, aid potential students in sorting through the minutiae of business school marketing materials, and suggest guidelines for future employers to use in selecting employee recruiting sites.

WHAT DOES IT TAKE TO BE EFFECTIVE?

The short answer suggests that effective organizations are those that can correctly interpret and respond to the nuances of a dynamic environment (Galbraith, Lawler, and Associates, 1993; Bowditch and Buono, 2001). That is, effective organizations anticipate the shifting demands of an environment filled with uncertainty, and they take risks by making anticipatory changes.

Birnbaum (1994) suggested three macro-views of institutional effectiveness—meritocratic, social, and individualistic. The meritocratic view dominates the media's perspective on quality and, as a consequence, drives the manner in which business schools tend to measure quality. Rankings are an excellent example of the media's approach to the meritocratic viewpoint. Taking into consideration reputation based on prestige, faculty quality, student quality, graduation placements, and the like, however, glosses over the way in which effective universities, schools, and programs exploit their unique qualities. It also assures the newcomer—perhaps the most innovative of them—of slow recognition by virtue of the retarded pace of change of reputation as expressed through rankings.

Birnbaum's (1994) social or community view of effectiveness revolves around the degree to which an institution meets the collective needs of those constituencies that it has an obligation to serve. In other words, environmental fit (with region, local community, students) is the crucial signal of effectiveness. The third view takes into account the impact institutions have on individuals, and in particular, how institutions help students. This perspective is traditionally most readily identified with the mission of community colleges with their frequently more intense view of students' needs. However, business schools at high-profile universities also pay close attention to student needs, particularly as they pertain to MBA students' satisfaction with faculty and program and employers' satisfaction with recruits and the recruiting process.

In contrast, Gibson, Ivancevich, and Donnelly (2000) delineated three micro-themes of organizational effectiveness, which they termed the goal, systems, and stakeholders approaches. The goal approach requires that organizations accomplish recognized objectives. The degree of accomplishment indicates the degree of effectiveness. Effective organizations that subscribe to the systems approach try to understand how and why people perform tasks and how the organization interfaces with other organizations. Because the survival of the organization depends on its ability to adapt to the demands of its environment, the total cycle of input-process-output takes on relevance. The stakeholder approach suggests that effective organizations balance the various parts of the system by satisfying the interests of the organization's constituencies. Most business schools engage in the goal approach by taking a systems or stakeholder view.

Whether we use Birnbaum's (1994) schema or the three approaches to which Gibson, Ivancevich, and Donnelly (2000) subscribe, environmental adaptation is key to effectiveness of business schools. But being effective is not as simple as mere static adaptation to the environment. Successful organizations—including effective business schools—necessarily must analyze their probable future environment. Then, through innovation, the truly effective business school moves a step beyond adaptation in the here and now to shape the future. Effective organizations create their own solutions to environmental challenges that they anticipate, which means they must be both persistent about the future environment and strategic about how they innovate in anticipation of it.

WHAT IT MEANS TO BE INNOVATIVE

Innovation refers to the creative process of seeing new applications for existing knowledge and the ability to combine different bits of knowledge to create new capabilities or solutions (Galbraith et al., 1993). It requires a blending of perspectives across constituencies and disciplines that links organizational members more tightly and binds the organization as a whole more closely to the external community it serves (Pinchot, 1985; Kanter, 1985; Quinn, 1980). The experiences of the business school at the University of Washington (Chapter 4) dramatically illustrate not only the creative aspects of innovation but also its collaborative nature.

Truly effective organizations encourage innovation when they are doing well as a strategy against complacency (Galbraith et al., 1993). Arizona State University (Chapter 15) is rethinking its successful approach of the 1990s with new strategic choices founded in its recent naming as the W. P. Carey School of Business. Using innovation as a strategy and being strategic about innovation, however, are different. In the first instance, organizations work with long, future-oriented time lines as they attempt to maintain clear visions of what they want to accomplish in the face of anticipated change. The exercise draws organization members together in pursuit of a clearly articulated direction. In the second, being strategic about innovation means anchoring institutional purpose in organizational strengths.

The anchoring point of a business school reflects its university's unique character and particular excellence (Rowley, Lujan, and Dolence, 1997). For instance, Purdue's Krannert Graduate School of Management (Chapter 12) defines one of its niches within the field of agriculture, and Georgia Tech's DuPree College of Management (Chapter 8) ties its identity to the Institute's dominant engineering culture. Similarly, the University of Florida (Chapter 14) defines faculty excellence in terms of publication quality because its Association of American Universities (AAU) standing dictates a focus on research.

Being strategic about innovation also means recognizing where to look for niches. Organizations can expend available monies more wisely and stand to profit more if they pay attention to those places their competitors overlook (Galbraith et al., 1993). The three Georgia-based business schools in the study provide excellent examples of what it means to search out hidden pockets of opportunity. All three operate in Atlanta, but Georgia State (Chapter 9) serves the downtown business community, the University of Georgia (Chapter 7) caters to the periphery ring of the city, and Georgia Tech (Chapter 8) targets a very narrow band of businesses that cross-fertilize technology with engineering. Both Arizona State University (Chapter 15) and the University of Maryland (Chapter 5), although on opposite sides of the country, have allied themselves very closely with high technology interests and have developed expertise in supply chain management.

Effective organizations that are strategic about innovation make innovation meaningful to organizational members because they understand that people want their work to count (Galbraith et al., 1993). In essence, effective organizations understand the dynamics of creativity. They give it enough time to bear fruit, but they implement any subsequent change rapidly to capitalize on healthy conflict in the first instance and avoid detrimental internal politics in the second (Bowditch and Buono, 2001). For example, Arizona State's (Chapter 15) expansion of its corporate online MBA with an online MBA for individuals capitalizes on the success of the first program in a relatively short period of time.

Einstein once commented that the significant problems with which we struggle cannot be solved at the same level of thinking with which we created them. Effective organizations rise to these challenges; in fact, the most highly effective among them anticipate these challenges and work to shape futures that clearly distinguish their efforts from those of others (Porter, 1985). In the next chapter, we explore the mechanisms that our case study business schools employ as they strategically embrace innovation in pursuit of effectiveness.

2

Strategically Embracing Innovation

Mimi Wolverton and Larry Edward Penley

The distinction between public and private universities has traditionally rested on two edges of the same sword: public funding for public service, in the first instance, and private spending for individual gain or enhancement, in the second. Today, public universities and the business schools that exist under their collective umbrella face an interesting dilemma. Charged with serving the public's needs, they now find themselves increasingly dependent on the same revenue base as private universities, that is, substantially higher tuition or fees and gifts, grants, and endowments. States confront growing demands for K–12 education and prison beds, both phenomena related to the baby boom "echo," as well as a growing health care burden, a phenomenon related to aging baby boomers. The result is that business schools will encounter the challenge of an increasingly privatized revenue environment but with a continuing demand from the state for responsiveness to the public agenda—an agenda that was formerly encouraged with proportionately much higher state allocations to higher education.

While states and students may have some inkling of what they want from public institutions, few possess the ability to envision programs that address their emerging needs. This requires highly systematic, innovative thinking, which hinges on the ability to harvest ideas from a wide variety of sources and the willingness to act on the information gathered (Goldenberg, Horowitz, Levav, and Mazursky, 2003; Wolpert, 2002). In short, it requires that public universities and their business schools understand what makes them strong and unique—as public institutions—and how, despite their increasingly privatized incentives, they can define unique and distinctive contributions to our future public welfare. Their special frame of reference demands that they rebuild and rethink themselves. They may dissect, add to, subtract from, or substitute vision, goals, and programs as a means to becoming stronger public business schools (Goldenberg et al., 2003). The process by which they become stronger enhances their competitive advantage. To embark on such a journey toward competitive advantage in this remade public environment requires forecasts of the future, admittedly with risk, ingenuity, and focus; in other words, these institutions must embrace innovation strategically (Drucker, 1985/2002).

COMPETITIVE ADVANTAGE: THE END RESULT OF STRATEGIC INNOVATION

In his classic work on competitive strategy, Porter (1985) suggests that organizations that survive and thrive in dynamic environments do so by engaging in one or more of three distinct strategies: cost leadership, differentiation, and focus. Although Porter based his conclusions on information garnered from profit-seeking firms, his work on competitiveness and strategic advantage has received wide application via the Institute for Strategy and Competitiveness at Harvard University.

Cost Leadership

Cost leadership refers to providing either superior value at lower prices or unique benefits that offset higher prices (Porter, 1985). The pricing of MBA programs at the case study institutions in this book certainly contributes to competitive advantage. Despite privatization, these public business schools continue to view one of their primary responsibilities as serving the residents of the states in which they are located. As a consequence, in-state tuition and fees for MBA programs at public universities tend to be low in comparison to those charged by their counterparts at private universities.

For instance, tuition and fees for Harvard University, the University of Pennsylvania, amd Northwestern University hover around $32,000

(AACSB Business School Questionnaire, 2000, 2001). Comparable tuition and fees for in-state residents at ten of the twelve institutions in this study amount to less than $20,000, with rates between $20,000 and $30,000 for the other two. At eight of the study schools, in-state tuition and fees fall below $15,000. These institutions definitely subscribe to the superior value at a lower price perspective, although they may be doing so because of state board constraints on tuition increases.

It seems that many of these institutions lose any competitive advantage based on normal comparative price when dealing with their out-of-state student prospects. Although private institutions do not differentiate cost by residency, business schools housed at public universities do. Six of the study institutions appear to charge out-of-state students higher tuition and fees than any of the three private university examples used for comparison, and costs at two others are within $5,000 of the amount charged by Harvard. Only four study schools hold their out-of-state tuition and fees under $25,000. The apparent price may disguise competitive strategy. These public schools may price their full-time MBAs at similar prices to private institutions as a means to position themselves in the same market space; yet, many appear to adopt heavy discounting of the nominal out-of-state tuition as a means to use cost as competitive advantage. They use assistantships (which usually include an out-of-state tuition waiver, as well as a stipend), scholarships, and fellowships to discount price. Clearly, cost leadership is employed as a strategy at most of these state institutions, but in a more subtle way than might be expected in a for-profit institution.

Several authors indicated that shortfalls in government spending on higher education in their states could jeopardize their ability to maintain cost leadership based on price. And this problem will manifest itself in subtle ways as well, for example, through a reduced number of scholarships, fellowships, and assistantships. Still, at the local level, where competition with leading business schools is often less keen, cost leadership is not the typical competitive strategy.

Already, the University of Maryland, Purdue, and Arizona State subscribe to a differentiated tuition strategy and level stepped-up tuition charges on their in- and out-of-state MBA students, and the University of Washington has petitioned its state legislature to do the same (see Table 2.1). Georgia State University sources suggested that future state budgetary uncertainty could necessitate the need to secure more external funding and engage in cost cutting measures coupled with aggressive marketing of premiere programs if the school is to contain tuition costs. The twenty-year downward trend in state funding at Purdue (not unusual, by the way, among public schools) signifies what some have called an ominous path from being state-funded to state-supported. Becoming far more typical is the stituation at the University of Washington, which has only 16

Table 2.1   Tuition and Fees in Descending Order

University	In-State	University	Out-of-State
Harvard University	$32,583	Purdue University	$38,688
University of Pennsylvania	$32,122	University of Maryland	$38,552
Northwestern University	$32,040	University of Pittsburgh	$37,117
University of Maryland	$27,014	Arizona State University	$36,708
University of Pittsburgh	$23,254	Georgia Institute	
Purdue University	$19,080	of Technology	$36,092
Arizona State University	$18,976	University of Washington	$34,116
University of Washington	$14,595	Harvard University	$32,583
University of		University of Pennsylvania	$32,122
South Carolina	$12,868	Northwestern University	$32,040
Georgia Institute		University of Florida	$27,399
of Technology	$10,256	University of Georgia	$27,220
Indiana University	$10,002	University of	
Texas A&M University	$9,020	South Carolina	$24,608
University of Georgia	$8,284	Georgia State University	$21,256
University of Florida	$7,856	Texas A&M University	$20,203
Georgia State University	$6,057	Indiana University	$20,006

Source: AACSB Business School Questionnaire, 2001–2002.

percent of its budget provided by the state. Growing demand on states for health care and K–12 expenditures as a function of the simultaneous demographic bulges from baby boomers and the baby boom echo will certainly dominate the early decades of the twenty-first century, with effects on states' expenditures in all areas, including higher education.

Differentiation

Differentiation has to do with discovering what is unique about a program or school that might be highly valued by students as they choose among schools and by future employers as they choose among schools and graduates. Each institution in the study identified some aspect that set it apart from its competitors.

The University of Washington recognized the overwhelming number of its alumni who still reside and work in the Seattle area as a valuable asset. Georgia State also sensed that its location in the heart of Atlanta's business district gave it an advantage over the University of Georgia or even Atlanta-based Georgia Tech, with its more narrow focus. It also quickly noted that serving a predominantly part-time constituency differentiated its primary MBA program from others in the area. Similarly, the University of Pittsburgh views the interconnectedness of the city, university, and business school as its true strength.

Over three decades ago, the University of South Carolina believed that it could differentiate itself from other programs by striking out in a direction that few in the region had taken, namely, international business. The University of Maryland saw its inability to differentiate itself as a type of differentiation in and of itself. A strong sense of history characterizes the business schools at the University of Georgia and Indiana University. And, although several universities in the study are land grant institutions, this line of distinction is most obvious at Purdue, which offers MBAs tied to both agribusiness and engineering. The Warrington School of Business takes the University of Florida's stature as an AAU member as its point of departure, and Texas A&M's code of honor underscores the Mays Business School's public image. Finally, each of the institutions in the study engages in entrepreneurial behavior to some degree, but the can-do spirit of Arizona State University as a whole permeates the actions of its W. P. Carey School of Business and connects its MBA specializations in services marketing and supply chain management into a larger entrepreneurial strategy.

Focus

Differentiation, like cost leadership, can be lost without focus. Focus determines the competitive scope within an industry, in this case, graduate business education. A focused organization targets a segment of potential clientele and tailors its strategies toward serving them to the exclusion of others. A business school, even a prestigious one, cannot be all things to all people. It must establish a position within the marketplace that provides an identifiable image, which differs from those projected by other colleges. While almost all of these schools offer what might be called a traditional MBA track, the primary foci of the schools remain clear.

The University of South Carolina, perhaps, offers the best example of what it means to maintain focus. Thirty years ago it developed a niche market—international business—and it seems not to have been tempted to defuse its focal point by embracing more recent emphases, such as technology and entrepreneurship. Interestingly, one or more of these themes—international business, entrepreneurship, and technology (particularly e-business)—run through all the schools in this study.

Georgia State, Georgia Tech, Purdue, Arizona State, and Washington subscribe to multifocal agendas. Even so, each interweaves a thread throughout its programs that ties it to what makes the school unique. Purdue, for instance, places a strong emphasis on industrial technology and

Georgia Tech on management of engineering-related enterprises. (Ironically, although Georgia Tech's mission statement mentions entrepreneurism and international business, it appears to place little emphasis on these two areas.) Georgia State, Arizona State, and Washington keyed off their local economies to determine their niches. Arizona State took advantage of the regional economy in two ways to define its emphases. First, it partnered with large manufacturing firms, for example Motorola and Intel, to develop a specialization in high-technology management, including supply chain and information management. This same industry–business school interface led to China-based programs; and it even influences its services marketing program. Similarly, the University of Washington enlisted alumni still living and working in the high-tech industries in the Seattle area in its efforts to reconceptualize its programs and implement needed changes. And Georgia State focused its attention on serving the full-time employee who works in downtown Atlanta. It also remains sensitive to the ethical dimensions of business because of its proximity to the corporate headquarters of many of the country's largest firms.

Texas A&M (TAMU) limits its thrust to two of these themes, technology and entrepreneurship. (As do most of the case study programs, TAMU does expose its students to the fundamentals of international business, but it is clearly not an emphasis.) Its strong emphasis on teaching ethics runs through its newly designed MBA program, clearly distinguishing it from others. The Universities of Georgia and Pittsburgh (Pitt) combine technology and global business. Georgia, with an Athens, Georgia location, drew on its long history as a leading higher education institution in the South as it repositioned itself to become a leader in graduate business education in metropolitan Atlanta. True to its image as a leader, it infuses a strong focus on leadership throughout its programs. Pitt, again because of its location in a city that headquarters numerous international corporations, sees ethics and interconnectedness as integral parts of doing business.

The dominant theme percolating through University of Florida and Indiana University programs is similar to that of the University of South Carolina. Indiana draws on a history of international engagement to continually shape its course offerings. Florida prides itself on it prominence in the international research community. The University of Maryland, too, has a single focus. In an arena ripe with geopolitical businesses, Maryland sought to differentiate itself from other Washington, D.C., programs by stressing technology (see Table 2.2).

COST LEADERSHIP, DIFFERENTIATION, AND FOCUS: ARE THEY ENOUGH?

Although these case institutions, for the most part, derive competitive advantage from all three of Porter's strategies—cost leadership, differenti-

Table 2.2   Differentiation and Focus

Institution	Differentiation	Focus
Arizona State University	Entrepreneurial culture	Technology, supply chain management, services, global
Georgia Institute of Technology	Engineering	Management of technology/engineering-related business
Georgia State University	Atlanta business community	Part-time MBA, emphasis on technology/entrepreneurship/global business
Indiana University	History	International business
Purdue University	Agribusiness/ engineering	Technology/entrepreneurship/global business
Texas A&M University	Institutional code of ethics	Technology/ entrepreneurship
University of Florida	AAU status	International business
University of Georgia	History	Technology/global business
University of Maryland	Lack of differentiation awareness	Technology
University of Pittsburgh	City/university interconnections	Technology/ global business
University of South Carolina	Long-standing belief in focus	International business
University of Washington	Seattle entrepreneurial spirit	Technology/entrepreneurship/global business (Asia only)

ation, and focus—clearly the cost leadership that public spending on higher education has historically provided these programs could wane with time, and it is apparent that cost leadership is of decreasing importance as a competitive strategy in these schools' local markets. Moreover, although these case study institutions still use it to their competitive advantage, especially at the national level via discounting, many see the dangers of overreliance on such a strategy to keep them at the top.

Differentiation, too, may become an inadequate strategy over time—at least as it is expressed as "first-mover advantage." Imitation is one of the highest forms of flattery that an aspiring business school can bestow on one that has achieved elite status. But it also eats away at the fundamental differentiation that distinguishes elite business schools from their competitors. As more business schools beat the ethical drum, for example, potential clientele may fail to distinguish the uniqueness grounded in historical precedent that a Texas A&M possesses from the image projected by institutions that only recently embraced ethical leadership as a differentiating cornerstone.

The views of the general public determine whether a strategy based on differentiation provides a business school with a competitive advantage. At the turn of the last century, unethical behavior was accepted as the price paid for moving the United States into the industrial forefront. During the one hundred years that followed, ethical behavior was either assumed or not a concern. Very few MBA programs fully integrated the topic into their curricula. Doing so made an institutuion unique. Today, the financial shenanigans of high-profile corporate leaders have brought ethics in business (or the lack thereof) to the attention of the general public. As a consequence, most MBA programs at least pay lip service to its inclusion. In some respects, what we see now is a standardization of what once made Texas A&M stand out from other programs.

Sustaining focus, over time, as a competitive strategy can also prove daunting. Again, imitators abound. Although the University of South Carolina may have established a niche in international business in the 1970s, many schools provide international experiences for their MBA students today. Likewise, perceived needs change. While entrepreneurship and entrepreneurial leadership are in vogue today, as newer industries such as telecommunications or electronics mature, the interest of potential employers could cycle back to a desire for solid general managerial talent that understands the fundamentals of business and possesses the means to lead strategically.

If neither cost leadership, differentiation, nor focus alone can guarantee competitive advantage, what can? The answer seems to be strategically embracing innovation in anticipation of environmental change. But this response shifts the question from *What?* to *How?*: How do elite business schools do it? That question is addressed in Chapter 3.

3

What It Takes to Be Strategically Innovative

Mimi Wolverton and Larry Edward Penley

Some public business schools have enabled themselves to be far more effective than other schools. Their approaches to strategic innovation and competitive advantage are told in their own words via the case studies. But there are common themes associated with these schools' strategic choices, and these themes give answer to the question, How do the elite public business schools embrace innovation in anticipation of environmental change? The first two themes discussed in this chapter establish the purpose and need for strategic innovation. The remaining themes highlight aspects of these organizations that permit them to realize the purpose of strategic innovation as they define it and to satisfy the need to accomplish it.

Strategic innovation requires a bedrock upon which to build. It provides the reason why we engage in the process at all. For the twelve business schools and colleges in this study, a fundamental commitment to excellence lies at the heart of their continued attempts at being the best at what they do. The second theme is the recognition that environmental change is a given. Nothing stays the same over time. These schools accepted the challenge of making change work for them. The remaining five themes—leadership, evidence of change, planning, community, and keeping an eye to the future—serve as building blocks for ongoing purposeful change through strategic innovation. Each building block is discussed from the perspective of the case study schools.

THE FOUNDATION: A COMMITMENT TO EXCELLENCE

We selected public business schools and colleges whose full-time MBA programs consistently rank in the top fifty programs nationwide. Such a distinction, in and of itself, suggests that these schools pay attention to issues of quality. To be sure, in telling their stories, the case study authors signaled their stature. Beyond numbers, however, lies a basic touchstone of sorts. For example, the University of Maryland and Arizona State aspire to be among the top schools in the country. Texas A&M speaks of high expectations; Georgia of leadership and excellence in its working adult programs; the University of Carolina, of quality; and Indiana University of its long and distinguished history. In a similar vein, the dean at Georgia State University (GSU) refers to his faculty as experts who make theory applicable in the real world.

Unabashedly, our authors tell us that Purdue's Krannert complex houses some of the finest graduate education programs in the world. Warrington at Florida describes itself as a small, high-quality research school. Likewise, the dean at Pittsburgh points out that the Katz School is located in a city with high environmental standards at one of the greatest research universities in the world, and that Katz faculty are the definition of the modern university scholar—distinguished researchers and excellent teachers. In other words, each of our case study institutions exudes a fundamental commitment to excellence.

In addition, all institutions subscribe to selective, or somewhat selective, student admissions criteria, admitting students to their programs who, in all likelihood, will represent their institutions well on graduation. Average Graduate Management Admission Test (GMAT) scores for students admitted into the MBA programs at case study schools range from 600 at Georgia State University to 670 at the University of Washington. All but four schools require GMAT scores in excess of 650. Acceptance rates vary from less than 25 percent to 60 percent, with Maryland exhibiting the greatest degree of selectivity and Georgia State the least (see Table 3.1).

RECOGNIZING THE NECESSITY OF CHANGE

Change confronts us at every turn today. In fact, colleges and schools of business have long faced change and dealt with it. But in the past, with

Table 3.1   Selectivity Based on Average GMAT Score and Acceptance Rate

Institution	Average GMAT Score	Acceptance Rate
Arizona State University	654	29%
Georgia Institute of Technology	640	40%
Georgia State University	600	60%
Indiana University	651	30%
Purdue University	651	26%
Texas A&M University	627	27%
University of Florida	660	23%
University of Georgia	659	26%
University of Maryland	656	23%
University of Pittsburgh	613	54%
University of South Carolina	629	54%
University of Washington	671	32%
More Selective Comparisons		
Harvard University	705	10%
Northwestern University	700	13%
University of Pennsylvania	703	13%
Less Selective Comparisons		
Florida State University	600	67%
Louisiana State University	588	43%
Virginia Commonwealth	525	61%

Source: Business Week Online, 2002.

change coming at a slower rate, they had the luxury of adapting at their own pace; and deans had the advantage of setting a direction that others more readily followed. Today, change bombards us and seems to envelop us. Instead of existing in an incrementally shifting environment, business colleges encounter dynamic complex worlds filled with expectant, yet unforgiving, constituents (including faculty), who demand a voice in the direction of the college (Wolverton and Gmelch, 2002; Wolverton, 1998). Developing a competitive strategy that not only responds to, but also anticipates, the environment becomes the mark of organizational effectiveness in a college. The kind of collective creativity required to accomplish such a feat, in turn, leads to innovative practice (Galbraith, Lawler, and Associatess, 1993).

Deans at the Universities of Maryland and Washington described their colleges as plateaued or as one put it "stuck at good" but wanting to be great. Washington's dean specifically talked about transformation and renewal and suggested that the school is a work in progress. Similarly, in the early 1990s, Arizona State University (ASU) adopted the mantra of the university itself—"A good university striving to be great." As the titles of their respective chapters suggest, Georgia Tech sensed that it was poised for opportunity and GSU believed its future depended on its ability to reinvent itself. As with Washington, the case author for Georgia State spoke of transforming the college. The University of Pittsburgh always knew that its strength lay in meeting the shifting needs of its students and in determining those needs by actively engaging with the corporations that hire their graduates. Pitt has a "promise to keep"—being the best.

Innovative change that strategically supports and reinforces college goals requires calculated risk taking. In 1997, Indiana University changed its view on what constituted viable funding resources and, in doing so, set fiscal development as its top priority. Florida took an entirely different tack—increasing graduate education and decreasing undergraduate education—as its route to maintaining both program integrity and prominence in the field. As priorities changed at the university level, the Indiana and Florida business schools found their environments altered.

A college must then stay the course or change direction. The University of South Carolina decided to strengthen its position as a leader in international business education (currently regarded as the best public school program of its kind in the nation) rather than develop a more diverse portfolio of education offerings. As a result, the school refocused its efforts.

In contrast, Texas A&M (TAMU) and Purdue both pushed the programmatic envelope, TAMU by reconceptualizing its MBA, Purdue by setting a direction that moved them beyond industrial management into technology and entrepreneurialism. TAMU provides a prime example of what it means to take calculated risks. Instead of "thinking anew outside the box" to design its program, the school redesigned from the inside out, applying lessons learned from a successful executive education program to the structure imposed on its full-time program. Finally, Georgia anticipated and matched two needs (a need for the college to expand its presence into an urban area, if it was to remain viable, and an unmet demand for MBA and executive education in Atlanta) that resulted in change and overall program revitalization.

BUILDING BLOCK 1: LEADERSHIP

School deans authored or coauthored five of the twelve case studies. In these studies, the dean as leader was never mentioned. Yet, the earmarks of leadership are clearly present, not only in those five chapters, but in the other seven as well.

Position Change

From a chronological perspective alone, a change in leadership seemed to be a watershed event at all twelve study schools. Deans at ten of the institutions took office in 1997 or later. The University of Florida and Arizona State University experienced change in their deanships during the 1990–1991 academic year. Each school rethought its focus under the new dean and moved up in stature as an elite institution almost immediately following the leadership change. ASU provides a dramatic illustration. In 1991, its MBA program ranked 197 out of 273. By 1994, *U.S. News & World Report* had included it in its list of the top fifty programs nationwide. Since that time it has moved steadily up in the rankings to seventeenth among MBA programs housed at public universities.

Catalyst for Change

New leadership, then, seems to be a crucial element. Indeed, Galbraith and colleagues (1993) equate leadership to being a catalyst for change. Others agree that producing change is a primary function of leadership (Carr, Hard, and Trahant, 1996; Kotter, 1990a, 1990b). If we think of change in terms of innovative practice, deans start by helping their colleges build visions of what they might look like if certain prescribed changes occur (Wolverton, Gmelch, Montez, and Nies, 2001). To do so, they must possess the ability to shape concerns raised by college constituents into conceptual pictures of change that are organizationally purposeful. They project this sense of direction and bring continuity to it. They provide stability by finding and securing untapped resources to further college efforts. They facilitate the planning, implementation, and evaluation of change efforts and demonstrate a bias for action (Wolverton et al., 2001; Conger, 1998; Guskin, 1996; O'Toole, 1995).

To be sure, change seemed to be a given for these deans, and they took their role as facilitators of change seriously. For instance, Georgia's dean understood how influential a dean can be in the evolution of a business school. Georgia State's dean came in believing that business schools have "to experiment now, to be innovators, to be willing to reinvent what worked yesterday." Such attitudes set the tone and serve as clarion calls for colleges.

Deans approached this responsibility differently. Some focused on vision, others on resource management, and still others on laying the groundwork for planning. The dean of the Smith School at Maryland took the position of dean with a direction already identified—to become the leading technology-oriented business school. The vision of Moore's dean (South Carolina) is to be consistently listed among the top international business school programs in the world. For the deans at Indiana University and Georgia Tech, the main concern was acquiring and deploying resources. Successive deans at Purdue built a track record of sparking purposeful change. At Washington, the dean facilitated the change process by asking, What do we want to be? Twice during his tenure, the dean at ASU enlisted high-profile business executives from the local community (first in the Business Partners Process and later in the E-Business Task Force) in determining the college's course. The dean at TAMU led the drive for program revision and laid the groundwork for successful change. Finally, the Pittsburgh and Florida case studies were written by their deans, both of whom focused on faculty and programs in their telling of the schools' stories. Doing so says much about the nature of their leadership.

BUILDING BLOCK 2: EVIDENCE OF CHANGE

Leadership sets the stage for change, but strategic innovation requires involvement in change initiatives over time. Evidence of change becomes a critical building block because it serves as a testament to progress and provides the impetus to continue to move forward. Measuring change as it relates to set targets ensures that actual outcomes are consistent with planned ones (Gibson, Ivancevich, and Donnelly, 2000). Evidence of change across all case institutions can be collapsed into four general categories: programmatic changes, influxes of funding, new or renovated facilities, and renewed or continued emphasis on faculty research productivity.

Program Changes

First, all study institutions engaged in major curricular and programmatic realignment. Maryland, Washington, Arizona State, and TAMU provide the most visible examples. Curricular reinvention at TAMU is so paramount that the chapter author explicitly details its creation and contents to the almost total exclusion of other aspects of the college. Both the Universities of Maryland and Washington and Arizona State so dramatically redirected their colleges toward technology that new MBA core curricula and elective options had to be put in place. In contrast, the University of South Carolina did not start anew but instead refocused what it already did in international business.

Influx of Funding

Second, these institutions experienced influxes of funding. In some instances, multimillion dollar gifts led to renovation, for example at the University of Pittsburgh, or they were associated with the naming of the schools at Maryland, Arizona State, and South Carolina. In others, major funding campaigns added (or will add) to the coffers. Other than the University of Florida, where no mention of funding was made, and the University of Pittsburgh, which spoke of a gift but no university- or college-initiated funding campaign, all case study institutions have either engaged in fund-raising efforts since a change in school or college leadership or anticipate that they will in the near future.

New or Renovated Facilities

In addition, between 2000 and 2002, eight of these business schools either built new buildings or completed extensive renovations to existing facilities. The Universities of South Carolina and Washington and Arizona State University anticipate major building projects within the near future.

Faculty Research Productivity

Finally, all case study schools placed a renewed emphasis on ensuring faculty research productivity. To do so, they implemented or modified one or more of five different, but complementary, strategies (centers, hiring, rewards, faculty support, and PhD education).

First, all schools and colleges developed new or realigned existing centers, institutes, or divisions so that they furthered the mission of the college or school and supported faculty research productivity. For example, the University of South Carolina has a research division that oversees and coordinates all its research efforts. Arizona State created a "holding company" for its research centers and named it the Seidman Institute after a former dean. Similarly, many centers and institutes at study schools reinforce the mission and focus of the institutions. For instance, Purdue and Indiana Universities and the Universities of Florida and Pittsburgh all house federally funded Centers for International Business Education and Research. Georgia's new Institute of Leadership Advancement complements its point of differentiation. Georgia Tech and the Universities of Pittsburgh and Washington have new technology centers that are centerpieces of their innovative strategic initiatives. Arizona State's information technology, supply chain research, and services leadership strengthen the school's areas of specialization. Georgia State's long-standing Economic Forecasting Center and its new Southern Institute of Business Ethics reflect its dedication to entrepreneurism and ethical business conduct. And TAMU's Center for New Ventures and Enterprise goes to the heart of entrepreneurialism.

Without a doubt, the University of Maryland provides a blueprint for schools and colleges to follow as they attempt to be strategic about innovation. Since the arrival of Smith's current dean, the school has created four centers that further faculty research at the intersection of business and technology. Each center started as a pilot with funding for three years from the dean's office, after which time they are expected to be self-sustaining.

Second, in instances where it was possible, schools targeted new hires to support the new direction of the college. Fifty percent of Georgia Tech's faculty has joined the college since 2000. Maryland has hired over sixty new faculty in the last four years. Several of Maryland's hires are categorized as teaching superstars, who carry heavier teaching loads in lieu of conducting research. This allows Smith to reduce the teaching loads of faculty who do engage in research. The dean at Washington sums it up nicely when he says: "Research will remain a high priority. And recruiting and retaining world-class faculty will be critical to our success."

Third, endowed positions at all study institutions help them attract the best and the brightest faculty in their fields. Arizona State added thirty endowed faculty positions in its late-1990s capital campaign. Research productivity as a primary vehicle for moving their schools toward their goals was mentioned by Florida, ASU, Washington, Maryland, and Pittsburgh. The University of Washington and Arizona State University have developed evaluation and merit pay protocols that explicitly recognize the value of research. Both examine teaching load in much the same manner as Maryland. Maryland and ASU also report providing summer research stipends. Others may use similar strategies but simply didn't mention them.

Fourth, some schools used teaching support as a means to provide faculty with flexibility and staff support. To support Maryland's technology orientation, it hired a full-time chief technology officer and tripled expenditures on staff and infrastructure. ASU made a major commitment to technology and eLearning (as they put it) as well. Over a decade its IT staff expanded from two to more than thirty, it raised its support for software and hardware many times over, and it developed a strong staff devoted specifically to eLearning and to technical assistance to support its faculty and enable them to be innovative teachers and recognized scholars. Such moves relieve faculty of tasks they had previously performed and help facilitate their research and teaching efforts with additional time and revenue from eLearning programs that were created.

Fifth, PhD programs designed to prepare the next generation of university faculty provide a special type of intellectual stimulation and research assistance to faculty at these schools. Programs are small. Each school enrolls less than 100 students—the elite of the elite. At Katz, these programs represent a vital part of the school where students work closely with faculty in one-to-one relationships. In fact, Pittsburgh's chapter author devotes considerable time to outlining the school's nine PhD fields. At GSU, 85 percent of its doctoral students publish prior to graduation, and the vast majority of them become academicians. Arizona State has focused on improving its placement of doctoral students at Carenegie-classified Research 1 institutions; this goal is viewed as instrumental to its support of a research faculty with doctoral students who are committed to

Table 3.2   The Nexus of Leadership Change and Evidence of Change

Institution	New Dean Year of Change	Evidence of Change		
		Program Changes	Influx of Funding	New Facilities
Arizona State University	1990-91	1992	1997-2003	2004-5 projected
Georgia Institute of Technology	1998	1999	1999 inferred	2000
Georgia State University	1997	1997	1997	2002
Indiana University	1997	2000	1997	2002
Purdue University	2000	1999	1998	2002
Texas A&M University	2001	2002	2003	2001
University of Florida	1990-91	2003	No mention	No mention
University of Georgia	1998	2002	2000	2000
University of Maryland	1997	1998	1998/2000-2	2002
University of Pittsburgh	1997	Ongoing	2000	2001
University of South Carolina	2000	2000	1998	Anticipated
University of Washington	1999	2000	Upcoming	Upcoming

careers in research. Both Indiana and Purdue referred to producing future faculty as a fundamental responsibility. Maryland and Georgia spoke of growing PhD program resources. In fact, five study schools—Maryland, Georgia, Florida, Purdue, and South Carolina—have engaged in strategies to limit undergraduate enrollments as a way to redirect resources to their PhD programs. Two statements capture the interconnectedness among doctoral education, MBA program vitality, and faculty research productivity. The dean of Warrington (Florida) stated, "Faculty research quality and innovation [are] the cornerstone[s] of quality doctoral programs." The dean of the school at the University of Washington noted that "strong PhD programs are a necessary element in building successful MBA programs."

Strengthening and maintaining a stellar cadre of productive research faculty takes time and cannot be tagged with a specific point in time. But program changes, large influxes of funds, the opening of new or renovated facilities, and the hiring of a dean are all time-specific. Table 3.2 presents these events side-by-side, to dramatic effect. Within a few years of leadership change, most schools and colleges experienced rapid changes in programs, resources, and facilities.

BUILDING BLOCK 3: PLANNING STRATEGICALLY

Three fundamental premises—maintain an external, environmental orientation; focus on the future; and never assume consensus where none exists—combine to make strategic planning instrumental to business schools' success and effectiveness. The potential challenge, however, lies in a reluctance to rethink basic strategies and the propensity to seek the path of least resistance by simply grafting additional pieces onto existing plans. As Mintzberg (1989) noted, "[They simply] leap onto [their] strategic horses and ride off in all directions" (p. 147).

Study institutions did not appear to take this tack. Instead, they viewed the plans that guided their actions as integrated, proactive processes driven by their basic missions. South Carolina is an excellent example. This school's decision makers also understood that most good ideas and plans surface because they are willing to simultaneously examine their clientele, competitors, and themselves (Pearson, 2002). But in looking outward, they have focused, not just on what the environment is like now, but on what leaders perceive the future will hold. To plan strategically means seeking opportunity (Rowley, Lujan, and Dolence, 1997). Case study institutions see strategic plans as mechanisms for prioritizing activities and ensuring that adequate resources are available to meet set goals (Keller, 1983). They also view them as a key mechanism for stretching their organizations—forcing them to move beyond the present, anticipate the future, and shape their own destinies. Those study institutions that spoke directly to planning strategically mentioned missions, visions, strategies, goals, and targets, all primary components of basic strategic planning.

Eight of the twelve study schools provided details of their planning processes and plans and addressed their importance. Georgia Tech provides one example. It aligned its programs, research, resource deployment, and strategic direction through planning. Although Pittsburgh, TAMU, Florida, and Indiana did not mention strategic planning, telltale signs nevertheless are evident. Indiana seeks to meet the needs of its constituents in a fast-paced and ever-changing environment because this is crucial to the school's continued success. Pittsburgh speaks of a century of continuous change. Historically, both institutions have engaged in change efforts that could only be sustained with some sort of planning. In the case of Florida, the reader senses a strategic agenda centered on the importance of research. And TAMU's curricular planning mimics traditional strategic planning, which starts with environmental scanning and conventional analyses of strengths, weaknesses, opportunities, and threats.

Of the remaining eight case study institutions, four in particular exemplify planning strategically. Their plans are clear and concise. Even a cursory examination yields a clear understanding of where these institutions are headed and of what they value as mainstays of excellence. Each one has an overriding vision or mission, which provides focus. All strategies, priorities, and targets tie directly back to that focus.

For instance, Krannert at Purdue "will be distinct from most business schools by having the highest quality expertise in the leadership and management of technology-intensive organizations." Its mission "to educate tomorrow's business leaders, increase the body of knowledge in management and economics, and provide outreach activities to various stakeholders of the school" is in complete accord with its vision. Its six strategies and twelve specific targets go to the heart of these two statements.

Similarly, a team of faculty, students, staff, advisory board members, alumni, and university central administrators at the University of Washington developed a mission to be entrepreneurial with specific emphasis on high-tech environments. This provided a powerful force for the school by exposing overarching issues that confronted it. Its five priorities—to improve the student experience; improve the work environment; reward activities that further the mission; provide the infrastructure to support faculty, staff, and student activities as they pertain to the mission; and find the fiscal resources to be able to compete—guide the school toward fulfillment of its mission.

Maryland, in its first experience with strategic planning, began by asking "what it means to be a leading technology-oriented business school"—the vision the dean set for the school. It then went on to examine its strengths and weaknesses in terms of the responses to this question. Then, and only then, did the school develop its plan, which centered on a dual strategy: to continue to develop first-rate academic areas and centers with distinguished research, teaching, and outreach and to differentiate Smith from other business schools.

ASU used what may have been one of the most extensive planning processes, called Business Partners, which was conducted over a two-year period and embedded in the relationship of the business school to the business community. The Business Partners plan provided long-lasting focus in a number of areas. It committed the school to a competitive full-time MBA degree, along with comparable high-quality MBA programs focused on the local business community. It controlled admissions to its undergraduate program, raising its quality while also redeploying resources to its MBA programs. It also recommitted the school to a doctoral program of high quality, a strong research faculty, and globalization of faculty and programs. The Business Partners process itself became very significant for the school, as it was used repeatedly to provide for ongoing, entrepreneurial, strategic change within the defined framework.

Although each school set some distinct goals for itself, such as promoting economic development in the case of Purdue, rewarding desired behaviors at Washington, responding to community needs while globalizing at Arizona Sate, and marketing at Maryland, many strategies and priorities of these four business schools fall within two themes. Each institution sees enhancing the learning environment, whether by ensuring program quality, developing innovative curricula, enhancing research excellence, or creating cross-functional programmatic linkages, as critical to realizing its mission. And each highlights the imperative to find the fiscal resources and provide the infrastructure necessary to accomplish their other goals.

BUILDING BLOCK 4: COMMUNITY

No business school is an island. Shaping one's environment through strategic innovation takes multilateral involvement of the business school and university communities as well as the community at large. Operationally, integrating multiple perspectives to inform change yields benefits. Involving community (faculty, staff, students, administrators, alumni, business, local, and state) enlarges the pool of ideas and concerns voiced, and at the same time builds trust. Trust, in turn, leads to new ideas and moral, financial, and political support. Structurally, change occurs only when its process becomes fully integrated into the way the college or school does business (Wolverton and Gmelch, 2002).

All case study schools mention extensive use of external advisory boards or community involvement, partnering with other colleges to develop hybrid programs, and actively involving faculty in change efforts. Some, like Purdue and ASU, add special twists. One of Purdue's programs, PL+S (Prepare Leaders and Stewards), for example, encourages community service among its students. Like Purdue, Arizona State places a heavy emphasis on the community through its programs and students with its new slogan, "Doing good while doing well." Many (Georgia State, Florida, South Carolina, Indiana, Pitt, Washington, ASU, and Purdue) expand the boundaries of community by stressing global connections.

Three schools in particular—the University of Pittsburgh's Katz, Arizona State University, and the school at the University of Washington—illustrate the power of community in pointed ways. The University of Pittsburgh provides a solid example of the importance that interconnections across the university and within the larger community play in sustaining program vitality. This school's relationship with the community is reciprocal in nature. Prominent executives and alumni participate in programmatic areas. In return, the Katz School has proved to be a "primary player in stimulating much of the dynamic growth that the city of Pittsburgh is experiencing."

Arizona State University demonstrates the significant impact of the business community on its strategic direction with its description of a turning point in its planning process. One business member of ASU's planning group challenged the school, "Don't focus on giving us the most graduates possible, but the best graduates possible." This engagement of the community had numerous positive consequences for ASU. It laid the foundation for its successful capital campaign. The business community members who had served on the planning group were influential with senior leaders at ASU in soliciting their support for the transformed strategic direction of the business school, including the growth and place of graduate business education.

The University of Washington offers an excellent example of what it means to involve multiple communities in the change process. As a precursor to planning, the school compiled a list of local alumni and overlapped it with a list of the most important business leaders in the Seattle area. The exercise was eye opening and allowed the school to tap two important communities (alumni and business) by engaging many of those who were common to both lists in determining the future of the college. Washington also realized that any new plan would demand the active participation of everyone in the school if it wanted to move forward. Prior to any planning, faculty were asked to complete a deceptively simple statement: "I would be proud of this school if . . ." The mere act of giving voice to faculty in this manner opened a floodgate of ideas and concerns, but more important, it laid a foundation upon which the new dean and his faculty could build a trusting relationship. The school also makes extensive use of business and community advisory boards. The comment, "I've never had an academic ask me how they could help us [before]," made by a local business executive, bears witness to extent to which Washington's business school partners with its external communities. And UW's unconventional corporate and school report cards send clear messages about the importance of reciprocal school-community involvement.

BUILDING BLOCK 5: KEEPING AN EYE TO THE FUTURE

Every one of the schools in this study set a direction for itself by developing a focus based on its anticipated environment. Direction, for these colleges, provides a kind of eye to the future, which, while grounded in realism, stretches them to reach beyond their comfort zones and take risks. At TAMU the concern is with shaping future direction through growth and change. At ASU, it is preparing for a technology-dependent and digital future where traditional schools use eLearning to compete with nontraditional business schools and where graduates of the MBA program are prepared to manage in a sophisticated, technology-enhanced world. Georgia Tech speaks about being "on the rise," and Georgia describes its determination to be "visible, powerful, and influential." Both the University of Washington and Purdue are building for the future as the twenty-first century unfolds. The dean at Maryland finishes his chapter with a list of goals that will propel his school into the future. He states that these goals are ambitious; in other words, they will stretch his school. His last statement: "Count on it!" (the goals being met), however, speaks volumes to the determination held by both the dean and the school.

But setting a direction and staying the course are sometimes very different challenges. Generating change initiatives can excite and drive initial involvement, but sustaining focused change over time can be a trying matter. Staying the course may require a regeneration of sorts when projected changes fail to result in taking the organization in an anticipated direction (Hilosky and Watswood, 1997) or when the forecasted environment is not realized. Pittsburgh regenerates change by anticipating and meeting its constituents' needs. Its dean speaks of the Katz School as one of the oldest and most evolved, yet one that is also continually flexible and responsive. ASU reviews its vision and mission each year as it revises annual strategic goals. The University of Washington reports that it worries about sustainability.

Indeed, organizational stability becomes a key determinant of whether organizations can handle change of this type over time. Today, when one change cycle bleeds into the next, organizations that retain their leaders from change inception to institutionalization stand less chance of becoming sidelined or derailed than do organizations that experience frequent leadership turnover (Carr, Hard, and Trahant, 1996; Cox, 1994; Guskin, 1996; O'Toole, 1995; Wolverton et al., 2002). Deans at eight of the twelve schools and colleges in this study had been in place for five years or more, with the deans at Florida and Arizona State in their positions for more than ten years. Such longevity provides consistency and helps guarantee purposeful change designed to move institutions in a desired direction.

DIVERSITY AND MARKETING: TWO ADDITIONAL UNDERSTATED, BUT NOT UNIMPORTANT, THEMES

Diversity as a strength and the need to market their programs surfaced in several of the case studies. As to diversity, in general, Americans believe that colleges and universities play significant roles in preparing people to function in a diverse workforce (Cook and Sorcinella, 1999). An increasingly global community demands it. As to marketing, out of necessity, some business schools see marketing as a vehicle through which they can distinguish themselves from their competitors, especially in the battle for students and resources.

Diversity: Mirroring Society

In the first instance, attention to diversity, all the study business schools, whether intentionally or not, interwove the need to engage and value diversity into their stories. They defined it broadly, paying particular attention to gender and racial/ethnicity balance and the presence of international students in their programs.

Women comprised anywhere from 25 percent to almost 40 percent of most entering MBA cohorts, and international students had a significant presence in these programs as well. U.S. racial and ethnic minority representation varied, with several study schools placing emphasis on attracting qualified students from this population segment. For instance, Georgia State received a gift for scholarships for students from underrepresented groups from the Bank of America. It is also part of the PhD Project, a program that promotes the recruitment and support of minority students in doctoral studies in business. Purdue and Indiana also participate in programs that target minority students, particularly African Americans. ASU uses its PepsiCo Scholars program to attract Hispanic students into its full-time MBA program. And Katz partners directly with historically African American institutions to encourage their students to enroll at the University of Pittsburgh.

In addition, all study schools either required or included optional international experiences in their programs. Many of them partner with universities in other countries, immersing both faculty and students in global business education. For example, recently Purdue awarded its first degrees on foreign soil to MBA students in Hannover, Germany. The University of Florida has tight Latin American ties, as does Georgia State University, whose master of international business requires proficiency in a second language. The Universities of Washington, South Carolina, and Arizona State have also built tailor-made programs taught jointly by case study institution faculty and host country faculty, in Korea, Mexico, and China, respectively. ASU's Corporate Online program reaches out to every region of the world with an MBA that blends traditional executive education with eLearning. Several schools offer international executive MBAs that bring international students to their campuses and place their faculties on foreign soil. The University of Georgia, in fact, owns a building at Oxford University in England.

Finally, many of these schools build their programs around team activities that encourage students to experience working with diversity. TAMU purposefully assigns its MBA students to teams designed to exploit the value of diversity, rotating them through at least four team member combinations over the length of their programs. ASU's cohort-driven, lockstep Evening MBA was redesigned to offer working adults the benefits of a full-time program with advantages like intensive teams, case analysis, and close collaboration with classmates.

Marketing: Putting Your Best Foot Forward

Marketing is, perhaps, a trend in the making. Its most visible element may be the rush toward naming of business schools with ASU providing the most recent example of this phenomenon. Marketing, however, surfaced as a specific concern for four of the schools—Maryland, Washington, Georgia Tech, and South Carolina—and it did so in the form of branding.

Branding helps an organization distinguish its offerings from those of others. Slogans, names, and symbols provide potential students and future employers with ways to identify a school or program. To be successful, branding efforts must delineate distinctiveness. Recognition must be immediate. The strategy employed must also convey to prospective students or employers the value of the programs through an understandable message that is easy to recall. Finally, an effective branding strategy is flexible enough to accommodate strategic change (Berry and Parasuraman, 1990).

Georgia Tech developed a tagline, "Prepare business leaders for changing technological environments," as a program identifier. Maryland and South Carolina spoke specifically about branding strategies. Maryland developed a comprehensive branding strategy that labels the school as an innovator in joining technology with business education. The Moore School at the University of South Carolina shortened its name to make it easier to remember and designed a new logo that features a globe as a symbol of its focus on international business education. Washington's dean spoke of "taking the brand upscale." A fifth school, ASU, weaves its case study around core values that it makes the central focus of its brand. A sixth, Robinson at GSU, sees marketing its premiere programs as a strategy as well.

ELITE PUBLIC BUSINESS SCHOOLS: WHAT MAKES THEM TICK?

All case institutions strongly subscribe to the necessity of focus but contend that it must be solidly grounded in what makes each one of them unique. In addition, for these institutions, determining and retaining that focus demands that they strategically embrace innovation. This means possessing an overarching commitment to excellence and the realization that they must change over time. Further, their consistent ability to embrace innovation strategically—that is, in a manner that moves them forward in their chosen directions—requires leadership, evidence of change as markers of progress, planning, community, keeping an eye on the future, capitalizing on diversity, and to a lesser extent, marketing what they do best.

Part II

Case Studies

4

A Work in Progress: Transforming the University of Washington Business School

Yash Gupta

Founded in 1917, the University of Washington (UW) Business School is the second oldest institution of management education on the West Coast. Throughout its eighty-five-year history, the school, led by twelve different deans, has always sought to provide students with the best business education possible and has earned a reputation as a premier educational institution, particularly in terms of research. In 2000, *The Academy of Management Journal* ranked the UW Business School's faculty as eleventh overall in research productivity.

It is tempting, at times, for an institution to rely on its good reputation. But in the arena of business, a world that, by its fiercely competitive nature, changes and evolves more quickly than perhaps any other sphere of human endeavor, a business school that does not keep abreast of new ideas, new strategies, and new technologies is destined to suffer.

The latest chapter in the ongoing story of the UW Business School is one of transformation and renewal. Students and faculty who were a part of the business school ten years ago—or even three years ago—might well call it a "reinvention" or a "rebirth," considering how dramatically we have refocused our mission and direction.

When I assumed the post of dean in 1999, the UW Business School was stuck at "good." Students, administrators, faculty, staff, and alumni all wanted the school to be great, but there was not a consensus on what that meant, and certainly not on how to get there. The various departments of the school were fractured, and communication among departments and programs was limited. The level of connection to the Seattle-area business community had languished, and in some cases had been all but lost. We wanted to be good at everything we did, a noble goal that was perhaps more romantic than practical. Meanwhile, the business world was becoming more technology and knowledge based, especially in the Seattle area. With these issues in mind, we set about defining who we were and how we could best serve our students and the business community.

With a lot of hard work and an equal amount of imagination we developed a new mission for the school and an ambitious, detailed plan to implement it. Parts of the plan are already in place, and the level of excitement and commitment among our stakeholders is impressive. We are proud to share the story of that transformation, which is very much a work in progress.

BRAINSTORMING OUR FUTURE

When we started the strategic planning process in early 2000, we enlisted the aid of expert facilitators Michael Moore and Michael Diamond of the Ernst & Young Strategic Planning Partnership, a duo with experience directing twenty-five such planning exercises at major business schools. The next step was to assemble a strategy team. We knew that including a broad mix of people and opinions was critical to giving the exercise both weight and legitimacy. Unlike prior attempts at producing a viable strategic plan, we made sure that all our stakeholders were well represented. When the team was in place, there were representatives from faculty, students, staff, the advisory board, alumni, and the UW central administration.

At the opening session the entire team discussed overarching issues—the entrepreneurial nature of the school, the internal climate, the level of connectivity to outside communities. What was most fascinating was the consistency of views about where we were and where we wanted to be. We had been risk averse; we wanted to be risk takers. We had been conventional; we wanted to be entrepreneurial. We had been isolated; we wanted to partner with academic, business, and alumni communities. Our scope had been broad; we wanted to be focused.

This concordant foundation was the departure point for months of discussion, hard decisions, and concrete plans. The team was split into five task forces sent to explore ways that our mission and values should shape the UW Business School in five critical areas: people, scholarship, academic programs, and external and internal relations. We devised mechanisms to gauge every action toward our objectives.

People had been open to change, but there had never before been a clearly defined mission that made them realize that change was not only acceptable, but *necessary*. Unlike prior planning efforts, the new strategic plan provided a clear road map for transformation.

THE CURTAIN RISES

What emerged from the process, what we unveiled for our stakeholders in the summer of 2000, were a mission statement and a list of strategic concepts for fulfilling that mission. While the complete planning document is too long to reproduce here, the mission and strategic priorities are worth noting.

Mission Statement
We are an entrepreneurial learning community dedicated to the creation, application, and sharing of knowledge that places special emphasis on high-technology business environments.

Top Five Priorities

- Improve student learning experience in all programs.
- Promote a collegial, supportive environment in which faculty, staff, and students are able to work together and develop to the fullest extent of their capabilities.
- Implement fair and equitable personnel policies that meaningfully reward activities that further the school's mission statement.
- Provide the necessary technology support for faculty, staff, and students to be current in their use of technology.
- Achieve sufficient resources to compete with peer institutions.

OUR TECHNOLOGY FOCUS

The technology focus reflected in our new mission statement was shaped by the needs of the local business community, as well as the revenue-generating strengths of the UW itself, which attracts more than $700 million in research grants each year. New technology developed by university researchers has long provided a catalyst for innovation in the local economy and helped strengthen Seattle's growing reputation as a technology center. Microsoft began here and remains the most innovative and dominant player in its industry. Seattle is a leader in the aerospace, biotech, software development, and wireless communications fields. There is a solid base of old-line manufacturing, such as PACCAR, as well as innovative retailers like Amazon.com and Starbucks. Several years ago, *Forbes* magazine ranked Seattle at the top of the list of 162 metropolitan areas in terms of technology growth, output, and jobs. The more we thought about Seattle as the nexus of technology and business, the clearer it became that technology must be our focus.

More specifically, we needed to be positioned at the intersection of technology and entrepreneurship—technology within the frame of entrepreneurship, not the other way around. The positioning mirrors the local economy, which is known for both its entrepreneurial spirit and innovative companies on the leading edge of emerging technologies. We wanted to be a school of national and international reach—especially in areas that are relevant to Seattle and the Pacific Northwest.

NEW SKILLS FOR MANAGING TECHNOLOGY

One program that embodies our new focus is the Technology Management MBA (TMMBA), which was developed for people already working in the high-tech industry and focuses on management issues faced in high-technology environments. Held on Seattle's tech-laden eastside, not far from Microsoft's headquarters, the eighteen-month TMMBA program blends the best analytical skills, management models, and decision tools of an MBA program with applications to the ever-changing and fast-paced fields of hardware design, software development, and cyberspace.

Beginning in January 2003, the school also offered a Master of Science in Information Systems (MSIS), designed for professionals interested in pursuing careers as consultants, business analysts, and project managers, positions that bridge the gap between information technology and business functions.

Both these new programs, the TMMBA and MSIS, indicate our commitment to equip business professionals with the management skills and technical expertise they need for positions of leadership in a knowledge-based economy driven by technological change.

CENTER OF ATTENTION

One of the best examples of the school's new emphasis on interdepartmental collaboration is the Center for Technology Entrepreneurship (CTE), a campus-wide resource designed to expose research faculty and students to the real-world challenges of turning innovative technology into viable companies. The program combines access to emerging technology developed by UW scientists and others with a multidisciplinary approach to research and teaching entrepreneurship. Members of every department are active in the program.

CTE involves students and faculty from the top-ranked UW schools of law, medicine, engineering, computer science, and others. In this way we are able to leverage the incredible assets of the UW and its cutting-edge research. The winning team for CTE's 2002 business plan competition provides an excellent example of our interdisciplinary focus. The team consisted of two second-year MBA students, a doctoral candidate in bioengineering, and a law student. Their combined expertise was essential in crafting a viable plan for Cogelix, a company that plans to distribute a patented radiation gel that targets cancer cells (technology developed by Battelle).

Similarly, through the WRF Capital/Gates Fellowship program, promising entrepreneurially minded graduate students from various disciplines can explore emerging technologies developed by the University of Washington and Battelle's Pacific Northwest National Laboratory. Current fellows include students from the business school, bioengineering, law, and chemical and mechanical engineering.

CTE's collaborative axis is the New Venture Creation Lab, in which multiple teams from diverse disciplines examine the market potential of emerging technologies, create business plans, and then pitch them to potential investors. Core areas of investigation include building new models for developing and commercializing emerging technologies, studying success and failure factors of high-tech start-ups, conducting market analyses for new ventures, and understanding organizational barriers to adopting new technology.

With CTE, we hope to create the leading national research center for developing and disseminating knowledge on technology entrepreneurship. CTE offers the first PhD program in the nation in Technology Entrepreneurship. Each year, starting in fall 2003, CTE admits two doctoral candidates, who will take approximately five years to graduate. These students will teach entrepreneurship courses at the undergraduate level and engage in research and support activities for the center.

As we look to the future, the CTE model, which integrates the business school with other disciplines and resources at the university, will become increasingly important. Our long-range vision is for the business school to operate less as an independent unit and more as a catalyst for innovation across the UW campus.

THE NORTHWEST MEETS THE FAR EAST

With Seattle as the closest major American port to the Pacific Rim, it is only natural that we continue to develop relationships with Asian businesses that have ties to our area's economy and business community. Thus, while we have connections around the world, we have chosen to focus our international outreach in Asia.

We already have an impressive start in that we have been developing many of these relationships for the last ten years. As a part of our Custom Executive Education program, we educate executives from Korea, Japan, China, and other countries and offer them the flexibility to customize the program to meet their needs, just as we do with domestic companies, such as Boeing. For example, we partner with a Korean institution, Yonsei University, where executives study for five months before coming to the UW for one year to complete a customized MBA curriculum. The program is populated primarily by a single Korean company, LG Corporation, whose mid- to senior-level managers benefit not only from the curriculum but also from the opportunity to share ideas with other MBA students.

These types of symbiotic partnerships are the heart of what we want to accomplish in our dealings with an array of companies, whether they are located in Seattle or in downtown Kyoto. We want to build long-term relationships, so that a UW Business School faculty member might visit a company to conduct research or write a case study, while an executive at that company might speak to our students, or even teach a class for an entire quarter. In seeking these partnerships, we know it is important to remember that we must be patient. But building such relationships creates trust and helps strengthen our reputation as a school that delivers on its long-term commitments.

ENGAGING OUR EXTERNAL STAKEHOLDERS

Our reimaging of the school also meant that we had to reintroduce ourselves to certain segments of the local business community. Some of these once-strong relationships had weakened, becoming dated or lost, and it was imperative to share with these business leaders our new desire for partnering with them and their companies. Some of these companies had wanted to help the school but did not know how, others had never even been asked for help, and still others had been approached but with no effective follow-through.

The importance of the Seattle business community's depth and breadth of knowledge in cutting-edge technology and the ever-changing knowledge-based economy became even more important to the school when we realized how many of these business leaders had a connection—in some cases a connection that had gone without being nurtured—to the UW Business School. With such a rich environment for business and with Seattle as a veritable incubator for new businesses (particularly high-tech businesses) many of our alumni stay in the area, drawn by the opportunities here and by the charm of the Northwest itself. In fact, 22,000 of the 35,000 UW Business School alumni live in the four counties that make up the Seattle metropolitan area.

When we started to overlay the list of local alumni with the most important business leaders of the area and the nation, the potential for partnering was startling. We were reminded that our alumni included the chief executive officer (CEO) of Starbucks, the chief financial officer (CFO) of Immunex, the chief information officer (CIO) of Microsoft, and many senior executives at Boeing.

We realized—and sought to make these alums understand—that resources, though always welcome, are far from the only way that alums can meaningfully give back to the school. Among the many other things they had to offer was their time, expertise, and advice, all of which can be more valuable than a financial gift. We also wanted them to understand that we were interested in an arrangement in which we could truly help each other.

The response to our new focus on technology—as well as the message that we were aiming to truly partner with local firms—was received warmly. When we met with Kerry Killinger, chairman, president, and CEO of Washington Mutual, one of the most successful banking networks in the United States, he laughed and said he would have to get back to us on the question of what needs the business school could help them meet. "I've never had an academic ask me how *they* could help *us* [before]," he exclaimed.

Local companies are seeing that the business school can help by allowing them to engage our award-winning faculty in consulting, research, and case studies. And many executives appreciate the opportunity to participate in the internal workings of the school, contributing their expertise to help shape our curriculum.

OUR INVALUABLE ADVISORY BOARDS

One of the many ways that local business leaders can help the school is to share their wisdom by serving on one of the UW Business School's many advisory boards. Their advice and expertise have been critical to the transformation process by going above and beyond the call of duty in many ways, like helping to shape our strategic plan, lobbying the Washington legislature for MBA tuition increases, and raising funds within the board and externally, as well as making significant investments of personal time in assessing and initiating technology enterprises, mentoring the business school leadership, and much more. Board members provide critical knowledge and decision-making skills, offer recommendations on curriculum, and educate the faculty and students of the school about critical issues impacting their fields—issues students will face soon upon graduation, issues and challenges that may well inform or even inspire faculty research.

Board members' involvement is not only appreciated but measured. When board members offer to help, we take them up on it, and not only that, we measure their company's commitment to the school in the form of what we call a corporate scorecard, which "grades" corporations on their involvement. Are they offering mentorships and internships to students? Are they hiring MBA graduates? Have they spoken to classes or engaged students in case studies or research projects? How involved have they been with their respective boards? With these kinds of questions, we track our benefactors and also show them ways that they can be of further help.

While board members may joke that we fill out "report cards" on their contributions, we measure our own dedication in much the same way by posing the following questions: Are we transforming the students' learning experience? Have we implemented personnel policies that will reward those people who are advancing the mission of the school? Are our faculty engaged with industry? What investments in technology infrastructure are we making that allow our students and faculty to implement mission? How are we moving to attract resources and to keep up with our peers?

As we move into the full-scale implementation of our strategic plan and realization of our mission statement, the answers to these questions (and the very act of asking them) will keep us on track with even our most long-range plans.

NEW CRITERIA FOR FACULTY EVALUATION

Closer to home, the new strategic plan and mission statement called for and created changes in the internal academic structure and workings of the school. We implemented important changes in the faculty compensation scheme to make it fairer and more transparent. We knew that we needed faculty to participate in the process in order to effect change, and the new direction made it exciting to serve as part of the process and make participation more than a duty or a chore.

The new spirit of cooperation not only emphasized service to the school, but it backed it up. New criteria for merit pay increased the emphasis on a faculty member's overall contribution to the school, not just his or her teaching or research accomplishments.

Our new strategic plan, to be successful, demands the active participation of everyone in the school, particularly faculty. Thus far, faculty have been more than willing to take on the challenge. Before, when the school was more department-based, some faculty resisted teaching in another department's program, and when they did teach, it was seen largely as a way to make extra money. Now, most faculty will agree to teach where their talents are most needed, without negotiating changes in salary. The mentality has gone from "me" to "we." The focus is not on personal gain but on the good of the school as a whole. As a result, the faculty are working more through programs than departments, reaching out to a wider set of colleagues than they would have thought possible just a few years ago. In the future we want to use our new vision and atmosphere of inclusiveness to retain and attract faculty. Already underway is a plan to reduce teaching loads for research-active faculty, and to make the faculty experience here a balance of teaching, research, and service.

Starting in the fall quarter of 2002, we reduced teaching loads from five to four quarter courses if certain research criteria are satisfied. We will also put more emphasis on overall service to the school, with service evaluations becoming a more important component of the merit review process and the awarding of faculty endowments (fellowships, professorships, and chairs).

THE TUITION CONTROVERSY

One of the UW Business School's primary sources of revenue, MBA tuition, is low when compared to the average tuition at peer institutions. The UW Office of Planning and Budgeting reported that UW MBA tuition for 2000–2001 was 57 percent lower than the average MBA tuition at twenty-four peer universities. Only 16 percent of the university's total budget is provided by the state general fund, but there is still political resistance to raising tuition. Although the situation is different than educating undergraduates, taxpayers still balk at raising tuition, arguing that higher tuition limits access.

With the strong advocacy of many influential members of our advisory board, including Orin Smith, CEO of Starbucks, and Ed Fritzky, the former CEO of Immunex, the state legislature in 2001 granted the University of Washington Regents authority to raise MBA tuition by 15 percent in 2001–2002 and 20 percent in 2002–2003. Because of public concern over issues of diversity and access, our moderate increase in tuition is being accompanied by a school commitment to increase our endowment for scholarships by $10 million. We are confident that this responsible stance toward tuition authority— incremental increases combined with more dollars available for scholarships—will allow us over time to set tuition at the levels of peer institutions and make our MBA program self-supporting.

It is clear that a quality MBA program cannot be sustained, much less transformed, when the school loses money on every student. Students ought to be charged at least the cost, if not the value, of the education they are receiving. With tuition on more of a self-supporting model, the school could implement more of its plans without constraints imposed by the state budget and without depending on private resources. Private resources, after all, cannot be the main means of sustenance in the long run. We want to offer a premium educational product. With products whose value is difficult to measure objectively, price can be a strong indicator of quality. Not only does low tuition result in a lack of resources, the low price itself can also create the perception that the school is low quality. Consequently, initiating a price increase—"taking the brand upscale"—may be essential to improving the school's reputation as well as its quality.

UNDERGRADUATE AND DOCTORAL PROGRAMS

Our undergraduate program serves over 1,600 students each year and has long been regarded as one of the nation's twenty best undergraduate business programs. We want to maintain and strengthen the quality of our undergraduate program—but have no plans to increase the numbers of students admitted.

UW BUSINESS SCHOOL FACTS

Faculty: 75 tenured and tenure-track faculty, 32 with endowed positions. (The number of endowed positions has increased more than 25 percent since 1999.)

Degree Programs:

- Undergraduate Program serves over 1,600 students each year and has long been regarded as one of the nation's 20 best undergraduate business programs.
- MBA Program has about 300 students in the two-year, full-time program. Working professionals can also complete a three-year Evening MBA program.
- Master of Professional Accounting (MPAcc) in taxation prepares students for careers in U.S. taxation.
- Executive MBA(EMBA): More than 400 Northwest firms have sent their management executives through the two-year EMBA program.
- Technology Management MBA: A new 18-month program.
- Global EMBA program: A collaboration between UW and Yonsei University in Seoul was custom-designed for Korean executives.
- Master of Science in Information Systems (MSIS): A new 18-month program designed for business and technology professionals.
- PhD Program: Primarily designed for those who want to pursue academic careers. About 65 students are in residence in eight fields of specialization. We are the first business school in the nation to offer a PhD in Technology Entrepreneurship.

Our PhD program, of course, is an extremely important component at a research university, such as the University of Washington. Nearly all of the top MBA programs in the nation are at business schools that have top-tier PhD programs—this is not a coincidence. Faculty research generates new knowledge that flows into the MBA curriculum. And a PhD program helps faculty in their research programs directly (with students as research assistants and coauthors), and by keeping abreast of the current academic literature. Since our PhD students receive, on average, about $27,000 to $29,000 per year (stipend and tuition), the program will never approach the self-sustaining model we would like to achieve in our MBA program, but students do make a significant contribution through their teaching and research activities. In short, we feel that maintaining a superior PhD program is a necessary element in building a successful MBA program.

LOOKING TO THE FUTURE

One of our main objectives is to have the learning environment reflect the values and the focus of our curriculum. We want all classrooms and offices in the business school to be as technologically advanced as possible. We must be an organization of the future. We aspire to better serve our students when they are here and after they have graduated, to better connect with our community stakeholders, and to operate more efficiently. We will only accomplish these goals if we "dream big" and follow through with a long-term commitment.

One of our major new initiatives is Project FutureTech, an information (IT) road map designed to identify and address the technology needs of the school's offices and classrooms. Thanks to the enthusiastic support of two members of our advisory boards, their firm offered its technology consulting services to us pro bono, to give us added expertise in developing our IT strategy. The FutureTech team (which involved faculty and staff from all departments) asked big questions, such as: "How can IT support the school's mission? How can it make life better for students, faculty, staff, and alumni? What does our perfect world look like?"

After a thorough study, the team made a comprehensive list of recommendations, many of which have already been implemented. All our classrooms, study areas, and library now offer wireless access to the Internet, transforming every learning space into a computer lab and allowing instructors to animate their lessons with the multimedia capability of the Web and interactive software. Five of the MBA classrooms are equipped with videoconferencing and recording equipment, which allows for interactive lessons with remote speakers.

Even more innovation is in the works. Portable video, projection, computer, and speaker systems will become standard for all other classrooms.

And the transformation will not benefit only students; the Technology Center provides training and software for all faculty and staff and teaches faculty how to improve the learning process with new technology. When our IT plan is fully implemented, technical support personnel will be added to better serve students, faculty, and staff; and the technology in use at the UW Business School will match the technology our students will find in the workplace at leading-edge companies.

Undoubtedly our most ambitious goal is to build a new state-of-the-art facility, a "convergence zone" for all of our new ideas and technologies, a physical embodiment of the new mission of the school and our focus on technology and entrepreneurship. It will be the first privately funded academic building on the UW campus. We have completed the predesign architectural study, which calls for a facility of approximately 260,000 square feet, incorporating classrooms, faculty/staff offices, study areas, laboratories, and an auditorium. The total cost of the project, which includes an underground parking structure, is approximately $100 million. Because of the substantial private dollars that must be raised, we do not expect to break ground on the building for several years.

In the near term we will continue to push for the right to set tuition at a rate that will benefit the school, the students, and the UW. In order to offer a premium product, our tuition rate must allow our important programs to be more nearly, if not totally, self-sustaining. We also will enlarge and develop the self-supporting programs, such as the TMMBA and the MSIS, Executive MBA, and Evening MBA programs. Further, we will evolve the state-supported day MBA program to be more self-supporting. All of this will help realize our goal of aligning the various MBA programs and specialties in terms of price and overall quality.

Research will remain a high priority. And recruiting and retaining world-class research faculty will be critical to our success, as will maintaining and improving the doctoral degree programs.

MBA CLASS ENTERING FALL OF 2002 PROFILE	
Entering class size	124
Full-time students	258
Average age	29
Average years of work experience	5.2
Average GMAT	671
Average undergraduate grade point average (GPA)	3.46
Women	31%
International	28%

We began the process by completing a seeminlgy simple statement: "I would be proud of this school if . . ." As we embark on the first leg of the journey from transforming a good business school into a great one, we face uncountable challenges and obstacles ahead, but with the energy and help of every student, faculty member, staff member, and alum, we can and will continue to make our dream a resounding reality.

5

The Robert H. Smith School of Business at the University of Maryland: Building a Technology Powerhouse

Howard Frank

In 1996, the University of Maryland Business School was a "nice," but relatively unknown, school, both nationally and regionally. Even though it was less than twenty miles from Washington, D.C., it was unable to leverage the political and international forces of the capital area in the same way that neighboring business schools at George Washington University and Georgetown could. To complicate matters further, because the school is part of the College Park campus and not located in Baltimore or another Maryland industrial center, Maryland residents did not think of it as "their" school; and consequently, it had little, if any, natural constituency base within the region.

   The core faculty possessed respectable research reputations and teaching credentials. But, in the main, its academic departments and school centers charted their own courses; and faculty had the freedom to follow their own goals, which revolved primarily around research. The school had established a solid foundation of core competencies across a range of business school offerings, including an MBA that had been transformed by the previous dean into a "current," well-structured program. The resulting curriculum was diverse and incorporated many approaches to business education including cases, teamwork, and experiential modules. In essence, however, Smith had not articulated a long-range vision.

In the absence of a unifying vision, the school attempted to be all things to all people. Faculty and staff often considered potential visions, such as becoming a school that emphasized the interaction of business with policy and regulation or taking on an international focus, but no theme was compelling and powerful enough to rally the school. However, in 1997, things changed.

THE STARTING POINT—SEPTEMBER 1997

During the recruiting process for a new dean in early 1997, interviewers asked, "What would your strategy for the school be if you were dean?" One candidate answered: "I'll make it the leading 'technology-oriented' business school in the nation." At the time, instinct motivated the response, but as the selection process continued, it became clear to this potential dean that such an approach was perhaps the only viable way that the school could build a national and global prominence.

Once in the position, this new dean acted on his instincts. As part of his initiation to Smith, he met with individual faculty and departmental groups to gain an understanding of their individual strengths and weaknesses. He quickly noticed that many departments identified similar weaknesses and often reported very similar strengths. Almost without intent, the individual meetings moved from "get acquainted" sessions to strategic planning sessions, often revolving around the questions: What does it mean to be the leading technologically oriented business school? And what would such an orientation mean in terms of rankings, environment, and students?

Early in this process, answers to these questions generated three specific targets for the school:

- Ascend to the top fifteen business schools in the nation.
- Provide a superb research and teaching environment for faculty and students.
- Give our graduates a first-class return on investment (ROI) for their time and expense.

These goals would have to be achieved by building on the school's strengths, correcting its weaknesses, and transforming its activities and programs. The starting point was to take a hard look at strengths and weaknesses and develop initiatives to capitalize on the former and address the latter.

Maryland Business School Strengths—1997

Even though overall recognition remained low, certain programs, such as a nationally ranked MBA program (which had been ranked twenty-fifth three times in the previous ten years by *U.S. News & World Report*) and a renowned entrepreneurship program, provided the school with a modicum of identification. Smith had also initiated several innovative cross-functional "boutique" programs, such as Quest, a novel undergraduate joint program between business and engineering; the College Park Scholars Initiative; and an entrepreneurship undergraduate track. The result, in part, has been to garner a top twenty-five national ranking in undergraduate education. In addition, faculty research productivity was outstanding and several of its PhD specializations were sought after by prospective students for their program excellence. Some of its cross-functional programmatic efforts in logistics and supply chain management and in telecommunications also showed solid potential. Finally, the culture of the school supported teamwork and collaboration.

These strengths, although significant, were offset by a number of weaknesses, relating to inadequate resources, too many undergraduate students, and too few faculty. Further, there was little recognition of these weaknesses by the university's central administration and virtually no prospect of additional state funding to address them. As one university vice president, when confronted by the inequities in faculty versus student numbers, told the dean: "Business schools are supposed to be milked."

Maryland Business School Weaknesses—1997

From 1990 to 1997, school enrollments had increased by 67.4 percent, compared to state funding increases of only 32.4 percent over the same period. Virtually all of this growth was at the undergraduate level, where total enrollment had grown from about 2,000 to 3,500 (about 14 percent of the university's 24,000 undergraduate students). To make matters worse, student credit hours taught totaled 10 percent of the university's total credit hours, whereas school faculty represented 4.8 percent of the comparable campus total. The existing building did not have classrooms for all of the school's classes, and available office space could not accommodate foreseeable growth. In reality, faculty at business schools in the tier to which Smith aspired carried lower teaching loads, had greater financial support for summer research, and were paid higher salaries.

In addition, although the school's MBA program had been ranked twenty-fifth in a single national survey, none of the school's departments or specialty programs ranked as high. At the graduate level, recognition among business school deans, MBA directors, and corporate recruiters was low. As a consequence, job placement opportunities for graduates did not match the caliber and potential of the students. Similarly, inadequate financial support for doctoral students and high teaching loads affected the school's ability to attract the very best PhD students. Finally, the school's alumni base (some 30,000 strong) remained virtually untapped because efforts at alumni development were primitive and underfunded.

JANUARY 1998 STRATEGIC PLAN

The school's first strategic plan, adopted in January 1998, proposed a dual strategy to build distinction: to continue to develop first rate academic areas and centers with distinguished research, teaching, and outreach and to differentiate the Smith School with activities built around creation, management, and deployment of knowledge and information.

Implementing these strategies required acceptance by a large portion of faculty members, including those who had not yet bought into the technology-differentiation direction set by the new dean. The dual strategy was essential to the accomplishment of this new direction because technology differentiation without leadership in core business school functions could lead to mediocre programs whereas improving core functions without establishing technological differentiation meant business as usual.

Six key strategic priorities emerged from the plan: enhance research excellence, create academic program distinctions, extend the cross-functional linkages within the school and across the university, advance information technology as a core competency, market the distinctions of the school, and improve the school's resources and infrastructure. The plan delineated specific, targeted activities designed to move the school forward, and parties responsible for their implementation were identified. In some cases, individuals carried out the implementation; but in others, groups of department chairs and members of the dean's office were assigned tasks.

The first charge involved designing and implementing a new business school model around the creation, management, and deployment of knowledge and information. This included developing cross-cutting content innovations in the curriculum that drew on virtual research groups and linkages with other disciplines on campus. It also meant introducing a new series of MBA concentrations: telecommunications, technology management, electronic commerce, financial engineering, and supply chain and logistics management.

The second, to hire and retain top tenure-track faculty, was the key to building excellence in emerging thematic emphases. The third imperative dictated that the school address the teaching overload burden on tenured and tenure-track faculty using all available tools, including nontraditional hiring approaches. Strengthening undergraduate and MBA job placement statistics through an organized campaign to attract corporate recruiters and programs to enhance career mentoring for both graduate and undergraduate students was also important. Along similar lines, the school also set out to enhance external and corporate recognition by building a strategic marketing program centered on the technology-differentiation strategy. A sixth priority emphasized the need to increase financial support for top-quality master's and PhD students and improve national programmatic rankings through placement and student career skills advances, strategic marketing, and leadership in curriculum innovation. It also focused on enhancing the caliber of the undergraduate student body through quality controls by increasing the grade point average required for admission as a junior from 2.8 to 3.0 and adding new boutique programs, such as a university-wide citation in entrepreneurship. Finally, Smith was determined to generate additional revenues through innovative programs that leveraged existing strengths and by launching new partnerships with other units on campus and elsewhere.

Each department, business unit, and the school, as a whole, undertook activities that spanned all phases of the school's operations. Each of the initiatives impacted the school's ability to generate revenue, student enrollment, program development, faculty hiring and retention (salaries), marketing strategies, facilities, and the need to mobilize alumni.

Importantly, the implementation of the strategic plan was given credibility as well as momentum by the announcement of a $15 million naming gift for the school in April 1998 when the school was formally named the Robert H. Smith School of Business. Coupled to this naming gift was an agreement with the university to support the expansion of the school's physical facility, Van Munching Hall.

THE PLAN IN ACTION

Over the next five years, Smith took steps toward realizing its strategic plan by concentrating on revenue generation, program innovation, faculty hiring, reorganization, facilities expansion, and alumni engagement.

Revenue Generation

Increasing revenues was essential if the plan was to be anything more than wishful thinking. Without additional revenues, the school had no way to increase the competitiveness of offers to outstanding potential new hires, correct salary compression problems, increase summer research support for new and current faculty, retain key faculty, augment financial support and travel funds for PhD students, enhance MBA financial aid, or improve the information technology infrastructure.

The school began a series of entrepreneurial ventures to build revenues. Ventures included launching a Baltimore-based, part-time MBA program in January 1999, expanding to other locations as identified by marketing studies, and generating additional revenues by "market pricing" MBA tuition. In the latter effort, the school, with the agreement of the university, developed a "differential tuition" plan, whereby MBA tuition is priced at the market rather than at the relatively low rates charged for the University of Maryland's general graduate programs. The school retains 75 percent of the incremental tuition generated for its College Park based, full-time MBA program and virtually all the revenues generated off campus.

The school, however, needed a "jump start." Faculty hiring, increases in compensation, and new programs all had to be put in place before the school had generated sustainable revenues to pay for them. As a stopgap measure, the school borrowed $2.5 million from the university. With these additional resources, it undertook several major efforts. It expanded the evening part-time MBA programs, first to Baltimore (1999) and then, a year later, to Washington, D.C., which increased the total number of evening tracks from three to five. The following year, the school launched a weekend program in Washington, starting with one track in 2001 and adding a second in 2002. By 2005, the school estimates that the number of part-time students will have grown from 400–450 in 1998 to about 1,100 with quality comparable to the initial group. These students, with GMATs averaging about 630 and six years of work experience, are the elite part-time MBA students in the region. Current master's-level enrollment sits at 1,100, 60 percent of which attends part-time. If full-time attendance remains stable, master's-level enrollment will surpass 1,500 in 2005.

Today, revenue sources beyond the base level of state support include market priced part-time MBA student tuition, executive education fees, center grants and contracts, private donations, and endowment proceeds. Figure 5.1 shows the growth in actual business school revenues from 1998 to 2002 and the School's 2003–2005 revenue forecast.

Caliber and Characteristics of Students

The school introduced innovative MBA cross-functional programs (including an executive MBA and joint MBA/JD [doctor of jurisprudence] and MBA/MPM [master's in public management] degrees) to attract top-quality students and to enhance job placement through market responsiveness to uniquely trained students. Current acceptance rates hover around 23 percent of those who apply for admission to the full-time, two-year master's programs. About 70 percent of the students accepted into one of the programs attends. The average GMAT score of enrolled full-

Figure 5.1
Robert H. Smith School of Business Revernues: Actual and Forecast from 1998 to 2005 (in thousands of dollars)

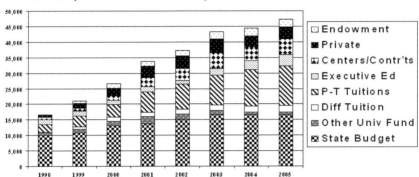

time students in 2002–2003 is 656. At the master's level, 34 percent of the students are women; 33 percent of the total enrollment are international students; and about 14 percent are either African American, Asian American, or Hispanic. Average age is 28 years and years of professional experience prior to entering the program is roughly five years.

In addition, the school admits 20 to 25 PhD students per year from an applicant pool that exceeds 800. These individuals score, on average, over 700 on the GMAT. In total, about 100 PhD students spend four to five years in the program.

New undergraduate admission requirements to the business school aimed at increasing quality and decreasing the number of students have also been negotiated with the university. Although easily said, this was a laborious process requiring a combination of patience, negotiation, and barely veiled threats. Existing business students not meeting standards were removed from the program; "provisional" admissions were discontinued; and a new, freshman direct-admit program was initiated for highly talented students. Over the three-year period since this process began, the number of undergraduate business students has decreased from about 3,300 to about 1,700, which is the approximate goal of the school. In 2002, entering freshmen had Scholastic Aptitude Test (SAT) scores averaging 1,360 and high school grade point averages of 3.85. Retention of the 2001–2002 freshman class was 94.4 percent.

Innovative Programming

In 1998, the school began a comprehensive restructuring of the MBA program to introduce curriculum innovation and distinctiveness. A portfolio of programs with significant scheduling, geographic, and delivery

flexibility was put in place. Elective offerings were redesigned and introduced the following fall. Specifically, the new program included scheduling options for full-time and fully employed students and offerings across
multiple part-time tracks. Expansion of program options across time and
location assured access to the very best members of the candidate pool.

The curriculum was transformed along the technological lines out-
lined in the initial strategic plan. Following the redesign of the elective
options, an entirely new MBA core was developed and implemented in
2001. Resources to strengthen the school's technology infrastructure
were increased. The school hired a chief technology officer, and expenditures for staff and technology infrastructure more than tripled. The
school developed laboratories in supply chain and financial markets,
and rolled out four centers—Supply Chain Management; E-Service;
Electronic Markets and Enterprises; and Human Capital, Technology,
and Innovation—aimed at supporting research at the intersection of
business and technology. Each center was created with pilot funding for
three years from the dean's office with the expectation that the centers
would be self-sufficient thereafter. This strategy has been very successful. Funded, center-based research expanded from virtually $0 in 1999 to
about $5 million in 2002.

Faculty Hiring and Salaries

The dean's office announced a three-year program to bring faculty
salaries to parity with aspirational peers. It adopted the goal that the top
25 percent of the faculty would be paid at the 75th percentile of the target
schools (defined as the ten U.S. schools paying the highest salaries). In the
first year of the program, salary increases averaged 10 percent, with over
20 faculty members receiving raises greater than 15 percent. Salary
increases were based on academic performance rather than longevity or
whether particular faculty members endorsed the technology differentiation direction the school had taken. Four years after its initiation, faculty
salaries were at the 100th percentile of all public schools and matched
those of faculty at the top ten private business schools at both the 50th and
75th percentiles. Academic year 2002–2003 salaries for full professors,
associate professors, and assistant professors and instructors averaged
$153,000, $121,000, and $109,000, respectively. (Comparison provides
some insight into the gains made at Smith. It must be noted, however, that
comparing averages among different schools can be risky because faculty
salaries vary considerably across disciplines and the exact functional com-
position of each rank can significantly affect the school-wide average
salary.)

In addition, the school developed a long-range hiring plan, aimed at
expanding the number of top faculty in each department. Targeted hires

accelerated the school's progress in shifting to a technology and management focus and helped it implement initiatives that bring distinction to the school. Groups were created in targeted areas to support teaching and research in these new areas not only by adding faculty with appropriate applied interests and skills but by capitalizing on existing faculty strengths. To do this, the school structured incentives for faculty to invest in cross-functional teaching and research collaborations. For instance, summer funds for faculty research in targeted areas were increased to encourage alignment with the differentiation strategy.

Faculty at all ranks were recruited and only the very best scholars were considered. Over the last four years, approximately 60 new faculty members have joined the school. In the same period, about ten existing faculty retired and a few others left the school for other reasons. In all, the permanent faculty has grown from about 75 to over 120. This expansion of school faculty represents one of the most successful business-school recruiting programs in the country to date. And the quality of this new pool has been noted. In each of the last three years, the *Financial Times* has ranked the school in the top ten in research (seventh in 2003) in the world (as measured by the number of papers published in top business journals over the most recent three-year period, adjusted by the number of faculty) and the 2002 *Business Week* MBA rankings placed faculty teaching seventh. (The other schools with top ten ratings in both categories were Chicago, Stanford, Northwestern, MIT, and University of California at Berkeley.)

A final strategic move where faculty are concerned came with the creation of a new faculty category. A limited number of non–tenure track, permanent, "superstar," teaching faculty were hired to address teaching needs across all programs. These teachers, termed teaching professors, hold terminal degrees (PhDs and the like) and possess outstanding teaching skills. Because no research is expected, teaching professors carry heavier course loads than tenure-track faculty and assist in various service and student support activities. Teaching professors hold three-year renewable contracts and are part of the life of the school. As such, they manage programs, advise students, and contribute to the general well-being of the school. Not only has the quality of teaching in the undergraduate program improved, but the overload teaching burden of the tenure-track faculty has also been reduced. Undergraduate student reductions along with the successful use of a teaching professor position (we now have eighteen faculty who fall under this category) and the increase in the total number of faculty enabled the school to decrease tenure-track teaching loads while at the same time increasing the number of sections taught by full-time faculty. Actual teaching load and class coverage statistics are given in Figures 5.2 and 5.3.

Figure 5.2
Average Credit Hours Taught by Tenured, Tenure Track, Teaching Professors, PhD Students, Adjuncts, and Visitors

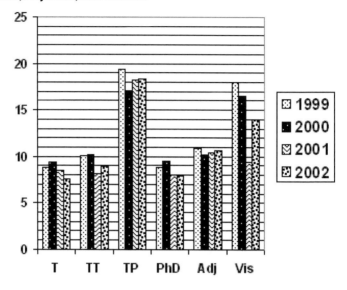

Figure 5.3
Percentage of Course Sections Taught by Full-Time Faculty

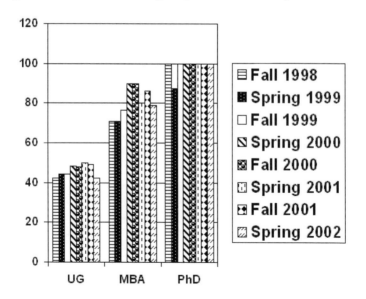

Today, more than 175 faculty work in the school. This includes about 100 tenure-track faculty (over 30 of whom hold endowed chair or endowed professorships), 18 teaching professors, about a dozen visitors and full-time lecturers, and a variety of adjuncts and PhD student graduate assistants.

Organizing for Effectiveness

At the outset, another significant strategic move provided a platform for the school's technology direction. A small, but aspiring, Information Systems Department was merged with a larger, relatively mature Management Sciences and Statistics Department. The new department, Decision and Information Technologies, has become the school's largest department, with thirty-five faculty members. The department, which contains key behavioral, information technology, computer sciences, telecommunications, and operations research and statistics capabilities, is in the process of building an entirely new field blending the "behavioral" aspects of information systems with the more technological nature of work in the mature specialties housed in the department. Moreover, this department has established itself as a leader in both information systems and operations research with the research of both groups of faculty being ranked at the very top of the profession.

At about the same time, the dean's office conducted an extensive review of existing units and operations with the aim of streamlining its operations to those with strategic impact. One center, deemed not strategic, was transferred to another part of the university along with two major contracts. The administrative and financial support units of the school were restructured and its Office of Executive Programs redesigned. In particular, the administrative and finance organization is now headed by the former chief operating officer of a commercial organization and an entirely new staff has been put in place. The Office of Executive Programs is now under the supervision of a former senior manager from the Wharton School; a new staff was recruited; and new programs, including an Executive Master of Business Administration (EMBA) degree, have been launched.

Current senior administration staffing includes the dean, three associate and five assistant deans (with responsibilities ranging from development and marketing communications to management of the academic and career management programs). There are also six department chairs, eight center directors and codirectors, and faculty directors for research, master's programs and other special programs, such as honors and joint programs with engineering and other campus units. In addition, several faculty committees focus on teaching enhancement and undergraduate, master's, and PhD programs. In total, the college has about 275 faculty and staff.

Marketing: Getting the Word Out

The school developed a comprehensive strategy to market its sources of distinction and the new business education model. With the decision to market the school extensively, an assistant dean for communications was recruited; the communications group staff built from a single person to a six-person team; and the communications budget tripled over a four-year period (to about $1 million per year). By *"branding"* the school as an innovator in joining technology with business education, the Smith School of Business differentiated itself from the competition. This created an immediate image for the school, and all marketing communications were integrated to deliver that message. Everything from department and school brochures to marketing themes were redesigned to have a common "look-and-feel" to support the message.

A variety of direct mail, advertising, and public relations programs have been used to promote the expansion of the part-time programs and to increase name recognition, regionally, nationally, and with deans and MBA and undergraduate program directors from other business schools. Not only has enrollment increased but recognition-based rankings have risen as well. For example, the *U.S. News & World Report* ranking of the part-time MBA jumped from 22 to 13, and its estimation of undergraduate education at Smith moved its ranking from 22 to 18. (Both ranking systems are based solely on reputation.) Regionally, the school is highly regarded with frequent press coverage and rapidly increasing regional student applications for all of its programs. Further, virtually every major national or international survey now places Maryland in the top 10 in the technology categories of supply chain, e-commerce, information technology, and information systems, and there are frequent top 25 rankings for most of the school's academic departments. And, prior to *Computer World's* decision to discontinue its numerical ranking of the top 25 programs, the school rose from being unlisted (1996) to third on the list (1999).

Facilities: Making Them Work for You

The business school is housed in a modern facility, Van Munching Hall, first built and occupied in the early 1990s. Within a few years, however, the building proved far too small for the school; faculty found themselves teaching undergraduate courses in as many as 15 buildings on campus in any given year. In addition, the school ran out of office space, and while every faculty member had a private office, many other functions were crammed into tight and inadequate spaces. There was little room for visitors or adjuncts. Corporate recruiters were forced into tiny interview spaces. Numerous PhD students were packed into one office. To make matters worse, the university's ten-year facilities master plan provided for no additional business school facilities through 2008.

Needless to say, correcting the facilities problems by getting additional space became a top priority. In the summer 2002, the school took occupancy of a new 103,000 square foot wing of Van Munching Hall. The addition is being paid for through a combination of state funding, a contribution by the university, a major donation by Leo Van Munching (a 1950 alumnus), smaller donations by other alumni, and $15 million of debt with principal and interest to be paid by the business school.

Mobilizing the Alumni

Active members of Smith's 30,000 alumni association mentor current students through an organized program of professional shadowing and ongoing communication. They participate in an online network whose goal is to maximize the value of the Smith School experience by enabling students to interact with alums in discussion groups and other networking events. This network was originally started as a network for MBA students and is now being merged into a new on-line system, called "Terps On-Line," being deployed by the university for all alumni. Alumni actively support the school through contributions to the Dean's Fund for Excellence, the Clock Tower Club, and a variety of endowed funds.

Engagement and integration of the alumni into a powerful support network for the school is perhaps the greatest challenge. The university and the business school started late in cultivating alumni. In fact, the Alumni Association was not founded until 1988. While it is working hard to close the gap, substantial future efforts are required to develop an alumni network appropriate to the school's programmatic, student, and faculty quality.

THE FUTURE: STRATEGIC GOALS TO 2006

The continuing strategy of the Smith School has been to provide focus and drive from the dean's office in a constant effort to expand the school along the lines of its strategy. Creating an environment where the vision comes from the top, but bottom-up innovation is encouraged, is perhaps the key to Smith's success.

Top leadership of the school, while outlining a distinct vision, does not micromanage every aspect of implementing the vision. Providing faculty members and staff with the freedom and resources to define, extend, and implement the vision in their own areas of specialization enables the generation of a great many new ideas. All of the school's new centers and laboratories have been faculty- or department-proposed concepts with the

dean's office playing the role of selecting, prioritizing, and finding funding for new initiatives. The process typically proceeds as follows: one (or a
few) faculty proposes an initiative. They test the idea for feasibility with
their department chairs and the Dean's Office. Next, they gain support in
their department to make their initiative a part of the department's strategic plan. The department plan is then integrated into the school-wide
plan, which incorporates it into the school's budget and five-year financial
forecast. For instance, in 2003, the school created a behavioral research laboratory, which was proposed by faculty in 2002; and the Center for Entrepreneurship closed a $20 million venture capital fund, first proposed by
that center's director and staff in 2000.

As to the future, the Robert H. Smith School of Business continues to
expand and articulate its vision. Five years from now, the school, through
its research, curricula, and outreach programs, will be viewed globally as
a leading center of excellence for the advancement of business knowledge
and critical competency in the management of knowledge and information in the netcentric era. It will be known for targeted sources of academic
distinction that support the overarching theme of knowledge and information management (e.g., entrepreneurship, management of technology,
telecommunications and information technology, electronic financial markets, information security, supply chain management, electronic commerce, and so forth).

The school's status in the national rankings will continue to rise with the
goal of housing a top fifteen MBA program, a top ten undergraduate experience, and a top ten PhD program, as measured by a combination of external rankings and criteria, such as research, placement, and teaching quality.

At least four of the school's academic departments will be among the top
fifteen in research in the country; and overall, the school will rank among
the top five in research. The end result will manifest itself in student job
placements and salaries at or above those of graduates from Smith's peer
institutions. To help promote recruiting and placement efforts, Smith established a Board of Visitors aimed at building partnerships with firms external to the university. This group also serves as a strategy advisory panel.
Programmatically, the school, as part of a strong research university with a
strategy of inter-unit collaboration among business, engineering, and the
sciences, will have expanded partnerships with other colleges to capitalize
on netcentric developments in the marketplace.

The school will hold a dominant regional position in a broad family of
programs and activities and national recognition in outreach efforts
geared toward executive and management development and entrepreneurship. Finally, state-of-the-art physical and technology facilities will
continue to add to Smith's attraction and continue to offer the technical
capabilities that support the school's netcentric agenda.

Will this ambitious set of goals be met? Count on it!

NOTE

Several comments and observations in this chapter are taken from a school project, "Change Management in Academia," by Macrena Janninck, Pamela Mandeville, Fanny Salaverry, and Segev Tsfati, May 2001, prepared for a second-year MBA strategic management course.

6

Aggies, Integrity, and MBAs: The Mays MBA Program at Texas A&M University

Dan H. Robertson

Texas A&M University is the fifth largest university in the nation with over 45,000 students enrolled, almost all of whom are full-time students. Founded in 1876, the university is a land-grant, sea-grant, and space-grant institution and is one of few universities to hold all three designations. The mission of Texas A&M revolves around the discovery, development, communication, and application of knowledge in diverse professional and academic fields. Academic programs are offered through ten colleges—agriculture, architecture, business administration, education, engineering, geosciences, liberal arts, medicine, science, and veterinary medicine. Renowned for quality of teaching, commitment to public service, and research, Texas A&M ranks in the top fifteen institutions nationwide in research and development spending. It is an institution steeped in rich traditions, perhaps the most important of which is the Aggie Code of Honor, which unifies Texas A&M men and women in pursuit of a high code of ethics, dignity, and personal integrity. The Aggie Code of Honor functions as a symbol to all Aggies, promoting understanding, loyalty,

FACULTY RESEARCH PRODUCTIVITY AT THE MAYS BUSINESS SCHOOL

The faculty of the Mays MBA program are widely acclaimed for their research productivity and excellence in classroom teaching. Some of the research rankings and honors from each of the five departments in the Mays Business School follows:

The Department of Management has been ranked tenth overall in research productivity by the *Academy of Management Journal*. In addition, several management department faculty serve as members of the editorial board on publications such as the *Academy of Management Journal*, *Human Resource Journal*, *Academy of Management Review*, *Journal of Organizational Behavior*, *Journal of Management*, *Journal of Applied Psychology*, and *Personnel Psychology*.

The Department of Marketing is ranked among the top twenty universities in research productivity in a recent study by the American Marketing Association. Marketing faculty have served or are currently serving as editors of the *Journal of Marketing*, *Journal of the Academy of Marketing Science*, *Marketing Educator*, and *Journal of Current Issues and Research in Advertising*. Members have also served as president of the American Marketing Association, on the Board of Governors of the Academy of Marketing Science, and as chairman of the Board of Trustees of the Graduate Management Admissions Council.

The Accounting Department has had its masters programs ranked fourteenth by the *CPA Personnel Report* and has had faculty members in editorial board positions for seventeen accounting journals, including as editor of the *Journal of Information Systems*. Accounting faculty are also involved in leadership positions, such as president of the Federation of Schools of Accountancy.

The Department of Finance has had published research selected as the best paper by the Financial Management Association and faculty selected for the International Business Director of the Year Award given by the Academy of International Business. Finance faculty participate on a wide range of editorial boards for financial publications.

The Department of Information and Operations Management also has a very active research faculty. These individuals have had research papers selected as the outstanding paper at various conferences including the Economics of Information Systems Conference. Currently, department faculty serve as senior editor of *Organization Science* and associate editor of *Information Systems Research*, *Naval Research Logistics*, and *Operations Research*.

truth, and confidence in others. Simply stated, this Code is: " Aggies do not lie, cheat, or steal nor do they tolerate those who do." This Honor Code has permeated the university throughout its history and has helped to set the tone for individual behavior and academic programs alike. It is a code that faculty and students proudly follow and share with future Aggies. It is also a code that serves our current students well in this time of ethical business crises and upheaval.

The MBA program at Texas A&M University shares this rich tradition. Some forty years old, the program began with only one specialization (accounting) but has rapidly matured into the distinct program it is today. But rather than dwelling on the rich history and tradition of the MBA Program, this chapter seeks to discuss the forces leading to change and to share the innovatively new and uniquely different MBA curriculum, which we initiated in fall 2002. In addition, this chapter touches on a major controversy in the current press concerning the value of an MBA degree. It also highlights other graduate management degrees offered in the Mays College of Business at Texas A&M University. Finally, this chapter provides a brief overview of some of the changes occurring in the Mays College of Business that will help shape the future direction of the college.

MBAS THE AGGIE WAY

Five major forces helped shape the evolution of the TAMU MBA program. The globalization of business and of the Texas economy, the continuing evolution of technology, the rapidly growing and culturally diverse state population, the high importance of oral and written business communication skills, and the pervasive nature of teamwork within the corporate business community comprise the forces driving changes in the curriculum. Today, the Mays MBA curriculum combines a comprehensive core curriculum with the flexibility for students to tailor or customize programs to their own individual needs. Although it retains some elements of a traditional curriculum, the new curriculum incorporates features and courses suggested by a diverse group of corporate representatives who together comprise the Mays MBA Corporate Advisory Board.

While many MBA programs draw upon internal resources, such as faculty, staff, and current students, for suggestions to improve their academic programs, the Mays MBA Program has gone one step further. In addition to these obvious traditional sources of information, our Corporate Advisory Board helped broaden the scope of suggestions for change. In addition, the overwhelming success of our Executive MBA program colored our thinking as we prepared to reinvent Mays' MBA. Most executive MBA programs use a curriculum patterned after the campus MBA. We reversed this approach to curriculum revision.

A new dean, Dr. Jerry Strawser, who joined the college in summer 2001, led the drive for program revision and laid the ground work for successful change. His suggestions, ideas, and experiences served as a piece of the base upon which we built. An environmental scan revealed a pervasive trend in MBA education: the majority of MBA students were enrolling in part-time programs, a fact that we also had to keep in mind as we developed a full-time program.

PROGRAM DETAILS

Figure 6.1 provides a visual depiction of the general design of the new Mays MBA curriculum. This program is sixteen months in length with students following a "lockstep" curriculum to graduation in December of the second year of the program. Entry to the program is restricted to one period in the fall of each year.

General Design

The Mays MBA program is based on a comprehensive curriculum completed in four, ten-week terms covering a sixteen-month time period. The fifteen-course, forty-eight credit-hour, lockstepped sequence places particular emphasis on small teams and teamwork. The expanded core includes: a portfolio approach to business communication spanning the entire program, a business negotiations course, an international business course, and a semester-long Business Consulting Project linking the program concepts to current business organization issues. The curriculum adopts a ten-week format within the semester long format of the university.

The Core Courses

One of the core courses (the business consulting course) is a six credit hour course while all others are three credit hours. Other core courses include financial and managerial accounting, marketing management, finance, microeconomics, corporate strategy, quantitative analysis, management of people in organizations, operations management, business computing, international business, business negotiations, business communications, and a specialization course selected by the student.

In the first year of the program, students choose a specialization course from among four options: marketing services, financial management, e-commerce, and supply chain management. The flow of these courses can be seen in Figure 6.1. Note that the business communications course is designed to further enhance students' oral and written communication

Figure 6.1
Mays MBA Curriculum

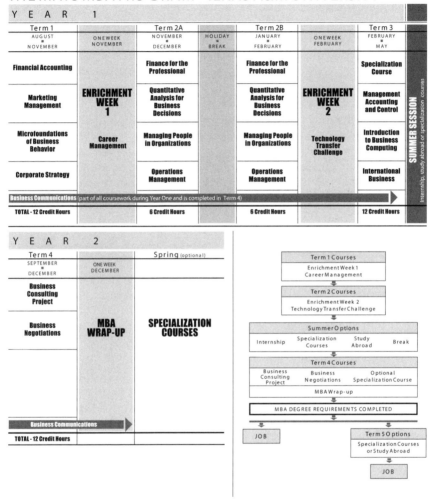

THE MAYS MBA PROGRAM • TEXAS A&M UNIVERSITY

skills and extends throughout the entire sixteen-month curriculum. Written and oral presentations are tied to subject matter from various core courses but graded and reviewed by faculty with expertise in written and oral communications.

Specialization

It is impossible for any university to design an MBA curriculum that is "right" for all students. The needs of students vary directly in relationship to such factors as their previous academic background and current and future career interests. The Mays MBA curriculum provides four opportunities for specialization. Three of these options occur during the sixteen months of the program, and one immediately follows the completion of the MBA program. The first option for specialization occurs during Term 3. A second option for specialization takes place in summer. No program course work is required of Mays MBA students during the summer, so those who wish to add a specialization can carry a full load of graduate courses (up to twelve graduate hours) if they choose to do so. These courses can be concentrated within one discipline or can cut across academic departments and disciplines. For example, students with an interest in international business can take four graduate courses during the summer in the Bush School of Government and Public Service. Chosen in concert with the graduate faculty of the Bush School, students completing this option qualify for a Certificate in Advanced International Affairs conferred at graduation. Other certificate programs are currently in various stages of development.

Yet another summer option involves participation in one of the university's Study Abroad programs. In partnership with the Center for International Business Studies (CIBS), which is housed in the business college, the program offers study opportunities in thirteen European, Asian, and southern hemisphere countries. Selected students often provide feedback indicating that their learning experiences abroad include both academic learning from participation in the classroom and added value obtained through hands-on experience in another culture.

The third alternative for specialization occurs in Term 4. Purposely designed to include a "reduced" academic load to facilitate time for employment interviews, Term 4 requires only two core courses. Thus, it is entirely possible for students to add one or two additional specialization courses of their choosing. A final specialization choice occurs after the MBA degree is granted. This self-designed option involves an extension of the sixteen-month program to include an additional semester.

Program Enhancements

One of the advantages of the ten-week course format is the opportunity to expose students to a wide variety of experiences. Enrichment Sessions take place between terms and provide students with interactive learning experiences outside of the traditional classroom environment. These Enrichment Sessions involve business practitioners, as well as faculty, and give our students opportunities to "bridge" the gap between classroom theory and application in today's business world. These interactions include company hosted on-site visits in various locations, such as New York, and interactions with corporate executives as guest speakers in on-campus sessions. The culmination of these Enrichment Sessions takes place at the end of the academic year in May with a little friendly competition.

May 2003 saw the first Technology Transfer Competition. This competition gives every Mays MBA student the opportunity to work in student-selected small teams of four or five with actual businesses to develop a commercialization plan for a technology. This plan is based on a full week of interaction with a firm chosen by the students and includes a written plan as well as a presentation of the plan to a panel of corporate judges. The competition draws upon the business communications skill sets developed and refined by students throughout the year. In addition to the academic learning experience provided, winning student-teams selected by corporate judges split cash prizes totaling several thousand dollars. To date, members of the MBA Corporate Advisory Board have pledged over $10,000 for this competition in an effort to underscore the value they place upon the importance of excellence in business communication skills.

The firms participating in this competition are current clients of the TAMU Technology Licensing Office (TLO) and are typically small, start-up firms with an existing or proposed business technology. TLO client firms who volunteer to be subjects in the Technology Transfer Competition receive free advice from the team of students. Such student contributions to the welfare and success of small business firms further the public service and community mission of the University and provide vivid illustrations of the synergy possible through careful planning and coordination of curriculum, student learning, and institutional mission.

The Mays MBA program "partners" with the Center for New Ventures and Entrepreneurship in the Management Department to make this project possible. The "troika" composed of the Mays MBA Program, the TLO, and the Center for New Ventures and Entrepreneurship promises to be a powerful and effective combination of resources that can significantly leverage such year-long learning experiences.

Capstone Experience

The Business Consulting Project is the capstone of the Mays MBA program. Working with company sponsors, teams of four or five MBAs tackle a company-defined issue over a fifteen-week period. Each team works with a faculty mentor and company sponsor to bring the full content of the MBA program to bear upon the company-chosen issue. The Business Consulting Project culminates with a presentation to the company and a written report that is evaluated as a component of the business communication course.

A VALUE-ADDING APPROACH

The Mays MBA Program prepares students to face the challenges of today's globally oriented businesses interested in employing individuals with varied academic backgrounds, expertise, and experience; who are strategic thinkers and accomplished communicators; and who are hardworking, committed, prepared, ethical, globally aware, and team-oriented. We seek to provide our students with more than a mere degree. We seek to give their investment in an MBA degree a high return on educational investment. These two statements are not mere rhetoric. Consider the following points.

Strategic Thinkers

This program is, by design, not for the faint of heart. It demands the full and complete attention and wholehearted involvement of each student. To be successful, students must exhibit excellent time management skills and sacrifice much of their leisure time in the pursuit of excellence in their classes.

Preparation

Mays MBAs complete virtually all of the core during the first year except for the business consulting and business negotiations course. Thus, they are well prepared for the challenges they encounter whether they engage in summer internships or add on-campus course work in business ethics, international business, or some other area of interest. The opportunity to enrich their backgrounds with multicultural exposures through study abroad represents an additional method of preparing students for the challenges of tomorrow's global business environment.

Accomplished Communicators

Throughout the sixteen-month long curriculum, various written communications and oral presentations are added to a Communications Portfolio for each student. Continuous feedback and suggestions for change enhance the learning experience. Students complete seventeen writing assignments and make a minimum of ten oral presentations during their first year of study. This ongoing focus on business communication skill sets emphasizes in continual, powerful, and meaningful ways the importance of communications in today's business world.

One of the major reasons for being able to accomplish this goal is our commitment to small class sizes. Each year, entering students are broken into three cohorts. With just over 100 new MBA students admitted annually, we offer three sections of approximately 35 students for each core course. For purposes of quality control, all three sections are taught by the same faculty member. Multiple opportunities arise for any one student to speak or be called upon in each section of each MBA class. Students learn early the importance of preparation for class just as if they were preparing for a professional job commitment.

Experience

Building the requisite types of experience needed to be successful upon graduation takes several forms. On average, entering Mays MBA students have had over five years of full-time work experience before entering the program. This experience base greatly enhances their ability to take advantage of the other experiential opportunities available in the program. It also provides a tremendously rich footing for class discussion. One hallmark of any good MBA program is the degree to which students can learn from the experiences of each other. At Mays, the ability to learn from the experiences of fellow students is indeed a rich one, and much of the true student learning occurs outside of the classroom in collegial, small-team environments.

Ethics

The Aggie Honor Code provides a firmly entrenched behavioral and philosophical guide that is a strong part of the local culture. With this Code of Ethics as a backdrop, the Mays MBA program has sought to further enhance student learning about business ethics with six different modules of ethics included in core courses in accounting, marketing, economics, organizational behavior, international business, and business negotiations. By doing so, ethical concepts are related directly to disciplinary subject matter. For example, a marketing case can bring out the ethical dilemma faced by marketers when an opportunity for bribes or kickbacks arises. The case focuses on marketing, but the application of ethical principles and concepts is a major issue discussed by the class and faculty member.

Global Awareness

In addition to an entire course on international business, Mays MBAs enroll in international modules in their accounting, finance, marketing, economics, corporate strategy, organizational behavior, and operations management courses. A significant number of our students (roughly one-third of the entire class) also takes advantage of opportunities to participate in study-abroad programs during the summer.

Through the generous support of corporations, former students, and our Center for International Business Studies, the two traditional barriers to Study Abroad, expense and language, have been eliminated. Mays MBA students who study abroad pay only TAMU tuition, and all students selected receive supplemental scholarship support making the cost minimal. Likewise, all MBA courses offered during summer sessions at partner institutions abroad are taught in English. Thus, students who do not speak German can still study in Koblenz, Germany.

Further, we work very hard to make certain that there is continual exposure to diverse cultures in every classroom every day. Our entering class last Fall consisted of 102 students, 27 of whom were international students. These 27 students, who represent some fifteen different countries, bring a wide variety of cultural backgrounds to the program. Since student teams are appointed rather than selected, we make certain that there is at least one international student on every team.

Together, these steps do much to enhance the global awareness of Mays MBA students. Although a relatively small MBA program in size, we believe that it has much to offer, especially from an international perspective. The overall quality of our program has been recognized by business periodicals, such as the *Financial Times* (2003), which engage in annual rankings of the top 100 MBA programs worldwide.

Team Orientation

The emphasis on teams came about because of a suggestion from the corporate community and our MBA Corporate Advisory Board. The wisdom of their advice is already evident, and we believe this approach will further benefit our graduates as they enter the job market. All entering students go through a two-week MBA Orientation Program preceding the start of classes. This program is free of charge and includes several team-building skill sessions, as well as an orientation to the university, MBA Program, and specific courses.

Upon entering the program, Mays MBA students are assigned to a cohort and a team within that cohort. Many of their assignments and class projects are team-based. Cohorts and teams are changed each term so that by graduation, each student has participated in at least four different teams. The eclectic, rich, and varied background of our entering class makes this a challenging task. We seek to "balance" teams, taking into account factors such as quality, length and variety of work experience, gender, age, ethnicity, cultural background, previous undergraduate and other academic background/experience, academic qualifications (grades, test scores, etc.), and so on. This also accomplishes the goal of maximizing student familiarity and awareness of their fellow students. In short, we value diversity in the Mays MBA program, and team assignments are intended to be microcosms of the overall diversity within the program.

RETURN ON EDUCATIONAL INVESTMENT

One of the most important issues facing MBA applicants worldwide is the issue of affordability. Much has been written in the press about the investment in an MBA. Unfortunately many of the recent articles dealing with this subject conclude that an MBA is NOT a good investment—that indeed, many cost upwards of $100,000. At the Mays, we beg to differ! We challenge any objective observer to examine the facts and see for themselves. We believe we can easily make a compelling case that a Mays MBA offers one of the highest returns on educational investment available anywhere in the world.

Several recent articles in business periodicals support this contention (see, for example, *Business Week*, Oct. 21, 2002). We are a state university and our mission is to serve the residents of Texas, many of whom are not wealthy individuals. The challenge of delivering a quality graduate program that is competitive with the top programs in the world can be daunting. However, we believe that we have succeeded in dong so. Today, the TOTAL COST of tuition and fees for the MBA degree in the Mays MBA program for a Texas resident is less than $10,000. We also make the investment in an MBA an attractive one for nonresidents and international students, with current tuition and fees for these students at less than $22,000. In both instances, we believe that our degree is a worthy investment with a high return.

OTHER GRADUATE MANAGEMENT DEGREES

In the College of Business Administration at Texas A&M University, the MBA degree is only one of thirteen graduate degrees offered. In addition, Master of Science and PhD degrees are offered by the Departments of Accounting, Finance, Information and Operations Management, Marketing, and Management. Further, a Master of Land Economics and Real Estate is offered through the Finance Department; and the Accounting Department offers a five-year integrated professional program with options in accounting, financial management, and information systems. According to recently published statistics, Texas A&M is the third largest producer of Master's degree graduates in the entire country.

The MBA and the Master of Science program differ in this way. By design an MBA degree is a "horizontal" degree intended to provide background and exposure to all disciplines within business administration (e.g., accounting, finance, information and operations management, management, and marketing). MBA candidates often hold baccalaureate degrees in nonbusiness disciplines, such as engineering, agriculture, the sciences, liberal arts, education, geosciences, law, or architecture. In contrast, a Master of Science might be thought of as a "vertical" degree with a primary goal of specialization within a single discipline. Typically, an MS candidate will have completed a baccalaureate degree in Business Administration often in the same department as the desired MS degree.

GROWTH AND CHANGE IN THE MAYS COLLEGE OF BUSINESS

One of the new dean's first activities was the groundbreaking for the Cox wing on the Wehner Building of the College of Business. This new wing will add much needed space for MBA and undergraduate classrooms, as well as administrative offices. Recently, Texas A&M University announced a new Capital Campaign, only the second such campaign in the 127-year history of the university. This campaign has the potential to provide additional much needed resources that will enable Texas A&M to keep pace with peer universities and to maintain its well-deserved reputation for academic excellence.

In sum, we have a relatively new dean, a new wing with new MBA classrooms and offices, a new curriculum, a new director for the MBA program, and great possibilities. Together, these changes set the stage for an exciting future for the Mays MBA program and the Mays Business School.

True Aggies never forget the high expectations that have been set by the accomplishments of those proud Aggies who have gone before them. Their accomplishments, their Code of Honor, their sense of integrity, and their reputation inspire and motivate us all. As we prepare to meet the challenges of the future, we reflect on the words of Thomas Jefferson, a man who saw so much exciting growth and change in his beloved country in a short time. He wrote: "I love my dream for the future of my country even more than the history of its past." His words capture the anticipation and excitement of the new era that we sense at Texas A&M.

7

University of Georgia's Terry College of Business: Leadership Comes Naturally to the Oldest Business School in the South

Paul Karr

Atlanta's newest business school is creating a stir. Its flexible graduate programs, taught on an attractive, central corporate campus by energetic faculty—and supplemented by talks from prominent executives—are the talk of the town. Its innovative courses, which use interactive technology to the fullest, allow even full-time executives and mid-career professionals to find time to enroll and develop their careers and skills.

Still, many are surprised to learn that this talented new contender is actually an old friend. It is the University of Georgia's Terry College of Business—one of the nation's oldest and largest business schools, based in Athens approximately one hour east of Georgia's capital city of Atlanta—and it has recently returned to that city after an absence of more than four decades. Firms are quickly taking notice. Ed Baker, publisher of the city's most respected business journal, the *Atlanta Business Chronicle*, hears surprise and pride as he circulates among the city's business community. Baker has been impressed enough that the magazine relies on college data for its annual economic issue, cosponsors a speaker series, and draws on Terry

College faculty for expertise in its reporting. "I think what Dean [George] Benson has done is just incredible," he says, "everything from opening a new facility in Atlanta to reaching out to so many organizations and companies here. It has really been impressive. And it makes such good sense."

Certainly, Terry College is proud of its past achievements. Terry began ahead of the pack, opening its doors just four years after Harvard's business college did so, which means it has more teaching and research experience than most other business colleges in the nation. It is also broad: Terry College is one of the nation's five largest business colleges. And its faculty are consistently ranked among the nation's best in terms of publishing productivity. But Terry has even bigger plans.

More than ever, Terry College is reaching out to the region's, nation's, and world's corporate communities, moving into partnerships with private firms in Atlanta, Tampa, New York, Germany, and elsewhere. Terry has built bonds with top accounting, consulting, marketing, financial, and retail firms; its MBA students consult for top international businesses; its marketing research center turns out top-quality research and uses an innovative public-private partnership to fund and guide itself; its economic forecasting is the regional leader in the field; and its new business center in Atlanta's Buckhead neighborhood is training today's executive students to become tomorrow's top executives.

Terry is also excited about a new leadership institute that will develop leadership potential and skills in both its students and executives from across the Southeast. Terry's evening MBA and executive MBA programs are growing rapidly in both size and quality, while paying for themselves. Terry College has achieved top rankings, developed a widely publishing faculty, and set a new course to become a top-ten public business college: one with both a solid foothold in Atlanta and an impressive group of research faculty in Athens.

MAKING HISTORY: TERRY BREAKS BUSINESS SCHOOL GROUND IN THE SOUTH

Terry College is the oldest in the southern United States. Its seeds were sown back in 1912, when the University of Georgia (UGA) authorized a School of Commerce to begin instruction.

Then as now, Georgia was a large state—tenth in U.S. population at the time—but there was one key difference: It was a predominantly rural state, and most academic programs tilted heavily toward agricultural research. During the early days, majors (known then as concentration groups) included such topics as secretarial sciences, and an early business college dean's concern revolved around "the lack of adding machines and comptometers."

The college soon overcame its lack of comptometers and began steadily growing in size. In June 1947, it assumed responsibility for the Evening School of Commerce, a fast-growing night school in downtown Atlanta that was then without formal accreditation; with a single stroke of the pen, UGA had accomplished the tricky blending of a small-town business college with a big-city entity. However, this bold experiment lasted only eight years, doomed, in large part, by its own success. The Atlanta business college grew so rapidly that university regents soon decided to spin it off from UGA and create a new and separate state university, the Georgia State College of Business Administration (known today as Georgia State University). UGA's business school was once again relegated to the status of a distant satellite of Atlanta.

PREPARING FOR THE FUTURE:
ATLANTA ON TERRY'S MIND

During the 1960s and 1970s, Dean William Flewellen, Jr., trained his focus on faculty development, actively recruiting talented faculty from outside the Southeast with broader publishing, teaching, and cultural experience. As a result, the college's reputation for faculty excellence began to grow.

In 1977, the college created one of the first five Schools of Accounting in the nation. Five years later, the school was endowed and named the J. M. Tull School of Accounting. In 1979, the college became the first in the nation to offer a master's degree in Marketing Research. Both moves helped distinguish the college and set it apart from other Georgia-based and regional business colleges.

The state of Georgia was changing, as well, and swiftly. Atlanta's boom as a manufacturing, technology, and hospitality center during the 1980s and 1990s spawned an influx of workers, capital, resources, and economic growth. Suburban communities sprang up almost overnight—part of what would eventually prove to be one of the world's fastest recorded urban sprawls—and the demand for business undergraduate and graduate students surged dramatically.

The college was ready for the challenge. Dean Al Niemi created the Georgia Economic Outlook luncheon, an important early signal that UGA would someday be back in business in Atlanta. He also became the prime architect of a major capital campaign to increase the college's endowment. He grew the endowment from $3.5 million to $32.5 million. Today it stands at more than $54 million. In October 1991, the college was renamed the C. Herman and Mary Virginia Terry College of Business to honor two distinguished benefactors whose support made possible a series of endowed chairs, faculty fellowships, and scholarships. This renaming

WHERE TERRY STANDS

MBA PROGRAM (OVERALL)
#13 public university MBA program in the United States (*U.S. News & World Report*)
19th best return on investment (*Forbes*)
#22 public university MBA program in the United States (*The Financial Times*)
#34 MBA program in the United States (*U.S. News & World Report*)

UNDERGRADUATE PROGRAM (OVERALL)
#17 among U.S. public business colleges (*U.S. News & World Report*)
#25 among all U.S. business colleges (*U.S. News & World Report*)

RESEARCH PERFORMANCE (OVERALL)
16th most productive faculty among U.S. public business colleges (*Academy of Management Journal*)
28th most productive faculty among all U.S. business colleges (*Academy of Management Journal*)

DEPARTMENT PROGRAMS (INDIVIDUAL)
Accounting
#13 graduate program in the United States (*CPA Personnel Report*)
#16 undergraduate program in the United States (*CPA Personnel Report*)
#21 undergraduate program in the United States (*U.S. News & World Report*)
Economics
#2 most productive research department in the southern United States (*Applied Economics Letters*)
Entrepreneurship
#19 graduate department in the United States (*U.S. News & World Report*)
Finance
#16 research productivity in the top four finance journals among public universities in the United States (*U.S. News & World Report*)
#22 finance faculty in the United States (*Journal of Finance*)
Management Information Systems
#5 faculty in the United States (*Management Information Systems Quarterly*)
#17 undergraduate program in the United States (*U.S. News & World Report*)
#21 graduate program in the United States (*U.S. News & World Report*)
Real Estate
#6 undergraduate program in the United States (*U.S. News & World Report*)
Risk Management and Insurance
#3 undergraduate program in the United States (*U.S. News & World Report*)

elevated the visibility of the college, and the increased endowment helped fuel the transformation now taking place.

In 1995 a fire seriously damaged Brooks Hall, the home of Terry College since 1927. The building was beautifully restored and reopened in 1997. At the same time, alumni, friends, and the corporate community fully funded a new, high-tech classroom building named for University of Georgia graduate Charles S. Sanford, Jr., and his wife, Mary McRitchie Sanford. Today, the Terry College is home to approximately 6,000 students and more than 225 faculty and staff. A number of Terry programs and departments rank among the nation's best.

RESHAPING TO MEET URBAN NEEDS

Terry College may have begun life as a tiny, rural, publicly funded business college, but in modern Georgia, Terry grows in importance as it helps educate and train the business leaders of the present and future. To that end, the college has begun transforming itself. For instance, Terry's programs have increasingly moved toward graduate education and executive training. Atlanta's corporate community demands a combination of short- and long-term course work aimed at educating everyone from early- and mid-career employees to members of corporate boards of directors. To meet this need, Terry College has expanded its MBA programs and created several new ones to reflect the times.

In addition, the college has also established a leadership institute to help students and executives enhance their leadership potential and skills. Programs include an individualized leadership development program for undergraduate students, an executive leadership program teaching personal leadership for managers, and an MBA leadership program. The institute also promotes groundbreaking research on leadership.

Finally, Terry College is teaming up with Atlanta corporate partners to offer residencies, internships, training, consulting, and a monthly speaker series. These public-private partnerships have brought Terry very much into the corporate community, and they have likewise brought the corporate community into the college's classrooms. More than one hundred business executives speak at Terry each year.

In sum, Terry College does more and better research than ever, across all disciplines housed in its seven academic departments. The college is at the forefront in the use of distance learning in business education. The quality of its MBA student body is rising year by year. Terry currently ranks seventh among U.S. public business colleges, and twenty-second in the nation overall, with an average entrance GMAT score of 659. And the college's programs are moving toward self-sustainability by funding themselves through program fees.

TERRY COLLEGE OF BUSINESS SNAPSHOT (FALL 2002)

Main campus: Athens, Georgia
Founded: 1912
Endowment: $51 million+
Student body: 6,974
- Undergraduate program students: 4,478
- Master's degree program students: 727
    Full-time:
    GMAT: 659   Age: 27 years   Years Experience: 4.75
    21% female   4% U.S. minority   31% international
    Acceptance Rate: <27%;   Enrolled: 60% of those accepted
    Employed 3 months after graduation: 83%
    Evening:
    GMAT: 572   Age: 32 years   Years Experience: 7
    25% female   14% U.S. minority   6% international
- Doctoral program students: 70

Faculty and staff: 252
- Full-time tenure-track Faculty: 100
    20% female   12% U.S. minority   12% international
- Non-tenured instructors and lecturers: 40
- Executives in residence: 3
- Professional staff: 111

Degree programs:
- Bachelor of Business Administration (BBA)
- Executive Master of Business Administration (EMBA)
- Master of Business Administration (MBA)
- Master of Accountancy (MAcc)
- Master of Internet Technology (MIT)
- Master of Marketing Research (MMR)
- Doctor of Philosophy (PhD)

MAN WITH A PLAN: A NEW DEAN CALLS FOR A NEW COLLEGE VISION

The foregoing sketch of Terry College suggests that as it moves back into the heart of Atlanta's financial district, its inner workings are being reshaped as well. Here is how Terry is doing it.

In 1998, Terry College of Business Dean P. George Benson began his term by taking stock of the college. To gain a clear and accurate understanding of how (and how well) the college had been operating to that point, he called upon all past and present human resources of Terry College (including emeritus faculty).

As a faculty member at the University of Minnesota, the dean had helped develop the 1991–1992 strategic planning process and plan that propelled the Carlson School of Management to prominence. "That experience taught me how influential a well-crafted plan and a dean can be in the evolution of a business school," recalls Benson. As dean at Rutgers, he perfected the technique. "The success we enjoyed at Rutgers encouraged me to implement a similar planning process shortly after arriving here at Terry." Based on what he had learned, Benson began the process of building a specific vision for the college's future, one that focused all college energies toward the fulfillment of its newly stated purpose: to develop leaders for the world's private enterprise system.

The dean began by appointing eighteen college members—dean's-level administrators, at least two faculty members from each Terry department, academic program directors, and two students—to positions on the Dean's Leadership Council. These council members were charged with developing a strategic plan, which has since become the blueprint for the kind of college Terry desires to become, as well as a road map to achieving those goals within a reasonable time frame.

To create Terry's strategic plan, the Leadership Council took a series of steps. It required each administrative and academic unit of the college to assess its own strengths, weaknesses, opportunities, and threats. It conducted focus group meetings with approximately four hundred students, faculty, staff, administrators, and alumni throughout Georgia as well as in Jacksonville, Florida, and Charlotte, North Carolina. Finally, it examined competing business schools to compare and contrast programs and resources.

This in-depth analysis of Terry's current state of affairs uncovered six weaknesses that the council believed could provide pivotal strategic targets and a focused direction for future college development. First, Terry College's full-time MBA program was very small compared to similar public university business schools, and the preponderance of undergraduate students was drawing resources away from graduate education. Second, the college did not have a part-time MBA program, although most similar-sized public university business schools did. Third, the college did not have an Executive MBA program whereas every other similar business college studied already did. Fourth, the college lacked up-to-date workspaces, such as "team" (breakout) rooms, interview spaces for recruiters, large reception spaces, and an executive education learning space. Fifth, the college's endowment was the smallest of all the universities studied. And sixth, the college operated as a loose collection of relatively independent academic departments that did not communicate well with each another, or with the rest of the University of Georgia.

To turn these competitive disadvantages into opportunities for future success, the college arrived at a series of specific goals; and it determined what sort of infrastructure would be necessary in order to achieve them. Fourteen months of hard work later, in December 2000, college faculty approved the plan. The plan suggested several specific remedies. For example, the college needed to break down the "silos" of isolated departments and to emphasize its college-wide academic programs, particularly the MBA. To do so, the college developed cross-disciplinary research centers that required its departments to work together. In addition, it needed to be better integrated with the Atlanta business community and grow its endowment steadily and significantly.

To move closer to the business community, the college needed to create a range of new MBA programs suitable for working, mid-career professionals for whom it was not practical to move to Athens and return to school full time. Each new program needed to be self-supporting and generate surplus revenue to help buffer the ups and downs of tax revenue-based state support. The Terry College also had to place more emphasis on three of its strengths, or "centers of excellence": leadership, emerging technologies, and strategic risk management, all of which are in high demand in today's southeastern and global economies. To this end, leadership, in particular, needed to be emphasized through a new college-wide—rather than a department-level—institute reporting directly to the dean.

The plan stressed the urgent need for the Terry College to return to Atlanta's corporate community, integrating Terry programs more closely with Atlanta's corporate culture from which it had frankly become cut off by the seventy-mile physical separation. Indeed, as a college, Terry had decided to return again to Atlanta for good—and in force.

PROFITABLE RETURN: TERRY KEYS INTO ATLANTA'S CORPORATE CORE

One of the keys to this renewal of Terry College's ties with Atlanta has been its full utilization of the UGA Alumni Club Center, which is located centrally in Buckhead, the city's most prestigious neighborhood. This facility—more than 10,000 square feet on the second floor of the Atlanta Financial Center—opened in February 2000 and consists of offices, lounges, and six classroom or meeting spaces. It is here that the college established its first beachhead in its return to the South's economic nerve center.

To this end, the college has expanded its public service programs to address the needs of nontraditional students, especially professionals who wish to improve their knowledge of business and economics. For example, the Economic Outlook Luncheon, held at the World Congress Center in Atlanta each December to present the College's current economic forecasts for Georgia and the United States, continues to draw more than one thousand business professionals annually. The program has expanded to include similar luncheons in the smaller Georgia cities of Savannah, Brunswick, Augusta, Columbus, Albany, Macon, Thomasville, and Swainsboro; all told, the series is attended by more than three thousand business leaders and alumni annually, and future luncheons are planned for Jacksonville and Charlotte.

Similarly, the Terry Third Thursday speaker series at the Alumni Club Center in Atlanta has been exceptionally well received since its inception in March 2000. Once each month, a prominent executive or other well known, public figure—often, but not always, a graduate of Terry College—speaks off-the-cuff before a breakfast gathering of 70 to 120 Atlanta executives and alumni. Recent guests have included AFLAC CEO Daniel Amos, Delta Air Lines CFO Michele Burns, The Home Depot President and CEO Robert Nardelli, Georgia Lieutenant Governor Mark Taylor, Synovus Financial Corp. Chairman and CEO James Blanchard, Judge (and former U.S. Attorney General) Griffin Bell, and AOL Time Warner Controller James Barge.

In February 2002, the college launched the first annual General Motors/Terry College Marketing Research Competition, a ten-week event. The competition provided GM with an array of potential new Internet strategies from the perspective of Terry College MBA students as well as students from ten other top business schools, including Michigan, Harvard, MIT, Stanford, Northwestern, and Emory. "It's already making an impact," says Keith Denny, a business analyst with the automobile manufacturer. "This is definitely something we want to continue." In addition, Terry's executive education programs—particularly the MBA programs, leadership programs, and seminars for current and prospective corporate board directors—have expanded significantly, in a very short time.

Finally, the college's Master of Marketing Research program teams up with more than seventy high-profile national corporate partners to offer student scholarships and a high probability of job placement. The consequences of these partnerships are mutually beneficial. In 1980, the Terry College marketing faculty created the nation's first graduate program to award a Master's degree in Marketing Research. Administered by the Coca-Cola Center for Marketing Studies, and funded partly by generous grants from the Coca-Cola Foundation, this program has gone on to make a national mark in a critical field. One of the most innovative features of this center and master's program is the advisory board, a collection of more than seventy marketing professionals working for a wide range of companies across the United States and abroad, from the Coca-Cola Company to the E&J Gallo Winery, from IBM to General Motors, from Hallmark to Intel to Nokia. The board meets twice annually to discuss recruiting, the marketing curriculum, and other related issues. Most importantly, these advisory board members provide the financial support for student scholarships that pay for nine months of intensive course work in statistical methods, data collection, problem solving, ethics, multivariate methods, and other research topics. Later, most of these students are offered full-time employment by an advisory board firm.

In addition to publishing cutting-edge marketing research and turning out quality graduates, the college has also made a renewed effort to meet the changing needs of the marketing research industry. In March 2002, for example, the Terry College and the American Marketing Association hosted the first Customer Relationship Management (CRM) Leadership Program in Atlanta. Led by more than a dozen academic and executive speakers, the three-day program versed executives in the essentials of creating and shaping CRM strategic plans, data warehousing, and personalization technologies to more effectively serve customers.

REVITALIZING PROGRAMMING: ESTABLISHING TERRY'S SECOND BEACHHEAD

Beyond the need to gain a foothold in Atlanta, one of the central conclusions of Terry College's strategic plan was that an urgent need existed for a much broader and larger set of MBA programs in order to serve the city's growing corporate community. To meet this charge, the college has refocused its energy in three very specific graduate programs: the executive MBA, the evening MBA, and the Director's College.

Executive MBA Education

One of the primary needs identified in the Atlanta metropolitan region was for executive development of professionals with ten to twenty years of work experience. To serve them, Terry College created an eighteen-month program for working executives, which enrolled its first cohort in September of 2001. Fully one-half the coursework in the Executive MBA Program is delivered via the Internet. Participants attend classroom sessions all day Friday and Saturday one weekend per month and interact with faculty and fellow students between sessions via distance-learning technologies. The program has proven so popular that interest in the second year's program rose by 50 percent.

The program's unique course design involves completion of ten modules:

- seven nine-week modules in Core Business Knowledge and Application, which are taught both on-line and during twenty-one weekend sessions in Atlanta

- two week-long modules in Leadership, taught on the college's Athens campus
- a concluding two-week international residency, spent traveling through various foreign countries to familiarize students with the global marketplace

The on-line component is where Terry has really separated itself from most other executive programs. Using a series of electronic presentations, threaded group discussions, and synchronous chats, students learn one-half of the course content, which takes in such topics as managerial finance, Internet technology and strategy, economic analysis, and operations management.

Feedback from Atlanta-area executives has been overwhelmingly positive. "I researched a number of executive MBA programs in Atlanta and found the Terry EMBA to possess the ideal combination of convenient location and modern classroom technology," explains Tucker Ramsey, Director of International Sales for Nth Degree. "With my hectic schedule, every minute counts. The program's central location at the Atlanta Financial Center fits my needs perfectly."

Terry offers several custom-designed MBA programs for working professionals as well, including one for employees of IBM's consulting division and another for those at the U.S. Department of Energy's Savannah River Site near Aiken, South Carolina. The IBM MBA program illustrates the extent to which programs can be modified to meet student needs. In fall 1998, the Terry College launched a customized, revenue-generating, two-year MBA program for employees of PwC Consulting (at that time, a division of PricewaterhouseCoopers, which has subsequently been acquired by IBM) wishing to further develop their careers. The program disseminates specialized coursework through technology-enabled interactions among faculty and approximately forty students each year, from across North America, who learn in virtual teams.

Students begin by spending two weeks at the University of Georgia campus in Athens, building camaraderie and learning to work together in teams that are organized according to students' home time zones; this allows for smoother team communication. Over the next twelve months they learn interactively, via e-mail, chat groups, on-line case discussions, and other electronic communications. (They continue working as full-time IBM consultants throughout the degree program.) The teams return to Athens for three four-day weekends of classroom instruction. During the program's second year, students return to campus again for an intensive week of course work, plus four additional four-day weekends. The program has become so successful that Terry is applying its best features to the full-time MBA programs, as well.

Evening MBA Program

Gwinnett County, in the northeastern corner of the Atlanta metropolitan area, is one of Georgia's largest, fastest-growing, and most diverse counties. Yet, it lacks a four-year college or university. To address the need for graduate business education in the county, the Terry College started a part-time Evening MBA Program, which operates out of the new high-tech Gwinnett University Center campus near Lawrenceville. This campus is a joint venture between the University of Georgia and Georgia Perimeter College. Most students attend two three-hour classes each term, achieving the MBA in as little as eight semesters.

"While the other programs I researched were accommodating, they couldn't beat the deal or convenience of the Terry program," points out Ken Holbrooks, an Evening MBA student and executive at United General Industries/Touchstone Homes.

The Director's College

The summer before the Enron debacle, the Terry College, in conjunction with the National Association of Corporate Directors (NACD), began offering short courses for existing board members—as well as accomplished senior executives who aspire to board service—at the UGA Alumni Club Center in Atlanta's Buckhead neighborhood.

Aimed at helping current or prospective board members develop the skills and insight needed to effectively monitor and guide corporate performance, these semiannual, two-day seminars include plenary sessions on such issues as warning signs of a troubled company, quality of financial reporting, and emerging issues and litigation trends. Smaller groups break out for seminar sessions. Additional specialized one-day programs for Audit Committee and Compensation Committee members are also offered. While the initial program was well received, post-Enron sessions were wildly successful.

In January 2002, this program received accreditation from Institutional Shareholder Services (ISS), the nation's leading provider of proxy voting services and other corporate governance services, making it the first program of this kind in the South to receive such accreditation.

LEADING EXAMPLES: A NEW TERRY INSTITUTE DEVELOPS TOMORROW'S LEADERS

Closely linked to the quality of any institution's executive education is the quality of its leadership training. The Terry College believes that leadership, after all, is more than simply good management; it is a combination of strategic thinking, technical knowledge, tolerance for ambiguity, and an ability to communicate persuasively. Thus, an emphasis on leadership became Terry's third beachhead.

To operationalize its understanding of leadership, Terry created the Institute of Leadership Advancement (ILA) in May 2000 with the approval of the University of Georgia Board of Regents, and more than $6 million in generous gifts and pledges from alumni, friends, and foundations. The Institute's substantial undergraduate leadership development programs complement MBA-level courses, seminars, and a speaker series, as well as a program of research and publication. Taken as a whole, ILA is already proving to be a vital cross-departmental force in leadership education and research.

For example, the MBA Leadership Program includes seminars on such topics as team development, understanding personal leadership styles, and presentation skills. Similarly, the Executive Leadership Program, begun in October 2000, offers managers periodic four-day training programs on the Terry College campus in Athens. Team-taught by approximately ten faculty, each course combines instruction in leadership skills, team-building exercises, a "360-degree" evaluation of each attendee's unique leadership skills and challenges, and one-on-one coaching for each participant. "[This] was, without a doubt, the most worthwhile conference I have attended during my twenty-year business career," commented Marty Miller, a Coca-Cola executive and one of the participants in the fall 2000 pilot program. "[It] gave me insights about my own leadership style, as well as the styles of others, that I use every day both personally and professionally."

Likewise, the Leadership Speaker Series brings top executives from companies, such as Georgia Power, Primerica Financial Services, and Home Depot to campus for discussions about issues surrounding effective leadership in today's business environment. In addition, thanks to a generous gift from the Columbus, Georgia–based Bradley-Turner Foundation, the college recently created the newly endowed Synovus Chair in Servant Leadership, reflecting Terry's deep commitment to the idea that leaders must always strive to improve others' lives. And, very soon, the Leadership Research Consortium will begin disseminating new research. With help from ten to fifteen corporate partners, this research arm expects to publish a biannual newsletter and host roundtable seminars on current leadership topics. "What I see in this Institute is that it combines the expertise of the Terry College with a specific program to develop leadership at all levels," says Drew Hamilton, a retired State Farm Insurance executive. "That's very unusual and special."

TERRY'S FOURTH BEACHHEAD: HIGH TIME FOR HIGH TECH

Terry College has made extensive use of technology to infuse its programs with flexibility. For instance, it has created a new Master of Internet

Technology degree. This two-semester, full-time program is taught by an interdisciplinary team that draws on the faculty and resources of the college's top-ranked Department of Management Information Systems, as well as the University of Georgia's Computer Science Department. It's a good example of how to break down the silos of separated departments within a business college or university. This master's degree program requires students to complete team projects during which they develop Internet-based solutions for client organizations seeking to expand their business opportunities.

PLANNING FOR A BRIGHT FUTURE

Terry continues to expand upon the inroads it has made to date and look for ways to build on its strengths. For example, the college is transitioning to a professional school model of undergraduate education, whereby undergraduate students will be admitted on a competitive basis to the Terry College as juniors rather than as freshmen. At the same time, the college is managing enrollment more efficiently by decreasing the size of undergraduate business classes. This will enable Terry to improve the learning environment for undergraduate students and simultaneously transfer more resources to graduate programs and executive education. In the process, the total number of Terry juniors and seniors should decrease from 3,600 to approximately 2,000.

Similarly, the college's international program offerings continue to grow. The Terry@Oxford program brings twenty-five Terry undergraduates to one of the world's top universities each summer. The University of Georgia is the only public U.S. university to own a residence facility at Oxford. Students pursue international economics and also experience Europe through tours of cheese factories, diamond factories, flower auctions, and the like. Similarly, several programs in Spain integrate upper-level Spanish and business classes for approximately thirty Terry students each year. And a new program in Italy will explore the relationships among the recent economic development of Europe, changes in communications technology, and art history.

The Terry College is developing more MBA consulting projects with foreign corporations, similar to the successful pilot project with Deutsche Telekom (DT) in Germany. In May 2002, four Terry College MBA students traveled to Bonn, Germany, for three weeks to consult for the international telecommunications giant. The firm asked the students to help develop potential market strategies for wireless communications services in the United States. After fulfilling their residencies, members of the team returned home to execute a telecom market survey they developed and to run a series of focus groups before preparing a final report for DT.

"Deutsche Telekom really wanted an American point of view," said Marc Lipson, Director of Terry College International Programs, "and I think this program was useful to the company for that reason. Of course, it was also thrilling for our MBA students to sit at a table with top managers of such a large and important telecommunications company—and have those managers listen!" Based on successes like these, the college is developing faculty and student links with educational institutions in Asia and Latin America. Terry sees no end to the international opportunities. The principal challenge will be to continue cultivating only those exchanges and partnerships that prove greatly beneficial to Terry faculty and students.

Finally, the college plans to grow its PhD program's resources, particularly its fellowships and assistantships. The PhD is presently awarded in eight separate academic disciplines at Terry; the college plans to better regulate the flow of students and resources so that higher-performing departments are properly funded and rewarded.

Georgia's Terry College has come a long way in a relatively short period. As Andy Barksdale (MBA 1993), executive director of marketing for Cingular Wireless, puts it: "It is truly amazing what can happen when you combine a rich history, a wonderful faculty, a solid vision, and leadership support." Indeed, "The Terry College has never been as visible, influential, and powerful."

8

College of Management at Georgia Tech: A College Positioned for a Compelling Opportunity

Terry C. Blum and Nathan Bennett

Atlanta is a great city for business and business education. Students find it an exciting place to live. Faculty members and their families find the city very livable and supportive of dual-career households. Located in the heart of mid-town Atlanta, Georgia Institute of Technology is a bustling urban campus. But, unlike many metropolitan universities, where part-time enrollments often outpace full-time, some 15,000 students, for the most part, attend full-time. (Part-time enrollment typically includes fewer than 1,000 students.) University-wide, 4,500 graduate students participate in technologically focused master's and doctoral programs. Twenty-five to 30 percent of all students are women and 36 percent (5,340) are either international or U.S. minority students.

The College of Management in many ways mirrors this profile. In any given year, virtually all of our 1,400 undergraduate and 250 graduate students attend full-time. Our areas of curricular innovation and research—technological entrepreneurship and commercialization, management of change and innovation, financial performance and analysis, managing the extended value chain, and enterprise globalization—reflect the strong strategic alignment of our programs and research efforts with our strategic direction, which in turn reflects and supports that of Georgia Tech, as a whole.

Today, our college sits at the cusp of opportunity, poised for greatness. Since its establishment roughly ninety years ago, the college's focus has at least partially revolved around building an international reputation for its ability to prepare business leaders for changing technological environments. Over this same period of time, however, various combinations of limited resources, organizational impediments, and seemingly insurmountable leadership challenges kept the college from realizing its potential. All this has changed. A majority of alumni, students, and faculty agree that right now the alignment of strategy, structure, resources, and environmental characteristics provides an opportunity for our college that is both compelling and exciting.

Georgia Tech and our college are fortunate to have a strong faculty and very bright students. Over the past ten years, these faculty and students have cocreated a learning environment that produces sought-after graduates. This is our story. It is one of promise about a very good college on the rise.

CONTEXT: THE COLLEGE
OF MANAGEMENT TODAY

The College of Management is staffed by approximately forty-five tenure-track faculty and thirty-five professional staff. Faculty salaries and benefits are quite competitive, and the three-semester course per year teaching load is very attractive. The college is guided in many activities by its recently reconstructed Corporate Advisory Board. The Board numbers approximately forty-five members; most are from the Southeast, though others come from New York, Florida, Colorado, and California. Many are alumni of the college; others are alumni from other parts of Georgia Tech; some are also alumni of the nation's most prestigious MBA programs. Advisory board members serve on one of six subcommittees that focus on key aspects of the college: Alumni Relations, Career Services, Development, Public Relations/Marketing, Executive Education, and the new Building at Technology Square. Committees participate in two status sessions a year with faculty-staff liaisons to ensure consistent communication and that activities in these areas are in alignment with the college's strategic plan.

Because we are a state school, most of our teaching resources support our Bachelor of Science in Management (BSM) degree. We do not have separate admissions requirements for the college; students apply to and are admitted to the Institute. Though the numbers are increasing, we historically have enrolled relatively few freshmen as management majors; most come to us as transfers from other parts of the institute or from other universities. Over time, enrollment in the BSM program has been a bit cyclical. For instance in 1988, we had roughly 1,600 undergraduate majors. That number declined by some 200 students in 1989 because the economics major was taken away from the management school and became its own school. We experienced further declines in majors in subsequent years to a low point in 1994 when we had just over 900 majors. Since 1995, we have experienced consistent growth. Fall 2002 enrollment stood at 1,500 undergraduates.

In addition to the BSM, we offer several graduate degrees. Our primary graduate degree is the MBA. Until the summer of 2002, this degree was called the Master of Science in Management (MSM). At one point in time, the MSM designation was considered important in differentiating between the content and the nature of our curriculum and that offered by other schools. In fact, one of our most recognizable strengths, over time, has been that we graduate individuals who are highly skilled at identifying ways for their employers to turn technology into a sustainable source of competitive advantage.

However, since the MBA degree is now the internationally recognized "industry standard" for master's-level graduate business programs, the change to MBA seemed appropriate. The technical focus of our curriculum and our commitment to preparing business leaders for changing technological environments has not changed. Our MBA program focuses on the nexus of technology and management. It is a full-time, sixty-credit program that combines a broad-based graduate business education with extensive use and understanding of the high-tech environment. We encourage students with diverse academic and career experiences to apply for the program. For instance, recent classes include students with undergraduate degrees in art history, marketing, chemical engineering, and architecture. Because of this diversity, required classes provide students with a general business background that enables them to select their concentration and electives to complement their desired career paths. As a fundamental part of our approach to education, we encourage students to learn from each other's backgrounds and experiences as well as from the faculty and visiting business leaders in and out of the classroom.

The MBA enrolls roughly one hundred new students each year. The program acceptance rate is 40 percent, with about one-half of those accepted officially entering the program. Typically, the average new student has a 3.2 undergraduate GPA, the majority with degrees in engineering or basic sciences. The average GMAT score is 640, the typical work experience is just over four years; and roughly one-half of the students are from out of state. About 25 percent of our MBA students are women; 38 percent carry international status; 12 percent are minority students. Historically, our placement upon graduation and at three months after graduation are comparable with the best business schools in the country. At the same time, the return on investment for our students is extremely high. We have plans to aggressively grow this program, without compromising on student qualifications.

Key among the program's goals are an insistence that students leave the program with a solid understanding of the social, economic, and political environments of global business and what it takes to manage across international borders. In addition, the program encourages the development of social, ethical, legal, and professional standards upon which students can build after graduation. Faculty in this program also push students to refine their abilities to listen, speak, and write; to present information to others; to engage in constructive criticism and problem solving; and to hone their skills at working effectively and creatively in diverse groups as team members or leaders. Above all else, Georgia Tech programs leverage the technical and quantitative basis of education at the institution to provide students with an appreciation of the impact and implications of rapidly changing technology in organizations and on society, in general.

One of the ways this is accomplished is through interdisciplinary initiatives: The environment at Tech is extremely supportive of collaboration. The most recent evidence of this is the Master of Science in Quantitative and Computational Finance degree, offered jointly by the College of Management, the College of Science, and the School of Industrial and Systems Engineering.

The College of Management also involves MBA students in community service activities that are coordinated by the MBA Community Service Organization. For example, groups of MBA students have participated in Habitat for Humanity home construction projects and "Hands on Atlanta" volunteer projects.

In addition to the traditional MBA, the college began formally developing executive education offerings in the mid-1990s. An Office of Executive and Professional Programs was established in 1994 to offer nondegree, open enrollment programs and custom programs. Our first Executive Master of Science in the Management of Technology (EMSMOT) class was enrolled in 1995. In total, these programs produce revenues of about $4 million per year. The Executive Master's program includes a core curriculum that approximates one found in an executive MBA program, but with an emphasis on cases and applications that are oriented toward technology-driven enterprises. The course work beyond the core is focused on the management of technology and innovation. A typical EMSMOT class has approximately forty students. These students are thirty-five years old, on average, and possess thirteen years of professional experience. Women make up 14 percent; 21 percent carry minority status. Our executive programs are very important to us because of the role they play in developing relationships with the corporate world, producing discretionary income, and helping us establish and promote our reputation. As the college grows and moves forward, these programs will continue to be of strategic importance.

One important element of our strategy is to build on Georgia Tech's strong reputation in various engineering disciplines. To this end, we partner with colleagues in the College of Engineering on a number of initiatives. For example, we are striving to meet as much of the demand from their students for our classes as is possible. At this point, about 25 percent of the seats in management classes are taken as electives by students in engineering, sciences, computing, and architecture. We also enroll engineering graduates with internship or co-op experiences in our MBA program, with less full-time, permanent work experience than we would expect from other applicants. Finally, we are developing a specialized, joint-degree program, the Master of Science in Management and Engineering. Students in this program will take specially tailored management classes (thirty-nine credit-hours) and engineering classes (thirty hours) over the course of approximately sixteen months. Such interdisciplinary collaboration is a hallmark of Georgia Tech.

The College of Management's PhD program is designed to develop scholars who are capable of making original contributions to their chosen fields. The college offers a flexible program, involving in-depth study in the functional areas of finance, information technology, marketing, operations management, accounting, strategy, or organizational behavior. While most graduates undertake careers as teachers, scholars, and researchers working within academic environments, the doctoral degree can lead to careers in industry and government. The program is limited to full-time students and is strongly research oriented, emphasizing early and effective involvement in research. Students experience considerable personal attention as well as close interaction with faculty.

The college currently enrolls twenty-eight students in this program. Admissions standards are highly selective with students averaging 670 on the GMAT. A typical student is thirty-one years old and has 6.5 years work experience. Slightly fewer than one-third of the PhD cohort are female. Given its size, the tutorial model is the primary educational approach employed throughout the program. In sum, the PhD program plays an important role in developing a vibrant intellectual environment that encourages exploration, innovative thinking, and the creation and dissemination of new knowledge. As a result, the program is crucial to achieving our overall strategic goals.

IN THE BEGINNING: OUR ANCIENT HISTORY

Georgia Tech was established in 1888 as the Georgia School of Technology. That year, five professors and five shop supervisors began by offering a Bachelor in Mechanical Engineering to 129 students, one from each Georgia county. In 1912, a School of Commerce, the precursor to the current business school, was created to provide business education to Georgia Tech students. In 1933, the newly created Board of Regents consolidated Georgia's system of higher education, and the School of Commerce was moved to the University of Georgia in Athens. However, in response to student activism that culminated in a march downtown led by commerce student Ivan Allen (who later became the mayor of Atlanta during the civil rights era), an industrial management program was established at Georgia Tech to meet the need for management training in a technical environment. A Master of Science in Industrial Management, the first professional management degree in the state of Georgia, was established in 1945. In 1969, the School of Industrial Management was renamed the College of Industrial Management. The professional degree was renamed the Master of Science in Management (MSM) in 1985, and in fall 2002 became the MBA. The PhD program was established in 1970.

INTO TROUBLED WATERS: OUR MORE RECENT HISTORY

In 1989, the College of Management, along with the other nonengineering units on campus, was reorganized into one unit by the then university president. The College of Management became a school within the Ivan Allen College of Management, Policy, and International Affairs. Other academic units reorganized into the Ivan Allen College included economics (formerly part of the Management College), the humanities, and the social sciences. This structure was less than optimal for the aspirations of the different units in the new college. The structure was particularly problematic for the management school because the units with which the management school was now aligned carried little prestige in the engineering dominated environment. This amalgamation did not produce a whole greater than the sum of its parts. Rather, at best it led to a regression toward the mean. In essence, the reorganization seemed to have as its primary goal the combination of underresourced units, not the promotion of academic programs.

From 1989 to 1999, the School of Management had a dean in name only. The dean of the management school's position was analogous to that of the chairs in the other schools in the new college and school or department chairs in peer business colleges across the country. As a consequence, the Ivan Allen College dean had to manage relationships among a collection of school chairs and a uniquely titled, yet internally unrecognized, "school dean." This collection of school administrators was quite heterogeneous in terms of goals, aspirations, and needs; and the college dean found himself combating perpetual conflict over resource questions (e.g., the different market demands on new faculty salaries and research support and widely varied professional norms regarding tenure and promotion) and curriculum issues. Consequently, the management school dean and his faculty felt their views were not effectively communicated to the top administrative levels of the institute. They found it frustrating that decisions made locally tended to be suboptimal because of the diverse and fragmented collection of the units that together constituted the Ivan Allen College. An additional consequence of this flawed organizational structure was that the management school dean position was untenable and difficult to fill.

During this ten-year period, the School of Management was led for one year by an acting director, followed by an interim dean (who also served as the interim dean of the Ivan Allen College) with a two-year stint, a one-year interim dean (who also served as the dean of the Ivan Allen College), a permanent dean who took the position for three years, and, finally, an acting dean who served for three years. Despite the personal qualities, capabilities, and efforts of those who held the school dean position, a social construction of reality of "interim leadership" developed, whereby opportunities to advocate for students and faculty tended to at first not be seized and ultimately to not be available. Also, ongoing interim candidates and the uncertainties about the future created an environment where even the weakest oppositional force became a loud voice of dissention.

In spite of the turmoil and change, the faculty continuously provided high-quality educational programs, remained active in research, attracted bright, well-prepared students, and satisfied recruiters who were interested in our graduates. Fortunately, the professional staff that supports the graduate and undergraduate programs experienced little turnover. This contributed to program stability. Importantly, the directors of each program have remained in place for over fifteen years. Consequently, they were successful in protecting the programs for which they were responsible from the instability at the top of the organization.

That said, however, the chronic temporary leadership and the concomitant instability of resources led to a sense of being "home alone." The world of business education was not standing still, yet it was difficult to secure investments in our future when it was unclear whom or what the future would entail. There was also underlying conflict among the faculty and later the graduate students, which led to a final reorganization.

This last reorganization, marked by the restoration of the school to college status, served as a launching point for our future. In some ways, we view our present position as akin to that of a "spin-off" from an established organization in that we have considerable momentum and are well resourced, but at the same time we carry historical institutional baggage.

The positive consequence of our tumultuous past is that the long period of instability has made it all the more clear to constituents today that much time has already been wasted; that indeed, we must make all we can of the opportunity we have been given.

THE HISTORY WE ARE MAKING TODAY

In 1998, the College of Management joined Georgia Tech's five other colleges—the Colleges of Architecture, Sciences, Engineering, and Computing, and the Ivan Allen College—with equal standing. During summer 1999, a newly appointed dean convened the faculty to start a strategic planning process. In the first meeting, we assessed our strengths and weaknesses as well as our opportunities and threats. These were presented, along with the plans of the other five colleges, to all academic deans, Tech's president, and his direct reports at a retreat in August 1999.

Our mission statement, strategic plan, and tagline, although continually revisited and refined, were completed early in the new administration in part because of the looming deadline for the self-study for our AACSB reaccreditation. To accelerate the process and its acceptance, faculty were divided into four groups, which also included staff and student representatives. All faculty members were invited to participate in a group, though not all did. Four faculty members were recruited by the dean to lead the groups and serve as links in the overall coordination effort led through the dean's office. The plans were communicated to student leaders and to faculty through email, and efforts were made to gain constructive input. Before the plan was given to the public relations/communications office for printing and dissemination, meetings were held with the group leaders, as well as other representatives, including the college's external advisory board, to ensure that the plan was a consensus document and reflected the input of constituent groups.

The agreed-upon mission statement is as follows:

> The College of Management at Georgia Institute of Technology strives for excellence in traditional business education while focusing on the multi-disciplinary areas of management of technology, international business, and entrepreneurial and innovative processes. We pursue the creation of new knowledge and the training of scholars to further the science and practice of management. We are committed to being a recognized leader in developing business leaders to operate in changing technological environments.

Faculty, students, and staff also agreed on a tagline: "Preparing business leaders for changing technological environments."

It is already evident that a consistent focus on the now-refined niches of technological entrepreneurship and commercialization, management of change and innovation, financial performance and analysis, managing the extended value chain, and enterprise globalization is extremely useful in helping us evolve. These focus areas have affected the type of faculty that have been recruited and hired, the way we have designed and developed curriculum and certificate programs, the manner in which we have presented ourselves to students and recruiters, and the way we have educated students. Most importantly, there is consensus that we should achieve recognition through branding and a niche strategy of areas where we have strengths in our faculty and in the larger university. To this end, we have been able to effectively capitalize on access to corporate giants located in Atlanta, promote a technology incubator that is associated with the college, and actively engage collaboratively with members of five other Georgia universities in the Faculty Research Commercialization Program to increase the number of new businesses in the state.

In addition, we have been able to focus on acquiring and deploying resources consistent with the realization of our strategic plan, with faculty recruitment a high priority. Fifty percent of the tenure track/tenured faculty members have joined the college since fall 2000; and we anticipate faculty recruitment into the future at all ranks and in all areas. Currently, 14 percent of the faculty members are female; 27 percent can be classified as international or minority. In the 2001–2002 academic year, 20 percent of the management faculty held endowed chairs or professorships. Fundraising efforts in the future will focus on increasing the number of such positions, with a particular emphasis on providing support packages to retain outstanding associate professors. Finally, we have succeeded in planning and financing a new $53 million building, composed of the business college, an executive education center, and flexible space to accommodate emerging interdisciplinary research areas. The building was ready for occupancy in summer 2003.

THE FUTURE: TECHNOLOGY SQUARE

When the business school was elevated to college status and the new college leadership was established in summer 1999, we had no plans for a new building (although one was sorely needed), nor any potential for one on the horizon. Though the institute's vice president for business was interested in extending the Georgia Tech campus into the adjacent, booming Midtown area, any plans that were considered did not include the business school. Those plans that were being explored for the campus extension included a 250-room hotel, retail space, a conference center, and continuing education center, but no academic building.

In summer 1999, the situation changed. We invited the institute's business vice president to tour our current facility. He was the first member of the top administration to come to the building for many years. Surprised at the poor condition of the building's interior, he commented that our current facility did not look nearly as bad from the outside and suggested that it was no way for a quality business school to do business, especially one with high aspirations and expectations to do even better.

Even the initial project that he envisioned, without the business college, needed the support of management alumni who were in important positions at the Georgia Tech Foundation. This support was important because the trustees would have to float bonds to fund the project, which is being privately financed in its entirety. To gain their support, we agreed that Georgia Tech needed to incorporate the business college on the acreage.

In addition to helping the institution garner support from the Foundation, adding the business college to the site accomplished another objective. It provided a way to get enough students across the interstate to support retail that would be there and to create a vibrant, full-time extension of the campus.

The campus expansion project is now called Technology Square. The $210 million complex includes a hotel and conference center, a global learning center for continuing and distance education, the College of Management, the institute bookstore, other retail space, and parking. In quick order, its design was completed and ground was broken. We designed the new building while we were going through the process of developing and enhancing our strategic plan. We realized that we were in an interactive situation where the building and our programs together could be greater than the sum of their parts.

Our part of the project is built over retail space, including the campus bookstore, managed by Barnes and Noble. Our teaching and administrative area house undergraduate and graduate offices, faculty offices, classrooms, seminar rooms, lounges, serendipitous learning spaces, behavioral and communications labs, a trading floor, career services offices, and interview rooms. An astonishing executive education facility has tiered and subdividable classrooms, meeting and office space, and numerous breakout rooms. The third module houses the college's interdisciplinary research centers.

We are serious about our tagline of preparing business leaders for changing technological environments. Our mission has us focusing on excellence in the functional areas of business but also looking at the larger context of Georgia Tech for areas in which we can really excel. These include management of technology (which incorporates the extended enterprise and value chain under the rubric of business enhancement through technology); innovation and technology entrepreneurship, including change management and leadership; and global investments and analysis of financial performance, which encompasses our accounting risk analyses, the Center for International Business Education and Research, and the Georgia Tech/Fortis Conference on International Finance.

Our new home is the first Leadership in Energy and Environment Design (LEED) project certified by the U.S. Green Building Council on our campus. Nationally only a few hundred certified projects exist. Our design and construction eliminate the negative impact of buildings on the environment and building occupants by emphasizing sustainable site planning, safeguarding water, promoting energy efficiency and renewability, fostering conservation of materials and resources, and enhancing indoor environmental quality. This "green" building complements the larger strategic plan of Georgia Tech and also the state's plans for economic development in sustainable environmental technology. In addition, it also encourages interdisciplinary collaboration to create a curriculum that focuses on sustainability.

The design of the new building encourages collaborations that might not otherwise occur. The connective space between our faculty offices and the interdisciplinary spaces houses all of our interdisciplinary programs, which adjoin each other, a Shared-Idea Laboratory, and a program on interdisciplinary technology innovation. The space allotted for the interdisciplinary centers is proposed as rotating space. The notion is to continually update and upgrade the focus of these initiatives to enhance the mission, visibility, and reputation of the business college. The space will be heavily competed for, and that competition will push the envelope repeatedly as space wars on the campus continue.

Within the interdisciplinary space, we will house teams of management and law students, who will use us as their laboratory for studying and building intellectual property and business models. Doctoral students in engineering and science will also participate. These groups of students and faculty will develop a two-year innovation program that will enable engineering and science students to engage in dissertation topics with commercial possibilities but are not tied to industry-sponsored incremental research.

Finally, Technology Square is happening within the context of urban renewal in Atlanta's Midtown area. The area is becoming a technology corridor, with major businesses, as well as new technology start-ups, locating there. The university-affiliated incubator, the Advanced Technology Development Center, will be housed across the street from the college, along with the State of Georgia's "Yamacraw" facility, which will house the "State-wide Design on a Chip" initiative. In reality, the buildings next to the business college will become our laboratories and the businesses that occupy them our partners in student education through providing internships and engaging in sponsored projects.

CONCLUSION

The new facility we enthusiastically anticipate is more than a bricks and mortar vision. The strong statement made by the facility will do a great deal to get all on board; the story is really one about vision, heart, and soul. Inadequate space can sometimes limit the imagination and discourage access to those who are needed to fulfill the dreams. In contrast, new buildigns provide opportunities to do things in the curriculum, executive education, outreach, and interdisciplinary venues. The opportunities presented by the new building enable a new vision through a new lens that opens vistas with no boundaries.

9

Georgia State's J. Mack Robinson College of Business: Reinventing Business Education in the Twenty-first Century

Gary W. McKillips and Rhonda Mullen

The symbolic heart of Atlanta sits at a place where cattle paths once met at an artesian well. Five Points, as the area is known, has emerged as the hub of transportation and communications in the Southeast. Located near the southernmost terminus of the first rail line to Chattanooga, this epicenter now serves a network of road, rails, and air routes. Similarly, Atlanta, the financial and commercial capital of the Southeast, serves as a crossroads in the information superhighway. This metropolitan nexus is home to some of the nation's most successful companies, including Bell South, Coca-Cola, Equifax, Home Depot, and UPS. It is the place where the best ideas in business converge. It is also home to the J. Mack Robinson College of Business at Georgia State University.

Like Five Points itself, Robinson has a long history as a crossroads of business knowledge and education. Here, the brightest emerging students cross paths with a preeminent business faculty that the *Academy of Management Journal* ranks as the best in the nation for research productivity. Here, too, scholars who serve as consultants to the nation's top *Fortune* 500 companies interact with alumni who are themselves corporate CEOs, successful entrepreneurs, and government officials. At Robinson, the classroom, the boardroom, and the community converge to shape the future of business.

Robinson College of Business is the sixth largest business school in the United States with more than two hundred faculty and eight thousand students (roughly one-fourth of Georgia State's total student population). *BusinessWeek* calls Robinson College's Executive MBA the twentieth best in the world. *Forbes* lists the college as one of the best regional buys for schools that cost less than $95,000. *U.S. News & World Report*'s annual survey ranks the school's Flexible MBA program first among all public institutions and fifth among all institutions. The college has retained a place in this national survey's top ten programs since 1997.

Within the Robinson College, areas of excellence cross-fertilize the curriculum, producing a strong academic core. Specializations that have garnered national attention include Risk Management and Insurance, Accounting, Management Information Systems, Real Estate, eCommerce, Hospitality Administration, Marketing, Finance, Entrepreneurship, Management, and Health Services Administration. The college also makes available a variety of boundary-spanning courses known as career track concentrations. These options enable Robinson MBA students to select a combination of state-of-the-art courses that cut across traditional business disciplines (e.g., international business and information services or international entrepreneurship). In addition, universities and business schools around the world collaborate with the Robinson faculty to offer joint degrees and programs. And businesspeople with years of experience return to Robinson's classrooms when they need additional specialized training and updated business skills. Dean Sidney E. Harris describes the Robinson College as "results oriented. Our faculty are expert at teaching business models and concepts that can be immediately adapted for use in the real world of business."

MAKING THE MOVE TO GREATNESS

Harris joined the Robinson College as dean in 1997. During his tenure, he reformulated the strategic direction of the college, provided leadership for a fundraising campaign, and launched new research initiatives. Under his tutelage, two distinct qualities—programs that take an applied, practical approach to learning and organizational agility—came to distinguish Robinson from its competitors. In the first instance, Robinson faculty members are scholars with practical experience, which they share with students to enhance the learning experience. They network with colleagues throughout the world and produce a portfolio of internationally respected research in the fields of e-commerce, entrepreneurship, marketing, and others. They lecture regularly from the southern tip of the world to the economic capitals of Europe to the remote interior of Asia. In addition, a hallmark of all programs at the Robinson College is peer learning. Students themselves bring a wealth of managerial experience to the classroom, which they share with each other. They not only learn from peers but also develop long-lasting ties that become part of their business networks.

In the second instance, Robinson's leaders recognize that today's business environment is one of constant flux, affected by globalization, technology, changing markets, and shorter product life cycles. To retain its sharp business edge, the college encourages experimentation, knowledge sharing, and an outside focus. "Businesses, and business schools, too, have to experiment now, to be innovators, to be willing to reinvent what worked yesterday." This statement, made by Dean Harris, typifies sentiment on campus.

REINVENTING EXECUTIVE EDUCATION

Innovation and adaptation are trademarks of executive education at the Robinson College of Business. The Executive MBA (EMBA) program—designed for business professionals with at least seven to ten years of experience—brings together groundbreaking theories, case studies, technological skills, and practical, real-world contexts. The innovative and comprehensive curriculum gives executives a competitive advantage as they navigate today's complex business environment.

Recognizing the growing importance of globalization, each of the classes in the Executive MBA program includes discussions of international theories and practices. Supporting this international focus is a two-week study tour abroad. Prior to the learning visit, each study team prepares a paper on one of the companies featured on the tour in locations such as Japan, Malaysia, Singapore, Hong Kong, China, and Argentina. Hosting executives receive a copy of the paper before students arrive, and the contents of the paper are a subject of discussion during the visit.

The global component of the EMBA program is also enhanced by faculty who bring with them extraordinary levels of experience and expertise. One such faculty member is Bob Oxnam, Robinson Global Scholar and one of the world's leading authorities on the Far East. He is responsible for organizing and facilitating the international component of Robinson's Executive MBA program. Oxnam, director emeritus of the Asia Society in New York, is a teacher, scholar, novelist, and former television commentator (for the *MacNeil-Lehrer News Hour*). He was also chosen to escort Bill

Gates and Warren Buffet to Asia. He brings a unique dimension to the Robinson EMBA experience.

Robinson's nondegree executive education courses, geared to the working professional who does not have the time to devote to the pursuit of a traditional MBA, offer high-quality, innovative educational responses to challenging business problems. From project management, strategic planning, negotiation skills, and finance to e-business models and processes, these courses, which range from one to six days, offer the tools needed to help participants build, and continually rebuild, competitive advantage. All executive education programs are taught at the Georgia State Alpharetta Center, a state-of-the-art classroom facility in North Atlanta, which also hosts many of Robinson's MBA degree classes.

AN MBA FOR WORKING PROFESSIONALS

Robinson's highly ranked Flexible MBA program provides an exceptional blend of innovative instruction and professional experience that is focused on contemporary, real-world business problems and issues. With Atlanta's business center serving as a learning laboratory, the program of study is enriched by opportunities and relationships fostered among faculty, student colleagues, and the business community.

The Flex MBA degree program is designed for individuals with work experience who aspire to organizational or entrepreneurial leadership positions. The program enhances general management abilities and provides an opportunity to place emphasis on a functional area of expertise. The primary objectives of the program are for students to develop and integrate

1. analytical skills for decision making that incorporate global, ethical, and culturally diverse dimensions.
2. skills in assessing organizational performance and developing approaches for improvement.
3. leadership skills.
4. interpersonal skills that contribute to teamwork.

The program allows students to pursue a course of study in general management in eighteen areas. Day, evening, and Saturday courses are offered for both full- and part-time students. The course schedule and degree timetable fit personal needs, and students can begin in any semester. Robinson College also offers specialized master's degrees in nine majors, and students have an array of choices for in-depth focus on a particular business discipline from Decision Sciences or Marketing to Risk Management and Insurance. The college awards specialized degrees in

Actuarial Science, Health Administration, International Business, Professional Accountancy, Taxation, and Real Estate. It also offers dual concentrations, which provide students with a cohesive set of courses relevant to a specific career path.

LEARNING FOR ENTREPRENEURS

Executive education and training are important parts of the college's overall program as well. To this end, Robinson places a great deal of emphasis on the entrepreneur. *SUCCESS* magazine named Robinson's entrepreneurship program among the nation's best, ranking it thirty-seven out of a total of fifty. Among public universities, the program is nineteenth, and it is the only entrepreneurship program in Georgia to be recognized.

Improving the chances of success for twenty-first century entrepreneurs is the goal of the Herman J. Russell, Sr. International Center for Entrepreneurship. The Russell Center provides innovative teaching, outreach, and research programs that advance the theory and practice of entrepreneurship. Programs focus on the lifelong learning needs of entrepreneurs, practitioners, and entrepreneurial organizations. The faculty's award-winning research on entrepreneurs and their companies ensures not only the creation of worldwide knowledge about entrepreneurs but also cutting-edge information for classroom instruction.

The Russell Entrepreneurship Center forms a vital link between the business community and the university. Through the Society of Entrepreneurs, faculty meet monthly with Atlanta's most successful innovators and growth-oriented companies. These business representatives, in turn, participate in educational programs, teach on campus, serve as judges of university competitions, provide sites for student internships, and hire graduates for their companies. Each fall, approximately twenty students participate in the Entrepreneurship Field Study Course, which places them in internships with an entrepreneurial focus in local companies.

The Moses Lee Reid Entrepreneurship Award competition for students recognizes an original business plan that demonstrates excellence in entrepreneurial innovation. The honor rewards innovative business ideas with a $5,000 annual prize and seeks to propel those ideas into the marketplace.

Entrepreneurship at the Robinson College brings together the synergies of the Russell Entrepreneurship Center, the Institute of International Business, and the eCommerce Institute. These groups strive for excellence, benefiting from the Zwerner Chair of Entrepreneurship and Family Business, established in 1987, as well as the Ramsey Chair of Private Enterprise, the first academic chair in the United States to focus on the study of entrepreneurship.

REACHING THE PINNACLE:
ROBINSON'S PHD PROGRAMS

Among Robinson's most elite graduate offerings is its doctoral program. Yearly, two to five students are admitted into each major (some programs do not admit students every year). Nine major areas of study are offered: accountancy, computer information systems, decision sciences, e-commerce, finance, strategic management, marketing, real estate, and risk management and insurance. All doctoral programs are exclusively full time and are designed for individuals who seek to develop a high competency in conducting research and teaching. In fact, 85 percent of these students publish prior to graduation. Students take, on average, five years to complete their degrees. All students are given teaching or research assistantships that are nationally competitive. The majority of Robinson doctoral graduates become professors. In the 2001–2002 academic year, Robinson graduated twenty doctoral students. To date the program boasts over nine hundred doctoral alumni. Incoming students take courses in methodology and statistics during the first year along with course work in their major area. The second year of study consists of specialized seminars in their areas of concentration. Some departments require course work in the third year. In any given year, Robinson enrolls about one hundred doctoral students; slightly over 40 percent are women. Almost one-half of all doctoral students carry international status. Robinson is a major participant in the PhD Project, which actively promotes the recruitment and support of minority students in doctoral studies in business. About 14 percent of the doctoral candidates are minority students.

GLOBAL CONNECTIONS

Anticipating the far-reaching implications of globalization, the Robinson College has strengthened its international presence. Today, it exhibits growing international stature. *U.S. News & World Report* ranks Robinson's international business program as the tenth best in the nation among public universities and twenty-third among all universities.

Academic programs are the cornerstone of international business education at Robinson, and the Master of International Business (MIB) degree is one of the college's premier offerings. It prepares students to become successful managers in a variety of global business specializations, including multinational corporate finance, international marketing, technology, international entrepreneurship, and worldwide operations management. Degree candidates achieve proficiency in a second language, enabling them to communicate in business settings in another country. A paid, supervised, international internship bridges classroom experience with the real world by placing students in international business settings and allowing them to test their business skills in uncharted territory. Interns tackle substantive assignments that directly impact the host firm's global strategy.

Robinson also provides opportunities for study experiences abroad that range from meeting the head of a cross-cultural firm to touring major industries in other countries to talking with workers in China, South Africa, Russia, or Latin America. These firsthand encounters give students an intimate understanding of doing business in a foreign country. Classes on the social, cultural, political, legal, and technological aspects of a foreign country augment students' visits.

In addition, an emphasis on international outreach has made new inroads in locations where there has been little previous interaction with American business models. For example, Robinson College's MBA for working professionals in the Caucasus region brings advanced business education to a nation just coming to grips with a market-based economy. In other regions, Robinson's programs and students overlap and spiral through each other like busy interchanges on an interstate. For example, study-abroad students travel to South and Sub-Saharan Africa, where the college also has grant programs providing business education and development for people throughout the region.

Similarly, the international program partners with several universities around the globe to offer dual degrees, joint MBAs, and study-abroad opportunities. These partner institutions include the Sorbonne in Paris, Posnan University in Poland, Group Ecole Superieure de Commerce in Toulouse, the University of Pretoria in South Africa, the Rotterdam School of Economics at Erasmus University, the Universidad del Salvador in Argentina, Cairo University in Egypt, and the Azerbaijan State Oil Academy in the former Soviet Republic. Two examples, one well-established and the other brand-new, provide concrete models of this type of enterprise. In the first instance, Robinson began offering a joint MBA with Cairo University in 1998. This program is supported through the Fulbright University Partnership Program and by Egyptian business leaders. Students enroll in core courses at Cairo University and then come to the United States to take their electives at Georgia State. The second example is a new initiative that spans three continents. Robinson teamed with leading business schools in Paris (the Sorbonne) and Rio de Janeiro (the COPPEAD Graduate School of Business, Federal University of Rio de Janeiro) to offer a new "global partners" MBA. The partnership launched classes in January 2004.

Through its Expanding Horizons program, Robinson draws Latin American business executives to Atlanta to participate in a range of business courses. The program gives a small group of fifteen to twenty managers tailored instruction with expert teachers, access to executives at

Atlanta's premier international companies, case studies of American companies and programs, and simultaneous interpretation. Led by faculty member David Bruce, Expanding Horizons has hosted Executive MBA classes from the Federal Universities of Pernambuco and Parana in Brazil, among others.

Robinson College also exports its successful international business models. For example, the Ron H. Brown Institute in Sub-Saharan Africa offers business training and skill development for people already in business in the region and those who aspire to enter the business world. One priority of the Ron Brown Institute—supported by the Robinson College, the Andrew Young School of Policy Studies at Georgia State, the University of Pretoria, and the Center for Scientific and Industrial Research in South Africa—is business promotion through workshops and seminars. The institute provides technical support for those who wish to develop business plans, secure financing, and establish new businesses.

A second project in South Africa seeks to develop institutional programs and faculty at the University of Venda, which serves some 8 million people in two of the country's poorest provinces. The labor market demand in the area is high for graduates trained in computer information systems, entrepreneurship, and hospitality—three areas in which the Robinson College excels.

Also in Africa, the College has been selected as the lead recipient of a $5 million grant from the United States Agency for International Development (USAID). The grant provides for tourism capacity development for Ghana.

A mecca for international students, Robinson College enrolls people from more than forty-seven countries. The Flex MBA alone draws students from thirty-eight countries, with Egypt, India, Germany, Turkey, and South Korea leading the list. International students make up more than 28 percent of the enrollment in specialized master's programs, hailing from twenty-three countries, including China, South Korea, India, Germany, Colombia, Jamaica, Taiwan, and Turkey. Some 53 percent of our PhD students are foreign nationals.

The International Business Alliance is a student organization dedicated to increasing awareness of international business opportunities and creating long-term relationships necessary to nurture those opportunities. The Robinson College serves as the headquarters for this multi-institution student consortium. Drawing on the vast cultural diversity and experience of Atlanta's academic institutions, as well as the business community, the alliance offers forums where members can interact and network with international business organizations. It supports mentoring programs, speaking engagements, seminars, internships, and cultural events.

BUSINESS IN A BRAVE NEW E-WORLD

To prepare leaders to navigate the challenges of the new business landscape, the Robinson College eCommerce Institute serves as an innovative, interdisciplinary unit that oversees education, research, and incubation projects related to the strategic use of technology. It has as its mission to discover, assimilate, facilitate, and disseminate knowledge regarding all facets of e-commerce. The institute acts as an outreach resource, providing information and assistance regarding e-commerce to a broad audience.

The eCommerce Institute reaches out to the community through the Center for Digital Commerce. The center, which helps shape the direction of electronic commerce for Atlanta and the state of Georgia, provides educational programs and expertise for companies that conduct e-commerce and assists the state legislature in formulating effective policies in this area.

"The Robinson College is a pacesetter for tomorrow's electronic business environment," says Dean Harris. "From our academic programs in electronic commerce to our outreach efforts with the Center for Digital Commerce, the Institute is educating and informing future business leaders and our community partners in this increasingly strategic and explosive area."

SIGNATURE PROGRAMS: ROBINSON REACHES OUT TO THE COMMUNITY

Robinson College has a long history of developing avant-garde programs that intricately link the university to its community. For instance, the college is the home to the Business Hall of Fame, honoring leaders who have distinguished themselves in both business and community service. The list of Hall of Fame inductees reads like a "Who's Who" of business and community leaders in the state of Georgia and the nation. Included are such notables as the late Roberto Goizueta, chairman and CEO of the Coca-Cola Company; former United Nations Ambassador Andrew Young; media magnate Ted Turner; Pat Mitchell, president and CEO of Public Broadcasting Service; Senator Zell Miller; Arthur Blank, cofounder of Home Depot and current chairman, president and CEO of the Atlanta Falcons of the National Football League; and S. Truett Cathy, chairman and CEO of Chick-Fil-A restaurants. A total of 46 individuals have been honored since the event began in 1985. An induction ceremony is held each spring in downtown Atlanta.

Another well-known initiative is the annual Marketing Awards for Excellence (MAX) program. Co-sponsored with the *Atlanta Business Chronicle*, MAX recognizes the best new products, services, and marketing innovations developed and launched by Georgia-based companies. Recent awards have gone to UPS for its Returns on the Web program, Delta Airlines for an on-line travel service for small- to mid-sized businesses, and the Simmons Company for the redesign of its flagship mattress Beautyrest.

"RoundTables" are another popular and successful signature of the Robinson College. These forums bring together senior executives from Atlanta's business community to promote professional development, cultivate networking opportunities, and generate closer relationships between the university and business. Membership is limited to a select number of organizations to ensure ample possibilities for interaction. At meetings scheduled throughout the year, RoundTable participants hear a range of speakers, including faculty at Georgia State and other universities as well as nationally renowned business practitioners. The meetings give members a chance to test ideas and share problems informally with colleagues in other organizations. Interactions with faculty give members direct contact with university resources, such as access to faculty research and students for recruitment and internships. There are currently seven RoundTables in existence at the college. These provide opportunities for chief financial officers, controllers, human resources executives, information systems executives, marketing executives, retailers, and entrepreneurs. Also in the planning stages is an International Business Leaders Roundtable.

The Robinson College benefits from these strong links with the business community. The associations have led to a host of class projects, brought mentors from the business community to teach in classes, and given interns a variety of hands-on opportunities. The membership fees paid by the organizations provide the largest single source of discretionary income for the Robinson College. The Marketing RoundTable, for example, has enabled the endowment of five marketing professorships and two annual marketing scholarships for minority students. This is Robinson's original RoundTable, founded in 1989 by Regents' Professor of Marketing Ken Bernhardt.

ETHICAL PURSUITS

Among Robinson's foremost initiatives are those involving the matter of ethics in business. Not only does Robinson have a renowned faculty teaching ethics courses, the college is also active in promoting ethical practices throughout the Atlanta area. In conjunction with the Society of Financial Service Professionals, Robinson sponsors an annual Georgia Business Ethics Award presented to the Georgia business that best demonstrates high ethical standards and a commitment to community service. The award is presented annually in the Fall as part of a luncheon event held in downtown Atlanta. To promote the study of ethics in business among its students, the college offers the Carl R. Zwerner Prize in Ethics, a scholarship grant. Each year students involved with the college's ethics courses have the opportunity to apply for the award. Nominees submit essays highlighting their career aspirations, the importance of integrity and ethics in business, and a summary project focused on the ethical conduct of business. A third initiative, in conjunction with the Southern Institute for Business Ethics, brings well-known speakers to campus to address myriad issues related to corporate responsibility, specifically ethics in the workplace. The program was launched in 2004.

DIVERSITY MATTERS

The 2000 U.S. Census identified a number of trends, including a demographic shift in the population. Hispanic and Asian populations are growing faster than the African-American population, and all of those categories are growing faster than non-Hispanic whites. Diversity is a definite factor in America's future, and businesses will need to embrace this diversity to succeed.

The Robinson College is lucky to have highly diverse groups of students and faculty members who bring different thoughts, experiences, and outlooks to campus. The diverse mix of students—more than 5,300 undergraduates and nearly 2,500 MBA, master's, and doctoral students— represents forty-seven countries. In fall 2001, female undergraduates outnumbered their male counterparts; on the graduate level, 37 percent of the students were female. A total of 28 percent of the college's two hundred faculty members are female. Thirty-six percent of both the college's undergraduate and graduate level are minorities.

To continue to encourage opportunities for students of diverse backgrounds, Bank of America has made a substantial gift to Robinson College and Georgia State University. Part of the donation supports business scholarships for women and underrepresented graduate business students who show potential as business leaders. The goal of the Bank of America scholarships is to bring more diversity and talent into the business world. According to Dean Harris, "Bank of America has been a strong supporter of the Robinson College and this gift will have a significant impact on providing opportunities to many students for academic growth and enrichment who otherwise might never have the opportunity."

UNDERWRITING INNOVATION: A DRIVE
FOR EXTERNAL FUNDING

The results-oriented Robinson College undertook an ambitious fundraising campaign in 1997. The aptly named RESULTS Campaign has raised more than $25 million in private support to augment operating

POINTS OF PRIDE: HIGHLIGHTS OF EXCELLENCE FROM THE ROBINSON COLLEGE OF BUSINESS

School of Accountancy. In an annual survey of faculty of accounting programs nationwide by the *Public Accounting Report*, the School of Accountancy's graduate program ranked nineteenth in the nation. The school also ranked nineteenth in the *CPA Personnel Report*'s Twentieth Annual Survey of Accounting Professors.

Cecil B. Day School of Hospitality. In the first comprehensive ranking of hospitality programs since 1993, the *Journal of Hospitality and Tourism Education* listed the Cecil B. Day School of Hospitality at the Robinson College among the top twenty-five programs in the nation. The School of Hospitality ranked thirteenth overall, receiving top ten scores for curriculum, quality of faculty, and the student body. The School of Hospitality is the largest and only accredited program in Georgia.

Computer Information Systems (CIS). Led by Ephraim R. McLean, Georgia E. Smith Eminent Scholar and Regents Professor, Robinson's CIS department was named one of the top twenty-five technology MBA programs in the nation by *Computerworld*. CIS faculty members engage in futuristic technical research and wireless applications. They work with graduate students on projects examining the dependability of wireless networks, knowledge sharing in short-term computer projects, and evaluation of multimedia training systems, among other projects. Recently, a team of graduating seniors developed a Web site for the Atlanta mayor's Office of Community Technology, helping bridge the "digital divide" between citizens who have computers and those who do not. The Office of Community Technology built Cyber Centers in local Atlanta neighborhoods, allowing residents to learn computer technology and access the Internet.

The CIS department reaches out to executives in the business community through an affiliate program, which brings executives-in-residence to the department to attend colloquia and research meetings and regularly interact with faculty on a full-time basis. In turn, faculty internships with participating affiliates allow CIS faculty to return to practice and refresh their practical experience.

Finance. *CFO.com* has listed Robinson's Finance Department as one of the ten "most intriguing" programs in the country. Editors found the program intriguing primarily because of the innovative CFO RoundTable, which brings together chief financial officers from major corporations throughout Atlanta to share ideas and assist the College in keeping its curriculum current. The department was listed with other elite programs around the nation including NYU, Chicago, and Wharton.

Management. The Management Information Systems graduate program ranked seventh best in the nation among public universities and twelfth among all universities in the 2002 *U.S. News & World Report* survey. The undergraduate program ranked thirteenth in the nation among all universities. Recently, management professor Shaker Zahra captured the highest honors for his research from two of management's premier academic journals. He was the lead author of two articles, which won the Best Paper Award for 2000 in both the *Academy of Management Journal* and the *Journal of Management*.

Undergraduate Division. Robinson College moved into the top fifty in the nation in the 2003 survey of undergraduate programs by *U.S. News & World Report*, an improvement of fifteen places over the previous year. The insurance undergraduate program ranked first among public universities and second among all universities. The eCommerce Program ranked fifth best in the nation among public universities and eleventh among all universities. The Real Estate program ranked sixth best in the nation among public universities and eighth among all universities. Management Information Systems ranked thirteenth, and General Management ranked twenty-third.

Economic Forecasting Center. Forecasting is not in vogue today in the academic world due in part to the complexities of the economy and competition from financial experts at brokerage and consulting firms. However, the Economic Forecasting Center at the Robinson College, established in 1973, remains one of the few university-based, nationally reputable forecasting centers in the United States. In fact, it has become a major source for economic analysis. Dr. Rajeev Dhawan is director of the Economic Forecasting Center. As such, he develops U.S., southeast regional, and local metro economy forecasts, which are published and presented to business leaders and the media at quarterly forecast conferences. One of the country's leading economists, Dhawan has for the past two years been named to *Georgia Trend Magazine's* list of the "100 Most Influential Georgians" and is a regular contributor to the *Blue Chip Economic Indicators, USA Today Forecasters Survey, the Federal Reserve Bank of Philadelphia's Livingston Survey*, and the Consensus Economics forecast panel in the United Kingdom.

In addition to his quarterly forecasts, Dhawan serves as an advisor to educational institutions and local and state government agencies. He is frequently called upon to brief the boards of private companies and regularly gives keynote speeches at events and gatherings organized by various industry and trade groups. As a business consultant, he has been commissioned to prepare economic impact reports, home price forecast models, and suggest public policy recommendations.

funds from state sources. The drive behind this fundraising initiative lies in the college's desire to recruit and retain the best faculty, ensure superior academic programs, attract and support the best students, and strengthen annual support for college operations. Of the funds raised to date, 40 percent has been used to enhance academic programs, institutes, and research centers; 38 percent to support chairs and professorships; 20 percent to create scholarships and fellowships, and 2 percent to offset ongoing annual expenditures. Thanks to the campaign, the Robinson College has raised the number of endowed professorships from ten to twenty-nine.

One of the college's most generous donors is the man for whom it is named, J. Mack Robinson. An entrepreneur, philanthropist, and breeder of thoroughbred racehorses, Robinson has had a long career ranging from a car business to finance, from insurance to partnership in a Parisian fashion house. When the school was named after Robinson in 1998, he stated, "I hope to see my gift used to keep attracting top faculty because if you're going to be at the top of the competition, you have to attract the top people. I believe in this city and in this college's potential to be the finest business school in the nation."

Robinson's belief in GSU and the business college has fostered reality. Robinson College is one of the best business schools, not only in this nation, but in the world. Robinson, however, is not content with its current position as an academic business leader. In a world of constant flux, it looks for ways to reinvent classes, predict trends, and produce results. As issues and trends manifest themselves, Robinson constantly adapts to bring students and the community the best in educational program offerings. Agility and innovation are the mottos that continue to propel the Robinson College of Business to the pinnacle of business education excellence. They are what keep Robinson on the forefront and the factors that make a Robinson education unique. With strong leadership, a stellar faculty, high-quality students, and a proven ability to adapt and reinvent itself, the college seeks to retain and build on its current stature well into the future.

10

Local Interconnectedness and International Outlook: The Joseph M. Katz Graduate School of Business, University of Pittsburgh

Frederick W. Winter

The City of Pittsburgh, the University of Pittsburgh, and the Joseph M. Katz Graduate School of Business intertwine to the mutual benefit of all three. The story of Katz cannot be told without telling that of the city and the university.

THE CITY

Pittsburgh, Pennsylvania, is located within five hundred miles of the majority of the U.S. population. It has also been consistently rated by Rand McNally over the past two decades as one of America's Top Ten Livable Cities, with the cost of living among the lowest in the nation.

The City of Pittsburgh has undergone a complete renaissance since the 1960s. It developed some of the toughest air-quality environmental standards in the nation and vastly improved its waterways until today, its three rivers boast the second largest private ownership of pleasure boats in the nation. And the city is one of the top three urban-forested areas in

America. It is a city built and nestled into forests and dramatic hillsides, which form natural and unique neighborhood settings. The interconnectedness of the city is truly amazing.

The University of Pittsburgh is the central occupant of the Oakland neighborhood. Its campus is divided by Forbes Avenue; and in a mere ten-minute drive along Forbes, a traveler passes not only our university, but six other universities and colleges as well. With eighteen other colleges and universities in the Pittsburgh area, it is no wonder that education, itself, has become a big business throughout the region.

Once the heart of American heavy industry, Pittsburgh transformed itself (over the past thirty years) into an urban environmental model and a city known for high-tech engineering, education, health care, and finance. Pittsburgh ranks seventh in the nation as the home for *Fortune* 500 companies. Some of America's largest companies and North American or regional headquarters for scores of international companies are located here. Companies like Alcoa, H.J. Heinz, PPG Industries, and United States Steel have long had homes in Pittsburgh. They have been joined by others, including Bayer, iGate, and FreeMarkets, to name a few.

THE UNIVERSITY

The University of Pittsburgh is one of the oldest universities in America, founded in 1787. Since that time, the institution has become one of the most distinguished and comprehensive universities in the United States and one of the greatest research institutions in the world. It is a member of the Association of American Universities, an association comprised of sixty-one prestigious doctorate-granting research institutions.

The university enrolls approximately 32,000 students and employs 9,600 faculty and staff. Its 132-acre main campus in Pittsburgh has more than ninety academic, research, and administrative buildings. Among them is the forty-two-story Cathedral of Learning, one of the tallest academic buildings in the world. The Pittsburgh campus offers 285 different degree programs at the baccalaureate, master's, and doctoral levels. Four regional campuses in southwestern Pennsylvania complement the Pittsburgh campus. Each year the university confers 5,900 degrees, and it currently has more than 187,000 alumni.

A powerhouse of research, the University of Pittsburgh typically ranks first in funding from the National Institutes of Mental Health, in the top ten in funding from the National Institutes of Health, and in the top twenty in terms of total science and engineering funding. Its prominence in research, a first-rate medical center, and highly rated medical and engineering schools, coupled with an emerging biotechnology industry that is located in and around the city, afford the university the opportunity to participate in commercially promising endeavors. Such biomedical research efforts include cancer treatments through the University of Pittsburgh Cancer Institute, pharmaceuticals development via the Drug Discovery Program, artificial organ development at the McGowan Center for Artificial Organs, tissue engineering with the Pittsburgh Tissue Engineering Initiative, and advanced materials development at the Materials Research Center. Through its Office of Technology Management, the university aggressively and strategically explores opportunities for technology transfer via patent and licensing options that add to the resource base of the institution while stimulating regional economic activity.

In all, the university has become a major participant in helping shape the future of Pittsburgh and the surrounding region. The Katz School of Business is a primary player in stimulating the new, dynamic growth that Pittsburgh is experiencing. It annually attracts speakers from across the country like Paul O'Neill, former U.S. Secretary of the Treasury, and President and chief operating officer (COO) of Ford Motor Company Nick Scheele. But its richest corporate resources come from the corporate halls of Pittsburgh. The influence of almost every major local corporation can be seen at the university and the Katz School. In recent years, two Pittsburgh corporations were key donors in the Katz School's renovation. The Mellon Financial Corporation funded the creation of the Katz School's Mellon Financial Corporation Hall, and the PNC Foundation funded the creation of the PNC Team Technology Center, a full-service, self-contained, wired facility designed with the latest technology to educate MBAs in a team-learning environment.

THE SCHOOL OF BUSINESS

The City of Pittsburgh has long been an industrial and commercial center, and the managerial and leadership needs of this business hub drove business education at the university. Business courses were first offered at the university in 1907 under the auspices of the Evening School of Economics, Accounts, and Finance. The newly formed school offered evening classes to help working people advance professionally and also served those individuals who had already completed a general undergraduate degree but wanted additional courses that prepared them for business careers.

Prompted by the enthusiasm of the business community, in 1910 the university established the School of Economics, which brought the Evening School under its jurisdiction. The School of Economics offered a four-year program with a major focus on finance and accounting. The school became a charter member of the American Association of Collegiate Schools of Business in 1916; and in 1920, Beta Gamma Sigma, the national honorary scholastic society for students of business, was installed.

In 1921, a major reorganization of the School of Economics took place. The four-year general program was replaced by a two-year upper-division program that concentrated on business subjects. It required two full years of liberal arts and social sciences course work as a prerequisite to admission. In light of this change in emphasis, the School of Economics became the School of Business Administration in 1923.

By the mid-1920s, like other schools that belonged to the American Association of Collegiate Schools of Business, the University of Pittsburgh also began to develop a core curriculum within its program. The core consisted of required courses in accounting, business law, finance, statistics, and marketing. These courses were thought to be "the broad functions of a business enterprise." The development of the core was significant in giving coherence to business studies. During this era, we became the nation's fifth school of business. Another development at the University of Pittsburgh Business School during this time was the introduction of courses, such as business policy and business organization, that focused on a "company-wide managerial perspective." Managerial case analyses were also incorporated into the curriculum.

During the period up to World War II, the business school became highly departmentalized, with numerous undergraduate course offerings. After World War II, dramatic increases in enrollment occurred as large numbers of veterans returned to pursue management degrees. Curricular changes were also occurring in consonance with societal trends, and new majors were evolving.

During the immediate postwar period, the School of Business Administration continued to develop and build upon the foundation that was established before the War. By the late 1950s, the business school enrolled more than 1,200 students in specialized undergraduate business programs. In 1957, the school became an upper-division, two-year professional school and remained so until the undergraduate degree was eliminated, with the last undergraduate class graduating in 1965. This undergraduate degree was reinstated in 1995 and in a few short years has once again grown into a nationally ranked and dynamic program.

The mid-1950s was an era of unprecedented change for the School of Business Administration. A new administration at the school initiated a process of major revisions that resulted in the establishment of a new Master of Business Administration program in 1960. With the appointment of Dean Marshall A. Robinson in 1960, the School of Business Administration and the Graduate School of Retailing merged to form the Graduate School of Business.

The new MBA program consisted of three fifteen-week terms taken consecutively over a period of eleven months. The program featured an interdisciplinary approach, focused on the application of behavioral science, economics, and quantitative concepts to the functional areas. Unlike previous specialized programs, the new business curriculum offered a broad range of functional courses, such as financial management, marketing management, and the management of human resources.

From the 1960s on, the school continued to grow. Its part-time MBA continued to draw students from the region; and in the 1970s, the school initiated an Executive Master of Business Administration (EMBA) program. We were the second school in America to offer this program.

The school also developed a PhD program dedicated to creating the greatest scholars in their fields. Graduates have gone on to teach in the world's most prestigious universities from the London Business School to the University of Southern California. Today, our PhD students can plan a unique, individual course of study from any of nine majors: Accounting; Artificial Intelligence; Business, Environment, Ethics, and Public Policy; Finance; Information Systems; Marketing; Operations and Decision Sciences; Organizational Behavior and Human Resource Management; and Strategic Planning and Organizational Studies.

In 1987, because of a generous gift from Joseph M. Katz—philanthropist, corporate leader, entrepreneur, and pioneer innovator in the field of paper products—the school was renamed the Joseph M. Katz Graduate School of Business.

THE MODERN ERA—THE JOSEPH M. KATZ GRADUATE SCHOOL OF BUSINESS

The Katz School has always transformed itself to respond to its students' needs. It has evolved in every new era to keep pace with the changing world and the changing nature of business. Its one-year MBA program, instituted in 1960, was in large part a direct response to the corporate needs of that time. The school found a successful niche among students because of their desire to not be absent from the workplace for two years. Corporations and government agencies were also willing to give employees a one-year, but not a two-year absence, to earn their MBAs.

These reasons still draw many students to the one-year MBA program. In addition, during the past few years, students have come to us as independent entrepreneurs, who realize that they need MBAs to move their businesses to the next level. Many others come to Katz because they seek complete career changes. Today, the one-year program continues to be one of the top return-on-investment MBA programs in the world and the only one-year program consistently ranked among the nation's top 50 programs.

Similarly, we were among the first schools in the nation to offer a dual-degree program consisting of an MBA and a Master of Science in the Management of Information Systems (Techno-MBA). Our Techno-MBA is perennially ranked in the nation's top twenty-five. This type of dual-degree programming became one of the school's mainstays. Dual-degree programs have been offered in various fields since the 1980s; their completion usually takes the time of a traditional two-year MBA. Katz offers several options outside the Techno-MBA programs. Students can combine their MBAs with a Master in Public and International Affairs, Master in International Business, or JD.

The three current techno-MBA options, however, remain the most popular choices. The MBA and Master of Science in the Management of Information Systems gives a deep business background and level of knowledge about corporate IT issues, along with a broad outlook on corporate technological issues. It was designed to meet the needs of any students who see themselves as CIOs or managing technological innovation within a company.

The second Techno-MBA option is an MBA and Master in Industrial Engineering. It focuses on the design, development, and deployment of new products and services and the continuing management of a company's product line. It is a perfect career path for any future product manager or leader of a cross-functional product development team.

The third Techno-MBA option is an MBA and Master in Bioengineering. This is the newest dual-degree program offered in conjunction with the Schools of Medicine and Engineering. This program serves those who see themselves as future managers of emerging companies in the biotech and biomed fields. The high quality of this program is only possible because of the strengths of the three, separate schools and their willingness to join together in such a progressive venture.

In addition, for the first time in the school's history, a two-year program has been created and is now being offered. Like many innovations at Katz, it promises to be a bit different from most two-year programs. The Katz two-year program is built on the solid structure of the one-year program. Comprehensive course work leads to a summer internship. The student then completes additional managerial competencies through an executive Coaching Program. After finishing the core curriculum, students choose up to twenty-seven credits from electives across the school, customizing their MBA to their professional objectives.

FOCUS AND CHOICE

Katz programs have always been built upon focus and choice. Students determine their concentration or concentrations of professional focus. Traditional choices include accounting, finance, human resources, management of information systems, manufacturing and operations management, marketing, and strategy. They can choose one or two of these concentrations.

Katz Signature Programs combine a sequence of courses across academic areas for students desiring a multidisciplinary focus. Signature programs are in one of three areas: Marketing of Technology-Based Products and Services, Process Management and Integration, and Valuation and Corporate Finance. In essence, they expand traditional categories. For example, the Signature Program in Valuation and Corporate Finance pulls together six courses from Finance and Accounting to give a tool kit of professional knowledge in that critical area. Top faculty scholars work alongside industry leaders to make these programs work.

Katz also offers eighty-one electives for its students. In doing so, it provides one of the deepest and broadest sets of electives at any graduate school of business. They take students beyond the requirements of business school into key areas of interest and both current and cyclical areas of corporate needs. Such courses include: Creating Value through Corporate Restructuring, Marketing Research, Product Development, Strategic Leadership, Systems Analysis and Design, and Supply Chain Management.

GLOBAL OUTLOOK

Katz has strong global resources. It is home to one of the first federally funded Centers for International Business Research. Students have opportunities to study abroad. We were the first business school to establish joint teaching and research centers in the former Soviet Bloc. A sense of international business pervades nearly every class at Katz. Case studies and examples often focus on the global business environment. A high percentage of our faculty members are internationals or internationally born. In any given year, 40 percent of our students are from abroad. Students in any class in the full-time MBA program easily will be from more than a dozen countries. Each year roughly one hundred MBA students from around the world are in residence at Katz.

All of this gives Katz an unmistakable international flavor. But one of the main driving forces in the global outlook of the school has been the development of its International Executive MBA (IEMBA) programs. Currently these programs are offered in Europe and South America. For several years, Katz has worked with partner organizations in Prague, Czech Republic, and in São Paulo, Brazil, to deliver a fifteen-month U.S. Executive MBA degree. The classes abroad are taught by the same faculty teaching at the Katz School in Pittsburgh. The curriculum, entrance requirements, quality standards, and format of the IEMBA program mirror those of the program offered in Pittsburgh. The Katz EMBA program in Pittsburgh is consistently rated among the top twenty of EMBA programs. Recently one of Brazil's leading magazines ranked the Katz EMBA program in São Paulo as the third best in Brazil.

FACULTY

The men and women who teach at Katz are the definition of the modern university scholar: distinguished researchers and excellent teachers. Our students routinely rate the faculty as superb teachers. They make a sustained effort to give their best. We hear students commenting frequently, with surprise, "Katz professors know your name on the first day of class!" It's not unusual for our professors to become mentors to our students long after they have left our doors and are pursuing their careers. Dr. Donald Moser, one of our faculty, said it best when, recently, he was elected by both our full-time and part-time MBA students as the Outstanding Professor of the Year. In his words:

> I believe I have a responsibility, indeed an obligation, to provide our students with the highest quality experience I can. After all, our students have honored us by choosing the Katz School for an MBA degree and have demonstrated their commitment to our program by parting with their hard-earned dollars. I feel strongly that it is only right that we respond in kind by delivering the highest quality experience possible.

Our professors are accessible and approachable. First names are part of the Katz culture. During the first weeks our new students join us, we arrange small group dinners for them with faculty and staff at local restaurants. Throughout the year, our dean hosts roundtable dinners with a corporate CEO and groups of no more than twelve students.

Interaction is everywhere and every day with our faculty and students. During any given week our students might be joining our faculty

- for an annual visit to the New York Stock Exchange.
- traveling with them to research international economies.
- taking part in our faculty-sponsored Management Information Systems (IS) Club to develop a clear understanding of executive and managerial problems in IS.
- reviewing the modern manufacturing locations visited by the Operations Club.
- participating with them in sponsored teams to compete in Case Competitions throughout the United States.
- working alongside them in the Katz Volunteers as they run for the funding of research to help those who have epilepsy, multiple sclerosis, Lou Gehrig's disease, and diabetes.

Because Katz has built a reputation of rigor and efficiency in its one-year program, our faculty has become accustomed to supporting our students in a way that is found in few other schools.

As to research, Katz faculty members publish their work in the most prestigious academic journals in their disciplines. Our faculty includes the founding and current editor of the *Journal of Corporate Finance*, the editor of the *Journal of Management Account Research*, and associate editors of all the primary accounting and finance journals, from the *Accounting Review* to the *Review of Financial Economics.* The American Marketing Association has ranked the marketing faculty first in the nation in terms of per capita research productivity. This productivity is reflected in their presence on the editorial boards of the *Journal of Marketing Research*, the *Journal of Consumer Research*, the *Journal of Marketing*, and *Marketing Science* and by holding the associate editorship for the marketing area of *Management Science.*

Faculty members also include the editor-in-chief of *Information Systems Research* and associate editors of journals such as *IEEE Transactions on Software Engineering* and the *MIS Quarterly*. Others hold the positions of departmental editor and associate editor of the information systems area of *Management Science.*

A number of professors at Katz research the environment in which firms and service organizations frame strategic initiatives and maintain operations. The academic journal *Business and Society* ranked us first in the country for research in social issues and business. And we had the most research presented in the "social issues in management" division of the renowned Academy of Management.

In addition, Katz faculty serve as editors and editorial board members of numerous journals in the areas of strategy and organizations, including the *Competitive Intelligence Review,* the *Journal of Organizational Behavior,* the *Journal of Management Accounting,* and *Organizations and Society.*

Finally, we have focused on the international dimension of business for over forty years in our teaching, our student body, our presence abroad, and our research. That breadth and depth is reflected in editorial board membership on major international academic journals, from the *Journal of International Business Economics* to *Managing in Emerging Markets.*

STUDENTS

The Katz full-time MBA program (one-year program) delivers the same workload as most traditional two-year MBA programs. This has developed a driven student culture within the school. It also drives students together in a culture of cooperation to meet the pace. We are a school of midwestern work ethic and international outlook.

Full-time MBA students are already a worldly and experienced group. They learn from each other's cultural, professional, and personal experiences. In recent Katz classes, about 40 percent of our students were from outside the United States. In any given year, roughly a third of the full-time MBA students are women. To diversify our student body even more, we have joined forces with the presidents of historically black colleges and universities to create the Presidential Fellowship Program, designed to encourage graduates of those institutions to consider the advantages of the Katz MBA.

Because Katz has been traditionally fast paced, students quickly form close friendships, many of which last long after graduation. Those friendships flourish in every possible venue, from collaboration on projects to quick lunches between classes. There is a marked generosity of spirit, with an unusual willingness to help one another, from a CPA spending free hours tutoring a team member in some difficult accounting concepts to a former business owner working with a novice on a business plan. The first things our students learn are that they cannot be anonymous and they are going to make friends for life.

We foster collegiality in class through our long-standing emphasis on teams and collaborative projects. Also, although there is a strong emphasis on academics, students still find time to take part in a host of clubs, both professional and social. MBA students also volunteer at charitable organizations throughout Pittsburgh, including Habitat for Humanity and the Rainbow Kitchen.

As we evolve the Katz student culture into expanded dual-degree programs and a two-year MBA, we expect that the strong points of the current culture will continue to permeate the school. Collegiality, cooperation, and diversity will always be among the school's strongest foundation pillars.

THE KATZ PHD

The Katz PhD program is a vital part of the school. During any year there are approximately eighty PhD students conducting research, working with professors in tight one-to-one relationships, in pursuit of their doctoral goals. The professors we create teach throughout the nation and the world. Like our MBAs, they are a diverse group with varying interests and different professional strengths.

Within the framework of nine standard PhD fields, each student plans a unique individual course of study. A student may choose any of the nine areas as a major or minor. Minors based on courses from other departments are appropriate if they are distinctive and support the major area. The following is a brief overview of our doctoral programs.

Accounting

The doctoral program in Accounting provides an opportunity for study in a variety of specialties in managerial accounting, financial accounting, governmental and health care accounting, and auditing. Specific topics include: agency theory, auditing, behavioral accounting, field-based managerial accounting research, experimental economics, income tax compliance research, role of accounting in organizational control, quantitative models of managerial decisions, and international accounting. Doctoral graduate placements from this program include faculty at Carnegie Mellon, Illinois, Minnesota, Michigan State University, and Northwestern.

Artificial Intelligence

Artificial intelligence (AI) is an inherently interdisciplinary field of study that, in a business school environment, provides opportunities for research in a wide variety of functional areas. The Katz program offers a thorough grounding in the scientific and theoretical basics of AI. We have an empirical orientation and are particularly interested in research that combines artificial intelligence and management science and statistics. Core requirements include courses in artificial intelligence theory and programming, optimization, networks and graph theory, and cognitive processes and problem solving. Within this broad framework, there are high degrees of flexibility and research opportunities. Students construct programs of study that match their interest. They work with some of the best people in AI, both in academia and industry. The University of Pittsburgh has a large number of AI researchers in various departments throughout the school and elsewhere. These researchers are deeply involved in computer science, the cognitive sciences, and management science. Most graduates are placed in business schools and in functional-area departments, since it is still relatively rare for business schools to have AI programs. Katz placements have included New York University, Georgia Tech, Rice, and William and Mary.

Business Environment, Ethics, and Public Policy

The PhD in Business Environment, Ethics, and Public Policy is one of only a handful of such programs in the United States. We study the complex ways in which business organizations interact with, respond to, and actively manage their environments. This field addresses the basic problems of organizational governance, organization environment management, and related ethical and social issues. Students examine such areas as the value profiles of managers, the strategies used by firms to influence government, the structure and behaviors of public affairs departments, codes of conduct for multinational corporations, social accounting and auditing methods, the management of global competitiveness, and managerial responses to issues such as environmental protection and social justice. One of our former professors and a current professor are the cofounders of the International Association for Business and Society (IABS).

Finance

The finance program focuses on issues relating to the acquisition, allocation, and valuation of financial resources. It deals with corporate financial policy, optimal consumption-investment decisions, and the nature of capital market equilibrium in a world of uncertainty. In particular, it is concerned with analyzing portfolio decisions of individual investors, financing and investment decisions by firms, the determination of the market values of capital assets, and the behavior of security prices in efficient markets. The finance faculty emphasizes the formal modeling of these issues and empirical testing of the various theoretical developments. This PhD program has a strong research orientation and is intended to develop research capabilities in financial economics. Students gain a thorough understanding of contemporary issues in areas such as the theory of choice, asset pricing, capital structure policy, dividend policy, mergers and acquisitions, agency theory, information economics, and market microstructure. Course work, readings, and other work with the finance faculty emphasize the use of both theoretical and empirical approaches to define and analyze relevant issues. Courses in finance, economics, and econometrics are required in order to develop an in-depth understanding of the core knowledge in financial economics. Both our faculty and our alumni are widely published and widely cited. Some of our program placements include University of Missouri, Georgia Tech, Baruch, Memphis University, and the Hong Kong Institute of Science and Technology.

Information Systems

The PhD program in Informatin Systems (IS) focuses on the management and organizational uses of computerized information systems. Students can specialize in IS strategic planning, human-computer interaction, implementation of IS, management of software engineering, information systems development, decision support systems, strategic applications of IS, or knowledge management. All students are expected, by the end of their first year of study, to have basic competence in computer programming, systems analysis and design techniques, and database management systems. In addition, students must fulfill research methodology requirements, take six to eight doctoral seminars in their major area and three to four seminars in a related minor area. Katz IS programs both at the PhD and MBA levels are rated among the highest in the world by academic organizations and publications, and by popular ranking magazines. Our faculty members were instrumental in founding: the International Conference on Information Systems (the premier research conference in the field); *Information Systems Research* (a premier research journal in the field); and the Association for Information Systems (AIS, the key global professional organization for IS academics). Some of our placements include the London Business School, Syracuse, University of South Carolina, National University of Singapore, and University of California at Berkeley.

Marketing

This program is intended to give students both the substantive knowledge and the practical research skills necessary to make contributions to marketing thought and practice. After acquiring the fundamentals, students have considerable freedom in selecting advanced course work and a focus of study. Along with seminars offered by the marketing faculty, students are encouraged to take seminars in related areas. Students learn to formulate research ideas and pursue theories with state-of-the-art methodologies. They work closely with faculty on projects related to marketing management, consumer behavior, and research methods. The marketing faculty emphasizes collegial relationships with PhD students. They stress learning through collaborative research, often leading to joint publications and/or presentations at national conferences. Our marketing faculty is ranked among the highest in the world for research productivity. Some placements include Dartmouth, Boston College, Emory, Illinois, Southern California, Texas, Wisconsin, and Yonsei University, Korea.

Operations and Decision Sciences

This program addresses the role of quantitative models in managerial decision making, and covers the methodologies as well as the applications of management science. Because of the variety of faculty research interests, there is great flexibility in choosing a research topic, including disciplinary research on the methodology of operations research and interdisciplinary research with other areas, such as artificial intelligence, management information systems, finance, accounting, or marketing. The program emphasizes the addressing of complex decision problems, not only operational problems in production and distribution, but tactical and strategic decisions in the fields of finance, marketing, transportation, and energy resource management. Students have flexibility in advanced course work as well. Along with PhD seminars at the Katz School, they may take approved courses in other university departments, such as industrial engineering, economics, and statistics. This program is ranked among the highest in the nation. The faculty is widely published and does large-scale project work for some of America's biggest corporations. PhD students are involved regularly with faculty research and corporate consulting.

Organizational Behavior and Human Resource Management

This program focuses on the behavioral processes and strategies of organizations and how they affect individual, group, and organizational performance. Excellence in content knowledge and research skills are strongly emphasized. The program provides an overview of both organizational behavior and human resources management; students can choose to concentrate in either area. Faculty and students are involved in active research applying behavioral science theory and principles to organizational settings. This involves the study of issues, such as managing organizational restructuring and change, developing and integrating mechanisms for employee empowerment, building institutions in changing economies, international human resource systems, managing an increasingly diverse and multicultural workforce, fostering constructive labor relations, and managing and developing human resources to acquire and sustain competitive advantage. Faculty conduct leading-edge research in diverse areas including organizational restructuring in emerging market economies, high-performance work and manufacturing systems in multinational organizations, human resources issues in an age of corporate restructuring and reengineering, union financial resources and power, issues related to women and ethnic minorities in management, in-group members' perceptions of racism, union strategies to organize contingent workers, and drivers and consequences of organizational and technological change.

Strategic Planning and Organizational Studies

Students in this area study the problems and issues facing general managers who must formulate and implement strategic relationships between organizations and their environments. The program offers two tracks: Strategic Planning and Policy, and Organizational Studies. Strategic Planning and Policy focuses on the concepts and frameworks for formulating and implementing strategic decisions in complex organizations. The Organizational Studies track places emphasis on the systemwide dynamics that determine the effectiveness of the overall organization. Topics include organizational design, organizational change and development, organization power and conflict, and the nature of organizational effectiveness. Placements include Massachusetts Institute of Technology, New York University, and the Universities of Southern California and Illinois. Many of our graduates are also placed in corporate and governmental positions.

CLASSROOMS, TEAM ROOMS, AND REBUILDING A BUSINESS SCHOOL

In late September 2001, the Katz School of Business and PNC Financial Services Group held a ribbon cutting ceremony to celebrate the creation of the PNC Team Technology Center, a full-service, self-contained, wired facility designed with the latest technology to educate MBA students in a team-learning environment.

The state-of-the-art center is the cornerstone of extensive, ongoing renovation efforts at Katz. The renovations were made possible through generous gifts from alumni and the business community. It is located in Mervis Hall, the Katz School's headquarters building on the University of Pittsburgh campus. (Katz is also integrated into three other major buildings on campus.) The PNC Foundation helped to fund much of the renovation of the twelve-year-old Mervis Hall through a $1.3 million grant and an in-kind contribution of $300,000 in technology consulting.

The Team Technology Center features streamlined library facilities, conference rooms, and eighteen meeting rooms dedicated solely to MBA student-teams. The center provides day-to-day implementation of the team-learning model, with rooms that facilitate group learning, study sessions, project course work, and the opportunity to replicate real-world practices in real-world settings. Its library offers students access to 10,000 periodicals, 600 journals, and numerous on-line databases. These academic facilities are complimented by a comfortable student lounge that enhances student life and promotes the exchange of new ideas in an informal setting. The Mervis Hall renovations represent one of the latest steps in a long and ongoing commitment to building and enhancing facilities that support the changing needs of business education.

Shortly before the Mervis Hall renovation, the Katz School was part of an architectural triumph in the City of Pittsburgh, when it moved its Executive MBA Program and Executive Education Program into the newly renovated Alumni Hall. Alumni Hall is a nine-story, 110,000 square foot building constructed in 1915 on the design of a classical Greek temple. It served through most of its history as the Masonic temple for the Pittsburgh region and was purchased by the university in the 1990s as part of its building program.

The Katz School's Mellon Financial Corporation Hall fills its fifth floor with state-of-the-art tiered classrooms, conference rooms, team meeting rooms and administrative offices. The building hosts Katz's Global Executive forum, which is an annual meeting of its current EMBA students from around the world, and is the site of different full-time and part-time MBA activities throughout the year.

Wesley W. Posvar Hall, adjacent to the central, Mervis building, in addition to being the location for several of our key administrative offices, houses the Katz School's Institute of Entrepreneurial Excellence, its International Business Center, and the David Berg Center for Ethics and Leadership. Directly across from Posvar Hall, the new Sennott Square building, completed in 2002 and the University's newest classroom facility, houses our undergraduate College of Business Administration.

This progressive building program has been integrated with the ongoing needs of the business school and the university. Its ultimate result has been to furnish our entire student body, both undergraduate and graduate students, with the finest and most modern facilities the university possesses.

THE KATZ PROMISE

The Joseph M. Katz Graduate School of Business is one of the oldest business schools in the nation, and because of that, it has been one of the most evolved. It has evolved because of its drive to respond to the changing times of every era since the 1920s. Early on, change became a part of our culture. The twentieth century, perhaps the century that has seen the most continuous change, did not allow us to rest on our past accomplishments and victories.

We have continued to grow and evolve and are poised to move in any direction this new century brings. We are a small, intimate program that is flexible and responsive to our students' needs. Our promise to our students and alumni is that we will continue to be flexible and responsive, and that we will continue to change.

We will always change to meet the new needs of the business world and the needs of our individual students, who embrace that world with their energy and intelligence. This promise is a contract with our students that we began almost a hundred years ago. It is a promise we honored then, honor now, and will continue to honor into the future.

11

Defining a Niche: Moore School of Business, University of South Carolina

Catherine Hines Wills and Jan Collins

In the early 1970s, then-Dean James F. Kane had a brainstorm: Fashion a niche for the University of South Carolina's business school by creating a master's degree program in international business unlike anything in existence at the time. That idea became a reality in 1974 when the school's Master of International Business Studies (MIBS) program was launched.

Today, it has been updated and renamed the International Master of Business Administration (IMBA), but the program's initial vision, uniqueness, and quality remain. Indeed, for the past thirteen years, USC's graduate international business program has been ranked number one or two in the nation by *U.S. News & World Report* in its annual "America's Best Graduate Schools" issue. In spring 2002, the Moore School of Business was the only public university among the top five schools in this category, ahead of Harvard, the University of Pennsylvania, New York University, and Columbia University.

Moore School of Business has earned several other high rankings for its business programs during the past decade:

- In January 2003, the *Financial Times* of London ranked Moore forty-fifth in the world for its full-time, MBA-type programs.
- Moore School was ranked number 20 on *Success* magazine's list of "Best Entrepreneurial Schools" in spring 2001.
- In fall 2001, *Forbes* magazine ranked Moore School eighteenth among twenty-five regional business schools in return on investment. It took just 3½ years for Moore MBA students to break even after paying tuition and forgoing income when going back to school.
- Moore School's international business faculty was ranked number one in research productivity by the *Journal of International Business Studies*, the world's leading journal for research in global management.
- *U.S. News & World Report* ranked Moore's undergraduate business program first among undergraduate international business programs and forty-third in overall business. These rankings appeared in the magazine's annual "America's Best Colleges 2003" guide in September 2002. This places Moore in the top third nationally for undergraduate business education.
- *The Economist,* in its initial survey of MBA programs, ranked Moore ninety-seventh in the world, and forty-first among U.S. business schools.

HISTORY AND THE CURRENT DAY

The roots of Moore School of Business reach back to 1910, when a Department of Economics was established at the University of South Carolina (USC). Nine years later, funds were appropriated for a School of Commerce. Still later, in 1944, a Department of Retailing was created. It was not until 1946 that the Board of Trustees authorized establishment of a School of Business Administration at USC as the umbrella organization for work formerly done by faculty in the Department of Economics, the School of Commerce, and the Department of Retailing. In 1947, one year after the new business school opened its doors, sixty-six students earned Bachelor of Science in Business Administration degrees, and seven received degrees in commerce.

The University of South Carolina's School of Business Administration began offering a full-time MBA program in 1959. It was granted membership in, and accredited by, the AACSB in 1962. In 1970, USC's business school launched the first master's degree program in the country that was designed for working professionals and taught via television. Originally called the MBA-ETV, it is currently referred to as the Professional Master of Business Administration (PMBA) program. This program is for people who have an undergraduate degree in business. The total number of students enrolled in the PMBA program for the fall 2002 term was 276. The average age was 30, and the average work experience was six years.

Each year, the school awards approximately one thousand undergraduate and graduate degrees. Current students receive instruction from ninety-six tenure-track faculty members with degrees from fifty-nine leading universities. Most faculty also have extensive experience working for and with private and public organizations. The faculty is 74 percent white male, 16 percent female, 8 percent Asian male, and 2 percent black male. These professors are proficient in numerous languages other than English, including Spanish, French, German, Hindi, Japanese, Chinese, Russian, and Italian. The Moore School of Business has twelve endowed chairs.

Graduate degrees offered include the International Master of Business Administration, Professional Master of Business Administration, Master of Human Resources, Master of Accountancy, Master of Arts in Economics, joint law degree programs, Doctor of Philosophy in Business Administration, and Doctor of Philosophy in Economics. Students can specialize in the fields of accounting, economics, finance, international business, management, management science, and marketing.

The Daniel Management Center (DMC) at Moore School of Business provides executive education and is dedicated to improving management and leadership skills. The DMC has more than thirty years of experience offering both standardized courses and customized programs for its clients. The standardized courses are offered year-round and are constantly updated to ensure their timeliness. Customized programs have been developed for public companies in both the United States and overseas.

The Division of Research (DOR) at Moore School of Business coordinates research services and facilitates grant applications for faculty members. The DOR, which specializes in economic impact assessments, also conducts economic research studies for private companies and public agencies in South Carolina.

A LEAP TOWARD THE FUTURE: REGAINING FOCUS

In 1998, South Carolina native Darla Moore, a New York financier and University of South Carolina alumna, donated $25 million to the school, which was renamed in her honor. This endowed fund is being used to support faculty fellows, alumni programs, and branding and special initiatives. Darla Moore's donation, plus the hiring in October 2000 of a new dean, Joel A. Smith III, former President of Bank of America, East Region, have generated a new vision for the school. This vision, as expressed by

Dean Smith, is "to be consistently mentioned among the top business education programs in the world."

SIX STRATEGIES FOR THE FUTURE

To achieve this vision, six distinct strategies are being employed. One of the school's most important strategies is to update the International Master of Business Administration (IMBA) program. The program has been rethought and reworked to ensure that it prepares students to meet today's global challenges. This next-generation IMBA addresses the need for a global education, whether our graduates plan to work in the United States or a foreign country. It recognizes that all business is global, and that global business must be experienced. We have also built on the unique advantage of the former Master in International Business Studies program: its overseas internship. This program affords all students the opportunity to engage in a five-month out-of-country experience.

The IMBA curriculum has three components: a business core, an out-of-country internship, and advanced electives. The purpose of the business core is to build a fundamental knowledge base within a functional area of business. A unique aspect of the core is the emphasis on the global issues associated with each functional area. The global aspects of business are fully integrated into each class.

Students enroll in the core business courses full-time from the end of July to the middle of February. The classes are small, with fewer than fifty students in each class. All students take the same core courses, ensuring that all students are exposed to the same concepts and techniques. The core courses are rigorous, demanding, and, at the same time, practical. The emphasis in the first year is the development of analytical and functional skills. Models and problem-solving tools learned in class are applied to real-world business situations.

The IMBA program offers three distinct options that build on this common academic core:

- The Language Track is for those students who want to learn a foreign language. The Language Track requires immersion in the language and culture, as well as the business, of a foreign environment. This track arms students with the language skills in Chinese, French, German, Italian, Japanese, Portuguese, or Spanish needed to flourish in business and social settings.
- The Global Track is uniquely suited to students who may not need to study another language. Intensive course work centers on the business practices and economies of all regions of the world. Both the Language and the Global Tracks give the students the opportunity to

participate in a twenty-week internship in a foreign country. Unlike internships at other schools that might only involve becoming acquainted with a country and its people, this internship involves working in a company in a foreign country. It is the intent of the Moore School internship that *all* students spend their internship outside their native country. Students are paid for their internship work.

- The Vienna Program is a unique partnership between USC and Austria's most prestigious business school, Wirtschaftuniversität Wien, Vienna University of Economics and Business Administration. Students spend half their time in Vienna, where they experience the core academic curriculum with emphasis on the European business environment. Students spend the rest of the program on the University of South Carolina campus in Columbia, South Carolina, where they specialize in a particular area of study such as marketing, finance, or management.

There are significant fellowships available for the International Master of Business Administration degree to help students defray the cost of the program. This group of students is diverse, young, and bright.

In addition, Moore School of Business offers several other master's degrees: Master of Human Resources, Professional Master of Business Administration (part-time), Master of Accountancy (which includes a tax specialization), and Master of Arts in Economics.

Our second strategy involves branding for easy recognition in a way that capitalizes on the school's strengths. To ensure a clear, focused image, we have shortened our name to Moore School of Business for branding and advertising purposes. We have adopted a new logo design featuring a globe to symbolize the international education offered. All publications, including the Web site, have been reworked to ensure consistency and focus.

PROFILE FOR THE INCOMING **IMBA** CLASS OF **2002**	
Number of students	172
Male	70%
Female	30%
Average GMAT	629
Average work experience	3.83 years
Average age	27 years
South Carolina residents	27%
International	355
Ethnic minorities	13%

Our third strategy involves the school entering into a partnership with the Instituto Tecnologico y de Estudios Superiores de Monterrey, one of the premier university systems in Mexico, to offer an Executive International Master of Business Administration degree at the Guadalajara campus. The EIMBA programs will afford Moore School the opportunity to establish a presence in the Latin American market, which in turn will strengthen the school's branding strategy as one of the top providers of global business education. It will also leverage the expertise in international business education developed by Moore School faculty over the past three decades.

The EIMBA Program is unique in format since the students are senior-level managers expected to balance their full-time career and personal obligations while they are pursuing an MBA degree. A combination of Moore School and Tec de Monterrey faculty will be used in the program. Three full-week resident sessions are incorporated into the curriculum. Classes, taught in English, are held every third weekend on Fridays and Saturdays at Tec de Monterrey in Guadalajara. In between weekend classes, students and faculty are required to participate in online discussions with their classmates and professors to discuss the assigned projects. Moore's first cohort of thirty students enrolled in fall 2004.

Our fourth strategy involves offering a joint, accelerated BS/IMBA program in conjunction with the University of South Carolina's College of Engineering and Information Technology. Under this program, undergraduate students with three years (ninety hours) of undergraduate study in engineering, appropriate co-op work experience or other work experience, and a GPA of 3.40 (both overall and in their major field of study) may apply for admission. Scores on the GMAT comparable to those of other students are required. This joint degree program will take approximately six years to complete.

To complement and build on our international strength, Moore School plans to offer an international undergraduate degree as our fifth strategy. This undergraduate degree will involve a major in a functional area, such as finance or marketing, plus a major in international business. Moore School expects to enroll about fifty students per year in this program. The timing and selection criteria for this degree are not yet finalized.

Our sixth and final strategy is to stabilize undergraduate enrollment at Moore School of Business to ensure a quality education. Moore is the most sought-after school for undergraduates on campus. Limiting enrollment will make certain that only the best and the brightest are admitted, thereby raising the educational level of all students. The preliminary plan is to limit enrollment in the business school to 2,000 to 2,200 undergraduate students.

These six strategies are supported by a detailed plan that includes funding to hire and retain the brightest and most innovative faculty members, more money for undergraduate scholarships and graduate fellowships, and modernizing our facility and its infrastructure. The funding for this plan will come in large part from the school's Business Partnership Foundation (BPF), which has an endowment of $60 million. The BPF, which was established in 1968, provides a continuing partnership between the school and the state's business community to enhance and improve the Moore School of Business.

A SUCCESSFUL NICHE

It has been nearly thirty years since Dean Emeritus James F. Kane decided to carve out an international business niche for his school. His prescience was remarkable, considering that today it is a universally accepted maxim that "all business is global." The Moore School of Business continues to educate business researchers, economists, accountants, teachers, and human resources personnel while also capitalizing on its strength: international business. Nearly three decades after its inception, Moore School's international business program remains on the cutting edge, training the best and the brightest of the nation's next generation of global managers.

12

Krannert Graduate School of Management, Purdue University: Where Business and Technology Meet

Tim Newton

Purdue University's Krannert Graduate School of Management defines itself as a place "where business and technology meet." More than one-half of the participants in the Krannert School's professional master's degree programs have undergraduate degrees and background in science or engineering. Krannert places consistently in the top five schools in production/operations management in business school rankings and has also been ranked highly in finance, management information systems, and quantitative analysis. Although relatively young—less than fifty years old—the school has devised a plan to help it become a preeminent business school as the twenty-first century unfolds.

SETTING THE STAGE

The Krannert story involves the foresight of several visionary leaders, talent of superior faculty, recruitment of outstanding students, dedication of alumni, and a few sick cows. The saga began in 1953, when economics

---

ABOUT PURDUE

Purdue University was founded in West Lafayette, Indiana, in 1869 as a land grant institution. The land grant universities came out of the Morrill Act, signed by President Abraham Lincoln in 1862, which stated that the federal government would turn over public lands to any state that would use the proceeds from their sale to maintain a college that would teach agriculture and the "mechanic arts." In 1865, the Indiana General Assembly voted to participate in the plan and took steps to establish such an institution. In 1869, the assembly accepted $150,000 from local businessman John Purdue, $50,000 from Tippecanoe County, and one hundred acres of land from local residents. Legislators established the institution and named it Purdue University, with the first classes held in 1874. The campus is located about 65 miles northwest of Indianapolis and 125 miles southeast of Chicago. As a land grant school, Purdue has long had a strong reputation in agriculture and engineering. It also has high-caliber schools in consumer and family sciences, education, health sciences, liberal arts, management, nursing, pharmacy, science, technology, and veterinary medicine. There are more than 38,000 students on the West Lafayette campus, and more than 68,000 at all Purdue campuses in Indiana.

---

split from Purdue's Department of History, Economics, and Government, and became the Department of Economics in the School of Science, Education, and Humanities. Purdue President Frederick Hovde hired Emanuel Weiler from the University of Illinois to head the new department. Weiler's workload increased in 1956, when Purdue established the Department of Industrial Management and Transportation within the Schools of Engineering. Weiler headed the new department in addition to the economics department, giving him administrative responsibilities in two different schools.

In the same year, faculty initiated an eleven-month Master of Science degree in Industrial Management (MSIM), a precursor to Krannert's current Master of Science in Industrial Administration. The program's first class of thirty-four students included twenty-seven Purdue undergraduate alumni. One of the students in the class was Arnold Cooper, who later joined the Krannert faculty and became a widely quoted expert on entrepreneurism.

Weiler soon had a difficult choice to make. He was offered the deanship of the Wharton School, but told Hovde he would stay at Purdue on one condition. He proposed the formation of a new entity, the School of Industrial Management, which would be a combination of the departments that Weiler already headed. The proposal was accepted and Weiler was named dean of the newly created school, which was authorized to offer both graduate and undergraduate degrees. A doctoral program in economics and a Bachelor of Science degree in Industrial Management (BSIM) were created. As part of the master's program core, faculty added a "Managerial Policy Reports" course, making Purdue's graduate business program one of the first in the country to require a course specifically for the development of written communications skills.

Enter the sick cows. At about the same time that the School of Industrial Management was taking shape, industrialist Herman Krannert and his wife, Ellnora, were having trouble with a herd of prize Guernsey cows on their farm near Indianapolis. The Krannerts consulted Fred Andrews, a professor in Purdue's School of Agriculture, and Andrews was able to provide the right answers to nurse the herd back to health. When Herman Krannert mentioned that he could use help with his company, Inland Container Corporation, Andrews put him in touch with Weiler. Krannert and Weiler struck up a friendship, and in 1960, Krannert approved a management development course for his executives taught by Purdue faculty.

Krannert was so impressed with Weiler and Purdue that in 1962, he and Ellnora endowed the management school with a $2.73 million gift. The Krannert Graduate School of Industrial Administration was named (changed in 1976 to the Krannert Graduate School of Management and School of Management). The Krannert gift went toward a new building (opened in 1965) and a trust fund.

The American Assembly of Collegiate Schools of Business (AACSB) voted to accredit and grant full membership to the Krannert School in 1967. That year, Ellen Day became the first woman to enroll as a full-time student in the Master of Science in Industrial Administration (MSIA) program. Today, the MSIA is an accelerated program that emphasizes analytical and communication skills, management fundamentals, and change management. Course work includes both a traditional MBA core and a strong technology component. Students in this program can elect to participate in an eight-week study abroad exchange program housed in Hannover, Germany.

In the early 1970s, a new two-year Master of Science in Management (MSM) degree was added to the Krannert menu. The Master of Science in Management degree was renamed the Master of Business Administration (MBA) in 2001. The name change, which did not require any modification in curriculum, was made to conform to other top business schools. Students specialize in one of eight functional areas (accounting, finance, marketing, strategic management, operations management, information systems, e-business, or human resource management) or in three interdisciplinary options (general, international, or manufacturing management). The year 2001 also saw the MBA program ranked, based on a survey of corporate recruiters, sixth best in the world in the first rankings conducted by the *Wall Street Journal.*

The Krannert School supplements classroom teaching with outside expertise. First-year students in the MBA and Master of Science in Human Resource Management (MSHRM) program, as well as MSIA students, are required to attend a Management Development Series each Friday. Speakers come to West Lafayette to talk to students about a variety of topics, from ethics to etiquette to résumé preparation.

EXECUTIVE EDUCATION FLOURISHES

The first conversations about executive education took place under Emanuel Weiler in the 1960s, but the idea bore fruit under Dean Keith Smith. A Krannert alum, Smith was familiar with executive education structures through his previous position as associate dean at University of California at Los Angeles. In 1981, he approached Professor Dan Schendel about putting together a formal program. The Krannert faculty felt that face-to-face interaction was essential in master's education. While computers were used to bridge the distance to off-campus students, the executive education program required a series of two-week residencies on the Purdue campus, a format that still exists. The Krannert School enrolled a class of twenty-five General Electric employees in summer 1983, and later that year, the school started its first open-enrollment executive education class.

In October 1983, the school dedicated the Krannert Center for Executive Education and Research, a 30,000-square-foot facility adjacent to the Krannert Building. Professor Wilbur Lewellen succeeded Schendel as director of executive education programs in 1985, and remains in the position today. Nondegree executive education courses were also developed by the Krannert School, which teamed up with Purdue's School of Engineering to offer the Engineering/Management Program. The one-week short course is designed for experienced engineers, scientists, and technical specialists, and engineering managers who have a desire to update and/or enhance their technical skills and managerial abilities. Program participants have the opportunity to select from an integrated set of courses for the engineering manager, manager-to-be, or technical professional seeking a grounding in current business thinking and skills. Drawing upon the combined talents of Purdue's renowned engineering and management faculty, the Engineering/Management Program has served more than 1,200 professionals from more than 300 organizations since its inception in 1986. It has been honored with the Award for Excellence from the University Continuing Education Association and was named the Outstanding Non-Credit Program Award winner by the Association for Continuing Higher Education.

Krannert's focus as a place where business and technology meet was further solidified under Dean Ronald Frank in 1988 with the launching of the Center for the Management of Manufacturing Enterprises (CMME). The center fosters an educational program offering an undergraduate minor in manufacturing management, has a major research agenda, and provides a forum for the exchange of ideas between the Krannert School and industry. Center corporate partners have the opportunity to interface with Krannert manufacturing students beyond standard recruiting, and they can tap into Krannert faculty research and curriculum development. Students concentrating in the Manufacturing and Technology Management (MTM) option participate in manufacturing projects. They also can gain real-world experience through lean manufacturing classes, where they focus on how to eliminate waste from all manufacturing enterprise processes.

The efforts of the Krannert School were recognized in 1990 when the professional master's degree programs were ranked nineteenth by *U.S. News & World Report*. Krannert also ranked fifth among schools offering production management specializations. The following year, *Business Week* ranked Krannert's executive education programs thirteenth in the country, and the school was lauded for its computerized communications linkage between students and faculty.

PREPARING ACADEMIC LEADERS
FOR TOMORROW

Krannert prides itself on its doctoral programs in economics, management, and organizational behavior and human resource management. Doctoral programs are limited to full-time enrollment and take four to five years, including summers, to complete regardless of whether a student enters with an advanced degree. Financial aid is offered to doctoral students through teaching and research assistantships. Fellowships and supplemental awards also are available.

Students enrolled in the economics PhD can specialize in one of seven traditional tracks: macro/monetary, public, industrial organization, experimental, mathematical, labor, or international economics. A new specialty, applied international economics, involves working with the Global Trade Analysis Project (GTAP). The project aims to improve the quality of quantitative analysis of global economic issues within an economy-wide framework. GTAP offers data, models, and software, and also organizes courses and conferences. The PhD in management allows specialization in accounting, finance, management information systems, marketing, operations management, quantitative methods/management science, strategic management, and organizational behavior and human resource management. Doctoral students in organizational behavior and human resource management receive training in quantitative research methods and statistics. Students in this area benefit from a small program, with a better than one-to-one student/faculty ratio.

The Krannert doctoral programs have produced several prominent alumni, including Abel Jeuland, Charles H. Kellstadt Professor of Marketing, University of Chicago; Morton Kamien, Joseph and Carole Levy Distinguished Professor of Entrepreneurship and director of the Entrepreneurism and Innovation Program, Northwestern University; Donald Straszheim, president of the Milken Institute and past chief economist at Merrill Lynch & Co.; and Carolyn Woo, Martin J. Gillen Dean of Business Administration and Professor of Management, University of Notre Dame.

SEARCH FOR DIVERSITY

Krannert has a tradition of fostering diversity within its students and staff. In the 1960s when the United States was embroiled in racial turmoil, several Krannert faculty members approached Dean John Day, who had succeeded Emanuel Weiler, and suggested that something needed to be done to recruit African American students to Purdue and the Krannert School. The result was the Business Opportunity Program (BOP), which helps support and fund minority students' college educations. The program, one of the first of its kind at a major business school and the first at Purdue, includes a summer preparatory session for incoming freshmen, as well as scholarships and fellowships. Since its inception, BOP has provided opportunities for more than eight hundred undergraduate and graduate minority students. Cornell Bell, a former school principal from Gary, Indiana, was hired to lead the program in 1970 and remains its director today.

The Krannert School also participates with Purdue University in the Historically Black Institutions Visitation Program on the West Lafayette campus, which encourages minority undergraduate students to pursue advanced degrees, particularly at Purdue. In addition, Krannert works with Purdue's Society of Minority Engineers and Society of Hispanic Engineers to identify potential master's students. Krannert staff members also attend World MBA Tour events worldwide to educate international students about the school's programs. More than one-third of the Krannert MBA student body is comprised of international students.

CONNECTIONS TO THE COMMUNITY

Krannert School engages in a number of outreach efforts that capture the interconnectivity that exists between itself and its students, alumni, and the community at large. For example, one ongoing effort started in 1988 when Purdue alumnus Burton Morgan provided funds for the first Burton D. Morgan Entrepreneurial Competition. The winning prize of $5,000 went to a group of students who developed a proposal to establish day-care centers in shopping malls. The competition, which has grown over the past fifteen years, now offers more than $85,000 per year in prize money to student teams that develop new products and services.

In 1992, a pair of students created the Management Volunteer Program (MVP), which provided assistance to a number of charitable organizations in the Greater Lafayette area. For three straight years, Krannert students won the national "MBAs Make a Difference Day" award. MVP students have been involved in the Big Brothers/Big Sisters program, and each year they host a Halloween party for local Head Start children and assist the Salvation Army during the holidays.

Under the direction of Professor Steve Green, the Krannert School started the Preparing Leaders + Stewards program (PL+S). The program, which is closely aligned with the Management Volunteer Program, includes elective course work, a plan for leadership development, and work with community organizations. Students in the PL+S program must volunteer for university- or community-related activities and engage in self-directed learning activities, ranging from writing reports on leadership books to attending lectures.

In addition to community service, the Krannert School offers outreach to secondary schools around the state through the Indiana Council for Economic Education (ICEE). Founded in the 1950s, the nonprofit ICEE is headquartered at Purdue and has developed a comprehensive partnership of leaders from business, labor, agriculture, education, and government. The council is dedicated to increasing economic literacy in the state of Indiana.

The Krannert School has made a strong commitment to bring respected external speakers to campus. A flagship program in that regard is MGMT 401, known as the Krannert Executive Forum. It is an academic class for undergraduates (both management and nonmanagement majors) that features top-level corporate executives as guest lecturers. Held each semester, the Krannert Executive Forum brings an executive to campus every Friday to lecture and interact with more than 130 students. The program has been in existence since 1973.

The Krannert School also works with different areas on campus to expand its outreach. A cooperative venture between Krannert and Purdue's School of Agriculture resulted in the first distance-delivered executive MBA in agribusiness. In addition, more than fifty doctoral candidates from Purdue's schools of Agriculture, Engineering, Pharmacy, Science, Technology, and Veterinary Medicine come to the Krannert School each year for the Applied Management Principles (AMP) program, which provides business knowledge to technical PhD candidates.

An exciting new addition to the Purdue and Krannert School landscapes is Discovery Park, a $100 million complex for advanced interdisciplinary research and education. There are four components to Discovery Park: the Birck Nanotechnology Center, the Bindley Bioscience Center, an e-enterprises center, and the Burton D. Morgan Center for Entrepreneurship. Four program areas, including the Burton D. Morgan Enterprise Competition mentioned previously, fall under this umbrella. The other three include the Technology Transfer Initiative, the Purdue Engineering Projects in Community Service (EPICS) program, and the New Ventures Laboratory. The Technology Transfer Initiative pairs engineering and management students to research the issues industry encounters when it tries to license and market new technologies and products. The EPICS program provides students with opportunities to work with community service agencies to find ways to use technology to solve problems and improve services. The New Ventures Laboratory encourages entrepreneurs and venture capitalists to visit campus and conduct workshops, and also will provide students with the opportunity to administer a venture fund investing in new technologies.

A final connection with the community aligns alumni with master's students in the Alumni Mentor Program. Started in 1996, the program provides academic and professional guidance for current Krannert students. Mentors are recruited through various methods, including contacts in Krannert advisory groups. Students initiate contact with their mentors, and communicate via e-mail and telephone. During the 2001–2002 academic year, more than eighty alumni were matched with first- and second-year students.

EXPANDING THE COMMUNITY TO INCLUDE THE WORLD

Krannert made international strides when it became a site for the Center for International Business Education and Research (CIBER). The center serves as part of a national network focused on improving American competitiveness and providing services and programs that help U.S. businesses succeed in the global marketplace. The Krannert CIBER site conducts research, sponsors programs and conferences, and serves as a resource for a number of stakeholders.

The school exported its Master of Science in Industrial Administration program beyond the United States in 1999. A partnership between Purdue and a German foundation resulted in the German International Graduate School of Management and Administration (GISMA), located in Hannover, Germany. Under the agreement, Krannert professors travel to Germany to give students a U.S.-style MBA education. The foundation is supported by the state of Lower Saxony, individual donors, and corporate sponsors. Members of the first graduating GISMA class in 2000 received the first Purdue degrees ever granted on foreign soil. Today, the German program continues to grow. An executive MBA program is also offered in Hannover, and exchange opportunities exist for GISMA and Krannert students.

One of the degree programs offered through Krannert Executive Education Programs is the International Master's in Management (IMM). The program is similar to the flagship executive master's degree program in that it requires six on-campus residencies of two weeks each during its duration. The unique aspect of the IMM program is that the residencies rotate between Purdue's West Lafayette campus, Tilburg University in the Netherlands, IMC Graduate School of Management at Central European University in Budapest, Hungary, and the ESCP-EAP European School of Management in Paris. In addition to learning from Krannert's senior faculty members, IMM students learn in person from some of Europe's finest instructors.

First-year Krannert students can participate in a seminar called "Doing Business in the New Europe." Held in Paris at Groupe ISC, a leading European business school, the seminar takes a cross-disciplinary approach to understanding the particulars of doing business in and with the European Community. The two-week seminar takes place immediately after classes end in May, allowing students to return in time to complete a summer internship.

A NEW ERA

In 1998, the school announced the $55 million Krannert at the Frontier campaign. Richard Dauch, chairman of the board, chief executive officer, and president of American Axle & Manufacturing, and his family donated $5 million to serve as the campaign's anchor gift. In honor of the gift, the Center for the Management of Manufacturing Enterprises was renamed the Dauch Center for the Management of Manufacturing Enterprises (DCMME). A pinnacle piece of the Krannert campaign called for a new building to expand Krannert's facilities, faculty and outreach development, and student scholarships and programs.

In 2000, with Dean Rick Cosier leading the Krannert School, Jerry Rawls, president and chief executive officer of Finisar Corp. and a 1968 Krannert alum, gave $10 million to the Krannert for the Frontier Campaign. The gift was the largest in the history of the Krannert School and one of the largest at Purdue. In recognition of his generosity, the Purdue

Board of Trustees voted to name the new Krannert facility Jerry S. Rawls Hall. In addition, a new center was added to the Krannert School. Funding from IBM sponsored the formation of the Center for E-Business Education and Research (CEER), which helps companies adopt cutting-edge technology and thinking in e-business.

New endowed professorships have also been established as a result of the Krannert at the Frontier campaign, which was folded into the $1.3 billion Campaign for Purdue in 2002. Krannert alumni at Accenture donated funds for the Accenture Professorship in Information Technology, which was filled by Prabuddha De, a highly regarded professor in management information systems. Purdue alumna Susan Butler combined with fellow graduates Harold Greenberg and Al Schleicher to endow the Susan Bulkeley Butler Chair in Operations Management. In 2002, Krannert graduate Bill Bindley announced a gift to Purdue of $52.5 million, the largest individual gift in university history. A portion of the gift is earmarked for endowed chairs in the Krannert School.

The centerpiece for the Krannert campaign is Rawls Hall, a $35 million addition to the Krannert facilities. Equipped throughout with the latest in wireless technology and teaching equipment (the Krannert School is ranked among the top twenty-five technology MBA programs by *Computerworld*), Rawls Hall won an architectural award from *AS&U* magazine for its open design, even before construction was started.

TODAY AT KRANNERT

The Krannert complex houses some of the finest graduate management education programs in the world. In 2002, more than one hundred students were enrolled in doctoral education. The students receive ample opportunity to collaborate with faculty; the *Financial Times* ranked the Krannert School among the top fifteen management programs in the world in terms of research productivity.

Close to four hundred students currently enroll in the full-time MBA, MSIA, or MSHRM (Master of Science in Human Resource Management) programs. The MBA program has been ranked in the top thirty by the *Wall Street Journal, Business Week, U.S. News & World Report, Financial Times,* and others. Krannert's strength in the production and operations management area is displayed in consistent top five rankings in the area, and the finance faculty was ranked in the top ten in the world in an alumni survey.

With the assistance of Krannert's highly rated Graduate Career Services staff, Krannert graduates have numerous options as they reenter the workforce. The 2002 *Business Week* survey listed Krannert fourth among ranked schools in terms of job offers and tenth among ranked schools in

---

KRANNERT'S STUDENT BODY

The admitted Krannert MBA class of 2002 included 23 percent women, 16 percent minorities, and 36 percent international students representing twenty-four different countries. The average student was twenty-seven years old, with a GMAT score of 651, GPA of 3.23, and four years of work experience. One-fifth were Purdue undergraduates, although 140 undergraduate schools were represented in the admitted class. Almost one-half had undergraduate degrees in engineering, science, or technology. The average age for executive education students in the flagship program was in the mid-thirties, with work experience of more than twelve years. The vast majority of students in the program were sponsored by their employers.

---

placement. The 2002 *Financial Times* survey ranked the Krannert School fourth internationally in terms of placement success.

About three hundred students are enrolled in Krannert Executive Education Programs (KEEP) degree offerings. Krannert executive education programs have been ranked in the top twenty in the world by *Business Week* and *Financial Times*. In response to the requests of local business leaders, the Krannert School offers a weekend MBA, with classes meeting each Saturday on campus for three years. Nondegree executive programs offer specialty training to veterinarians, engineers, scientists, and others.

The Krannert School, which also offers a top fifteen undergraduate program in management according to *U.S. News & World Report*, has produced a number of successful master's alumni. In addition to the aforementioned Rawls, Joe Forehand, managing partner and chief executive officer of Accenture, earned an MSIA from Krannert. Other prominent graduates include Marge Magner, a senior executive vice president with Citigroup who was named one of the top twenty-five most powerful businesswomen in the world by *Fortune* magazine, and Karl Krapek, retired president and chief operating officer with United Technologies Corp.

Even though the state of Indiana struggles to make investments in higher education, the Krannert School has been able to steadily grow its budget. Twenty years ago, more than 80 percent of the school budget's income came from central university funds, largely supported by the state. Today, that figure is down to 50 percent.

Krannert had adapted to the decreased state funding by being entrepreneurial and efficient. Money has been raised through a differential tuition for the master's program, executive education programs, increased private and corporate fund raising, the GISMA program in Hannover, Germany, and Krannert's various centers. The school has become more efficient by using computer systems to distribute course work, registration information, and other communication material.

PLANNING FOR THE FUTURE

In 2000, a group of Krannert faculty, staff, and alumni began formulating a strategic plan to help propel the Krannert School into the next decade. The plan spells out a vision statement for the Krannert School that is consistent with its strengths:

> The Krannert School will be internationally recognized as a premier institution for management and economics education, scholarly research, and the development of career opportunities for those interested in becoming leaders of technology-driven enterprises. Krannert will be distinct from most business schools by having the highest-quality expertise in the leadership and management of technology-intensive organizations.

The vision is supported by the mission statement: "The Krannert School will educate tomorrow's business leaders, increase the body of knowledge in the various areas of management and economics, and provide outreach activities to the various stakeholders of the school." This includes ensuring that Krannert graduates have the ability to manage a technologically oriented business. They must also possess strong team leadership skills, global awareness, and the ability to apply knowledge from the basic functional areas of management (accounting, business law, finance, marketing, management information systems, operations management, organizational behavior and human resources, quantitative methods, strategic management) and economics. It also means that the school will continue to undertake and disseminate research that expands the frontiers of knowledge in management and economics. Finally, because Krannert is housed in a comprehensive land grant university, outreach efforts are central to realizing Krannert's mission. In sum, Krannert's strategic plan calls for it to continue to enhance the learning environment, ensure program quality, augment its resource base, operate efficiently and effectively, promote economic development, and increase the school's recognition and prestige.

The Krannert School wishes to move to a new level of prominence in the upcoming five to ten years. When it does, it will have met or surpassed the following milestones:

- The number of tenure-track faculty will increase over the 2001–2002 number by 35 percent.
- At least 10 percent of additional new faculty hires will be from underrepresented minority groups.

- Median faculty and staff salaries will be at least equal to the median salaries of our aspiration benchmark schools.
- The number of full-time professional master's students will increase to 20 percent.
- The number of undergraduate management majors will decline by 5 percent from the 2001–2002 level.
- Rawls Hall will be on-line, with wireless network connectivity throughout and the latest videoconferencing technology.
- The number of endowed faculty positions will increase to thirty.
- The percentage of undergraduate course sections taught by graduate teaching assistants will be no more than 20 percent.
- The amount of financial support from private designated funds for undergraduates and graduate students will increase by $1 million over the 2001–2002 level.
- PhD stipends will increase by 30 percent over the 2001–2002 level.
- Krannert will play an ongoing leadership role in the interdisciplinary entrepreneurship and e-business programs in the Purdue Discovery Park.
- Krannert will be consistently ranked in the top ten overall among public business schools.

With a new building, additional resources for endowed professorships and scholarships, and a continued sense of commitment from faculty, staff, and students, the Krannert School is poised to take its place among the preeminent business schools in the country.

13

Indiana University, Kelley School of Business: A Long History of Innovation

James C. Wimbush

The Kelley School of Business has a long and distinguished history. The development of its graduate programs intertwines with the histories of both Indiana University and the Kelley School in general; thus, a brief review of the origins of Indiana University and the school provides a fitting backdrop for the rest of the chapter.

On January 20, 1820, the Indiana General Assembly established a State Seminary in Bloomington, a rural, frontier backwoods at the time. Enrollment numbered ten students with a faculty of three. The seminary became a college in 1828 and in 1838 attained university status. A major reorganization of the university in 1974 added a second campus. The Indianapolis campus, known as Indiana University-Purdue University at Indianapolis (IUPUI), is jointly administered by the two partner universities. Today, combined campus, business school enrollment sits at 5,800 undergraduate and graduate level students. Kelley enrolls 4,600 undergraduate and graduate students on the Bloomington campus and 1,200 at the Indianapolis facility.

The seeds for business education were planted early in the history of Indiana University. The Kelley School of Business traces its beginning back to 1829 when four students enrolled in a course on the political economy. Upon this inauspicious foundation, the university built the School of Commerce and Finance, which eventually became the School of Business, which in turn matured into the premier school that it is today. Indiana's School of Business awarded its first master's degree in 1937 and its first doctorate in 1950. In 1961, students began taking MBA courses in Indianapolis. When IUPUI became an official state education entity in 1974, Kelly was transformed into one school with two locations, and the program on the Indianapolis campus became firmly entrenched as an integral part of Indiana University's business school program offerings. In the fall of 1997 as a new dean took its helm, the school was renamed the Kelley School of Business, after alumnus E.W. Kelley. His $23 million gift remains one of the largest in the history of Indiana University. This donation currently funds the Kelley Scholars program, which is aimed at attracting top-notch undergraduates to the school. In 2002, the school dedicated its newest facility, the Graduate and Executive Education Center.

KELLEY'S GRADUATE PROGRAMS

All of the school's programs adhere to a policy of continuous improvement and are designed to prepare students for the business challenges they will face two, five, or even ten years after graduation. To this end, Kelley was one of the first business schools to integrate core curricula and infuse skills building into course work. Each of its programs has a clear and distinctive personality and direction. These strategic directions are blended with the school's general principles of differentiation and supported by its unique cultural and structural environment to produce a positive and effective experience for students that is not only stimulating but demanding and rewarding as well.

MBA Program

In 1935, the University Board of Trustees approved the school's first advanced degree, the Master of Science in Business. Degree candidates had substantial undergraduate backgrounds in business and economics. In 1939, the Master of Commercial Science was developed as an alternative for students without much background in business and economics. Both of these degrees were abolished in 1946–1947, when a more general Master of Business Administration was established in their place. The length of the new program depended on the background in business and economics of the students. For those students with basic undergraduate training in business and economics, the MBA could be completed in an academic year and a summer session. Three and sometimes four semesters were required for those students without the basic undergraduate background. This early MBA required a thesis on some specific business problem and a comprehensive oral or written examination, or both. The thesis and oral examination were soon dropped, and a comprehensive written examination was administered at the end of the program on the candidate's field of specialization and on his or her general knowledge. A business case was used to measure general knowledge. This case exercise proved to be a traumatic experience for many MBA candidates.

During 1965–1966, the faculty approved a major revision of the MBA degree requirements. The ability to complete the program in three semesters was eliminated for any students. From this point on, candidates had to spend four semesters (forty-eight credit hours) on campus to complete the program and exhibit competence in the basic disciplines (economics, quantitative techniques, and social and behavioral sciences); proficiency in applying knowledge, concepts, and analytical methods to problems; and integration of the above in terms of administration and policy. A moderate degree of specialization was allowed.

From 1975 to 1977, the faculty again spent time revising the MBA program in Bloomington. Although the program required two years of study, it allowed a student to exempt out of appropriate first-year courses. First-year courses included work in mathematical tools, linear programming, computer programming, accounting, organizational behavior, managerial economics, statistical tools, marketing, production, and finance. Those students who received exemptions were allowed to add depth or breadth to their programs through the choice of electives. In the second year, students followed one of forty-five tracks within the business curriculum closely related to their career goals. Tracks involved a minimum of twelve credit hours of course work. Four additional courses were required in the final year of the program: analysis of business conditions, administration, administrative policy, and legal environment. Strict sequencing of MBA core courses and control of program size through more select admission standards were also put in place.

The program remained fairly constant and traditional in its approach to business education until the next major change became effective in fall 1992. Faculty teams put together a drastically new MBA structure and curriculum. The new program was described in the school's "Annual Report of the Dean":

> Driving the new program is integration of subject matter. Financial accounting, managerial economics, quantitative methods, and organizational behavior are merged in the first semester Foundations Core to give students the tools the contemporary manager needs. Contemporary business

issues—the globalization of business, quality assurance, environmental concerns, ethical problems—are incorporated within the overall course work. In the second semester, finance, marketing, and operations are integrated with managerial accounting and information systems to duplicate the way separate functions of business operate together. The interrelationship of the various business functions is dramatically demonstrated to students when they analyze management problems from different approaches. Teamwork is the second principle emphasized. From the start, students are assigned to cohorts of about 65 people. Within each cohort, students work on assignments as teams. Each cohort has its own faculty team throughout the semester. The effect is small group interaction within the structure of a larger program.

After a summer in which the students were encouraged to develop themselves professionally through internships and other activities, the second year consisted of the students pursuing courses of study through majors or other combinations. The new program allowed innovations in scheduling course work (for example, the use of shorter modules to convey subject matter rather than the traditional semester-long approach), and the holding of special events, such as the outdoor challenge held at Bradford Woods, Indiana University's 2,400-acre Outdoor and Leadership Center.

At the time, the new MBA program was quite innovative among graduate schools of business. The success of the program greatly influenced the ranking of the school in *Business Week*. Whereas the school had typically been ranked in the teens during the 1980s, early in the 1990s the school's MBA program was ranked eighth and then seventh among its peer institutions.

The MBA academy concept proved to be another unique idea among business schools when it was introduced in 1995. Academies are an optional, but intense, opportunity for MBA students in Bloomington. They are interactive combinations of high-level course work and senior practitioners that provide a window into a sector's key technologies, trends, dynamics, and trade-offs. Students are exposed to a sector in the first year, undertake an internship or project-based work during the summer, and take course work in the second year. Academy offerings available now are in the areas of consulting, entrepreneurship, global experience, health care administration, investment banking and capital markets, investment management, retailing and consumer marketing, and sports and entertainment.

The most recent MBA program revision efforts began in 2000, supported in part by a competitive grant of $150,000 from the Procter & Gamble Foundation. Students begin their MBA experience with a two-week orientation in the summer prior to entry into the formal program of study. This orientation, offered in partnership with the Leadership Development Institute, begins with an extensive assessment of each student's leadership skills. In addition, students get to know each other through team building exercises and social events, a day spent on career development issues, and jump-start sessions, which focus on accounting and quantitative skills. Following the orientation, the institute works with students to create personalized leadership development action plans. Students in the first-year of the program concentrate on business situations and problems instead of more compartmentalized functional areas (e.g., marketing, finance, operations). For the first twenty-four weeks of the program, students are engaged in three blocks of work. The first block deals with management and decision making. In the second block, evaluation and taking advantage of new business opportunities are covered. Students learn about managing ongoing operations in the third block. The final eight weeks of the first year allows students to pursue electives that prepare them for internship experiences during the summer before embarking on their second year of studies.

A 1976 alumnus, CISCO's CEO, John Chambers, recently donated $1 million for an innovative MBA internship program. The Chambers internship program affords students the rare opportunity to work alongside top executives in all phases of a company's operations. Eight interns work ten to twelve weeks with a COO, CIO, or CEO at an emerging company. In exchange for such exposure, students focus their energies on projects that are of value to the company.

In the second year, students follow a traditional major, a combination of major and minor, or an individually designed major. The academy concept has been carried over from the previous MBA program model. The new program is rich in application and integrative experiences, such as the one-week competitive simulation given half way into the first year and a similar experience at the end of the first-year core. This full-time program attracts roughly two thousand applicants each year, of which it accepts about 30 percent. Of those accepted into the program, about one-half finally enroll. Roughly three hundred students enroll yearly. GMAT scores for these students cluster in the mid-600s.

Change certainly has characterized the school's MBA program. The willingness to take risks that move the program forward has put it at the forefront of innovation among graduate programs in the country. The Educational Benchmarking Corporation recognizes this characteristic and includes the Kelley MBA program as one of five programs it uses in tracking programs and as a standard for curriculum innovation. The Kelley School remains committed to being an innovator in graduate business education.

MBA Courses in Indianapolis

In the 1961–1962 academic period, the first MBA classes were offered in Indianapolis. The classes were provided through closed-circuit TV and by

Bloomington faculty traveling to Indianapolis. Students finished the program in Bloomington. In 1964–1965, the first group of Indianapolis students received their MBA degrees from the Indianapolis program. At the time, five classes were offered through the TV format and four classes presented "live" in Indianapolis.

In 1971–1972, the concept of the MBA Career Integrated Program (CIP), specifically designed for part-time students, was instituted in Indianapolis. The MBA/CIP degree can be obtained in eight semesters after forty-seven to forty-nine semester hours of study. It consists of two phases. The first phase stresses the disciplines essential in business decision-making as well as the basic business functions. The second phase emphasizes integration of the business firm and the business environment and allows the student to develop an area of concentration.

After the reorganization of the university in the mid-1970s, Kelley realized substantial enrollment growth on the Indianapolis campus. The number of students in the MBA/CIP program grew from 182 in 1971 to 414 in 1980–1981. Enrollment growth provided the rationale for better and more permanent facilities to sustain this development. Groundbreaking ceremonies for a new building occurred in 1978, and the first classes were held in the new building in May 1981. Currently, 330 part-time students attend classes in this program.

Master of Professional Accountancy and Master of Business Administration in Accounting

During the 1970–1971 academic year, a structured honors program for undergraduate students was created. The program incorporated special honors classes both within and outside of the School of Business and offered a one-year MBA option. Honors students could complete the graduate degree by putting in an additional year of graduate work instead of the two years required for the regular MBA program. The MBA degree option for honors students was eventually phased out but was reincarnated in the late 1990s as a more functionally oriented MBA in Accounting degree.

The school actually launched two accounting graduate programs: the Master of Professional Accountancy (MPA) and the Master of Business Administration in Accounting. The MPA degree entails an intensive one-year program, beginning with an eight-week session in the summer. Here, the students are introduced to the basics of accounting and prepared for the following two semesters of course work with classes in business information systems, financial accounting, managerial accounting, taxation, auditing, finance, and business law. Students with an undergraduate degree in accounting can obtain the degree with just two semesters of course work. In both cases, a field study or research project is a part of the curriculum.

The MBA in Accounting is a two-year program for which students may apply in their third year as a Kelley School of Business accounting undergraduate. Students enroll in the first year of the program in lieu of their final undergraduate-degree year. This first year of the program provides the student with a broad understanding of business, including accounting. In the second year, students focus on a special track in accounting and an outside area of interest. There is a field study or research project component as well. At any one time, approximately ninety students take advantage of this programmatic option.

On-line MBA Program

The Kelley Direct Program puts technology to its full use. In collaboration with Kelley Executive Partners, the executive education arm of the school, an on-line MBA degree is offered to individuals and corporations. Unlike the flagship program in Bloomington, the two-year Kelley Direct Online MBA program is designed for professionals who wish to continue their employment while earning their MBA. The Kelley Direct program is the only such graduate management program offered by a top twenty business school that is delivered entirely over the Web. Among the tools used are discussion and debate forums, on-line testing, audio- and video-streaming, and simulations for case-based learning. Course materials, including audio and video presentations and virtual tours, can be accessed directly from the Web. The class interaction is asynchronous with some synchronous elements, allowing students the flexibility to balance family and career demands.

In addition to the on-line MBA program, which was opened to the public in 2000–2001, a tailored on-line MBA degree has been developed for General Motors. More specialized, on-line degree-programs have also been established with Deere & Company (on-line MBA in Finance), General Motors (MS in Finance), and United Technologies Corporation (MS in Global Supply Chain Management).

Kelley Executive Partners is now focusing on the development of non-credit on-line executive education courses for alumni and other individuals. Expectations are that there will be significant enrollment growth in on-line programs in the future.

Master of Science in Information Systems

The newest addition to the graduate education package at the Kelley School was launched in the 2000–2001 academic year. The Master of Science in Information Systems (MSIS) is an academic program reflecting the technological age. Students who enter the program with a background in business and systems complete thirty credit hours of additional work to obtain the degree. Individuals without this background are required to take additional courses or attend the program's intensive summer session before the beginning of the fall semester. Topics covered in the course sequence include: new e-commerce business models, redesign and integration of core business processes (e.g., customer relationship management), design and development of Web-based applications, architecture of enabling telecommunications infrastructure, project management of Internet-based systems, and pervasive computing (e.g., wireless communication, information applications, and collaborative computing).

PhD Program

Over 1,000 Indiana University doctoral graduates function in key university, business, and government positions, 80 percent in faculty positions. Today, seventy-six students major in one of nine fields and carry minors in a second field, such as international business, mathematics, psychology, sociology, political science, or any of the cultural and languages programs offered on campus. Admittance into the program is dependent in part on evidence of the applicant's interest in learning to conduct research (e.g., previous publications) or teaching (previous teaching experience at any level). A typical program of study includes two years of course work and another two to three years of dissertation research.

Students who receive funding from the doctoral programs typically teach two to four courses during their years at Indiana University. Early on, they enroll in a course on teaching effectiveness to hone their teaching skills. Students can also compete for research funds. These funds can be used for either predissertation or dissertation research.

The first phase focuses on assuring that each student demonstrates a proficiency in business operations (quantitative analysis, economic analysis, social and behavioral sciences) before being advanced to PhD candidacy in Phase II. Proficiency is demonstrated through examinations. Students admitted to Phase II prepare themselves in a major and a supporting field, engage in greater depth in either quantitative business analysis or in economics, and attend research seminars. Written examinations follow in the above areas. The degree requirements conclude in Phase III with an examination of the dissertation proposal, completion of the dissertation, and finally, its defense. Although Kelley offers both the PhD and the Doctor in Business Administration (DBA), 98 percent of its doctoral students pursue the PhD.

Executive Continuing Education

The Kelley School has been a leader in the field of executive education for over forty years. It was one of the early developers of general management programs for business executives, offering its first program in 1952. In a move to improve organizational flexibility and to stimulate innovation in its products and services, Kelly Executive Partners (KEP) was formed in 1999 as the operating umbrella for executive education. It is an autonomous business unit of the Indiana University Advanced Research and Technology Institute. It reports to a board of advisors with representation from the university, the Kelley School, and the Institute.

KEP focuses on strategic thinking and management education. It also offers change management services that include action research, assessment and analysis, decision support services, and consultation on the design and implementation of knowledge management and organizational learning systems. The Institute for Philosophy-in-Business represents an integral part of KEP's research and consulting service line. The institute, led by Peter Koestenbaum, generates studies, publications, and services that address whole system learning and conscious culture building. It partners with the Indian University Center on Philanthropy, headed by Peter Block, to promote conversation about learning and leadership as primary means for managing the polarity between wealth creation and advancement of human values in the emerging global economy.

STUDENTS, FACULTY, AND THE IMPORTANCE OF DIVERSITY

For almost forty years, Kelley School of Business has recognized the value of educating a diverse group of students. In 1966, the school was one of three that established the Consortium Program for Graduate Study in Business for Black Students. Washington University in St. Louis and the University of Wisconsin were the other two schools involved in this innovative program whose purpose was to prepare minorities for managerial positions in business. Shortly after the consortium's inception, the University of Southern California and the University of Rochester joined the group, and the program was expanded to include Latin and Native American students. Today, the Consortium for Graduate Study in Management hosts fourteen member schools. Since its inception, over 800 minority students have graduated from the Indiana MBA program. This program has been crucial in enabling us to maintain our diversity goals.

The profile of today's students reflects an ongoing commitment to diversity. For instance, students in the school's full-time MBA program represent broad sectors of a diverse, global economy. Twenty-seven percent of them are women, 30 percent come from countries other than the United States, and 16 percent belong to U.S. minority groups. On average they are twenty-nine years old and come to the program with five years' experience. Educationally, 41 percent hold degrees in business, 31 percent in liberal arts, and 27 percent in science and engineering.

Once on campus, students engage in activities outside their studies, which broaden their perspectives and expand their personal understanding and appreciation for diversity. In an attempt to facilitate such learning, the Leadership Development Institute serves as an umbrella organization under which the MBA Association functions. The MBAA is a network of student-run organizations: nine professional clubs, five networking clubs, four support clubs, and twenty-three committees. More than 90 percent of Kelley students participate in organizations as diverse as the International Business Society, Graduate Women in Business, the Graduate Entrepreneurial Club, the Asian MBA Association, and the Gay-Straight Business Alliance.

INTERNATIONALIZATION: THE WAVE OF THE FUTURE

Kelley has a long tradition of working with organizations around the world to better their education and business communities. The school's first major effort in the international area was the European Productivity Agency program, which began in 1955–1956. Sponsorship of the program consisted of the American Association of Collegiate Schools of Business, the International Cooperation Administration, and the European Productivity Agency. Other universities involved in implementing the program included the University of California at Berkeley, the Harvard Business School, the University of Illinois, and the Wharton School of Business at the University of Pennsylvania.

During the 1960s, with funds from a series of Ford Foundation grants, the school participated in a number of institution-building projects around the world. For instance, the school was able to establish a National Training Center for Office Administration in Djakarta, Indonesia. Four faculty members from the school spent 1963–1965 on site creating a successful center in cooperation with the National Institute of Public Administration, an entity of the Indonesian government. During the two-year period, several Indonesian faculty were trained at Indiana and then returned to their home country. The center was set up, and plans were made to extend the project another two years to build another center in Surabaja, Indonesia. However, because of deteriorating political conditions in Indonesia, the project ended.

A team of resident advisors from Indiana also established the Institute of Business Administration at the University of Dacca in East Pakistan (now Bangladesh), the first MBA program in that region. As part of their assignment, they served as administrators and faculty of the institute while nationals studied at the Indiana University School of Business for their MBA degrees. The institute opened its doors in 1966 and, in 1968, awarded the first MBA degrees in East Pakistan to twenty program graduates.

Beginning in 1966, the school also participated in the eleven-year development project that created Thailand's National Institute of Development Administration in Bangkok. The project was administered by the school for the Midwest Consortium for International Activities. With the help of other consortium universities, four schools were established at the institute in Thailand: Applied Statistics, Business Administration, Development Economics, and Public Administration.

In summer 1967, Kelley faculty assisted with the inauguration of the first executive development program ever held in Slovenia, then a part of Yugoslavia. Over a period of years, the IU School of Business faculty helped in the establishment of an MBA program through a series of short-term consultancies with the University of Ljubljana. Several faculty from Ljubljana, in turn, studied in Bloomington. The relationship has continued to the present time, taking a variety of forms.

The school continued its international involvement in a number of different directions during the 1980s and 1990s. During this period, both the undergraduate and MBA programs entered into numerous partnerships with universities in Eastern Europe and the former Soviet Union to create overseas studies opportunities for their students. These programs also initiated overseas recruiting activities to attract more international students to the Kelley School. It was felt that the presence of these students enriched the international environment of the school and contributed to the diversity of the student body.

A school-wide approach to internationalization both internally and abroad came about in 1985–1986 with the establishment of the Center for Global Business. The goals of the center were to provide opportunities and incentives to faculty to do more international research, to infuse more international content into business courses, to offer more specialized international courses, to enhance student interest in the international field, and to collect and synthesize information on the various international activities of the school of business. The latter information was used in grant applications and other promotional efforts of the school.

The outreach work of the center was assumed and continued in 1993 by the Global Business Information Network (GBIN). Emphasis in GBIN was on providing information on a fee basis to companies requiring research on their international markets and activities. GBIN conducted numerous brokering and consulting projects for businesses, completed major research reports, and held international business conferences. Up to four conferences a year were held in Indianapolis with speakers being drawn primarily from the business community.

In 1994, the School of Business was designated as a Center for International Business Education and Research (CIBER). One of twenty-eight federally funded CIBERs around the nation, the Indiana CIBER's mission is reflected in its "efforts to identify improvements in pedagogy and encourage and support faculty in using and creating cutting-edge tools to improve the delivery of international issues in business classrooms." This focus has been realized through pedagogy workshops, a newsletter, collection of international cases, and awarding of case writing travel grants, among many other activities.

A Global Program Office (GPO) was created in 1994. The GPO serves as an umbrella to cover and coordinate already-existing international efforts, such as GBIN, CIBER, and the various academic and administrative programs. A Global Policy Committee developed a strategic plan for the school in 1998, a blueprint for future activities of the Kelly School. The committee continues to monitor the current international initiatives of the school and provide direction.

FACILITIES: CREATING A PHYSICAL IMAGE

In fall 1994, the school identified the need for a building to house the school's graduate students, particularly the "flagship" MBA program, and also provide better executive education facilities. Officials presented a plan to the university's Capital Priorities Committee for consideration, and a proposal for a new business building was submitted in 1996 to the Indiana Legislature for funding approval, as the number one priority of the Bloomington campus.

The plan called for an addition to the existing building, which had become seriously outmoded and inadequate since construction in the mid-1960s. Ground was broken for the Graduate and Executive Education Center in June 2000. The $34 million project was funded with $22 million of private money and $12 million from the Indiana Legislature. It opened in fall 2002. The new building houses the school's graduate and executive education programs, graduate career services, external relations offices, dean's suite, and research centers. Space is divided among classrooms, breakout and conference rooms, a commons, computer labs, and an investment research laboratory where students can execute actual stock transactions.

Technology is one of the essential tools in top-quality business education today. It allows for the sophisticated manipulation and presentation of large amounts of data and for real-time interaction with colleagues near and far. A full range of state-of-the-art technology—including wired and wireless Internet access—is available in all classrooms, conference facilities, lounges, and other study areas. The investment research lab, which in effect is a simulated trading room, features a wide range of leading financial data sources and news retrieval systems. In the past three years alone, over $3.5 million was spent on technology improvements.

RELATIONSHIPS THAT FOSTER
ONGOING SUPPORT

In the late 1930s, a dozen businessmen were recognized as associate members of the business school faculty, a precursor of the present-day Dean's Advisory Council (DAC). The DAC provides advice, counsel, and support to the dean; it also serves as the key interface between the faculty and its business constituency and assists in fund-raising programs.

Over the years the DAC has grown in stature and size. Today, it consists of more than one hundred leading business practitioners dedicated to engaging in an ongoing effective and meaningful dialogue with faculty and school administrators. Among its members have been Randall L. Tobias, chairman emeritus, Eli Lilly and Company; Frank P. Popoff, president and CEO (retired), Dow Chemical Company; Richard L. Lesher, president, Chamber of Commerce of the United States of America; Harold A. Poling, chairman and CEO (retired), Ford Motor Company; and John T. Chambers, president and CEO, Cisco Systems.

Dean's Associates are generous alumni and friends who provide annual support for the school. Committed to quality business education, these individuals understand that private support is critical if the school is to maintain and enhance its margin of excellence. Although established in 1970, the Dean's Associates assumed a more formal organizational structure in early 1977, as private funding became increasingly important in the development of the business school. Giving started off slowly in the early years, with annual gifts amounting to $17,950, $29,805, and $42,786 in 1971, 1972, and 1973, respectively. Considerable growth in annual giving has occurred since then, with annual gifts from 3,500 donors amounting to $1.6 million in 2002.

Development has been a priority of the current dean. Since 1997, the Kelley School of Business has raised more than $130 million, which is more than had been raised in all the previous years of its existence. The money has come from a variety of sources: legislative allocation for facilities, gifts-in-kind, executive education, the Campaign for Indiana University, annual giving, and facilities campaigns. The Bloomington endowment campaign, which raised $42 million, made it possible for the Kelley School of Business to add thirty-seven chairs, professorships, and faculty fellowships. There are now sixty-five of these funded positions.

Kelley also prides itself on working with the local community to provide service and funding for community charitable initiatives. Many

Kelley students actively serve the Bloomington community via voluntary work in kitchens, shelters, and fundraising activities for charities. The Central Charity Challenge, an example of student fundraising, pits Kelley MBAs against their peers at other top business schools to see who can contribute the most in volunteer hours to the host community. Students also build houses for Habitat for Humanity, work at the Boys and Girls Club, and participate in a faculty auction designed to raise funds for inner-city youth. The Graduate Women in Business spearheaded a Career Development Mentoring Program for students at a local high school.

In closing, it is obvious that the Kelley School of Business has a proud history and tradition of accomplishment. As it looks toward the future, the challenge of meeting the needs of its constituents in a fast-paced and ever changing environment will be crucial to its continued success.

14

Warrington College of Business, University of Florida: The Path to Excellence

John Kraft

In 1990, the Warrington College of Business had three hundred graduate students distributed across three programs: a traditional two-year MBA program, a Master of Accounting program, and a PhD program. We currently have over 1,000 graduate students distributed across numerous programs, and our goal is to reach 1,500 graduate students. Today, we describe ourselves as a small, high-quality research school located in a nonurban area. The college has a budget of approximately $40 million and an endowment of about $95 million, which is used to support seventy business faculty plus twenty economics faculty.

The University of Florida is one of only three AAU public research universities in the South. As such, the university has a research mission and a responsibility for innovative, high-quality research, not only to the state of Florida, the nation's third largest state, but to the region. As part of the institution, the Warrington College of Business is committed to the same mission. Faculty research, quality, and innovation provide the cornerstones of the graduate programs within the college. Faculty quality and

THE UNIVERSITY OF FLORIDA

The University of Florida is a major, public, comprehensive, land grant, research university. The state's oldest, largest, and most comprehensive university, Florida is among the nation's most academically diverse public universities. Florida has a long history of established programs in international education, research, and service. It traces its origins back to 1853. It is one of only seventeen public, land-grant universities that belongs to the Association of American Universities. With more than 46,000 students, Florida is one of the five largest universities in the nation. It offers more programs on a single campus than all but a few U.S. universities. Florida has twenty-one colleges and schools and more than one hundred research, service and education centers, bureaus, and institutes and offers more than one hundred undergraduate majors and honors programs and almost two hundred graduate programs. Professional degree programs include dentistry, law, medicine, pharmacy, and veterinary medicine.

Approximately 90 percent of all entering freshmen score above the national average on standardized college entrance exams taken by college-bound students. The University of Florida ranks fourth in the nation among public universities and tenth among all universities in the number of freshmen National Merit Scholars in attendance. Florida also ranks second among all public universities and fourth among all institutions in the number of National Achievement Scholars in attendance.

Florida has more than 4,000 distinguished faculty members with outstanding reputations for their teaching, research, and service. The faculty attracted $379 million in research and training grants in 2000–2001. In 2000–2001, University of Florida-based technologies brought in a record $28.7 million in royalty and licensing income. Florida ranked seventh among all universities for licensing income.

University points of excellence include the following:

- Eighth among all universities in royalty income in 2000
- Thirteenth among all universities—public and private—in number of U.S. Patents awarded in 2000
- Fourth among public universities and tenth among all universities in number of National Merit Scholars in 2001 freshman class
- Second among public universities and fourth among all universities in number of National Achievement Scholars in 2001 freshman class
- Ninth among all public universities in 2002 rankings of "Top 10 Values in State Universities," according to *Kiplinger's Personal Finance* Magazine
- Eleventh straight SEC combined Men's/Women's All Sports Trophy

- Fourth largest student enrollment as of fall 2001
- Twelfth highest in alumni giving in 2000–2001 among AAU public universities
- Nineteenth among all public universities for endowment assets from private funds in 2000–2001
- Fourth among AAU public universities in number of Fulbright Awards made in 2000–2001.

productivity has been recognized through ranking authorities, such as *U.S. News & World Report*, academic journal rankings, and individual research studies. The college's research productivity per faculty in 1997–2000 places us in the top fifteen business schools and the top eight of public universities (Appendix 14.1). Seven key areas capture the essence of Warrington: faculty research, PhD programs, MBA programs, external MBA programs, specialized master's, distance learning, and international programs. As such, these foci provide a framework for discussing graduate education in the college.

FACULTY

Graduate program growth can take two directions. A common approach focuses on developing professional programs, usually at the expense of research programs. In contrast, we view having the highest-quality faculty research as the first step in expanding graduate education and attracting the best graduate students in both research-oriented and professional programs.

Indeed, having a recognized, research-oriented faculty supports the University of Florida's philosophy of graduate program growth. As a consequence, a central emphasis of the business college revolves around recruiting, retaining, and supporting such faculty endeavors. While research can be measured in a number of ways, we prefer to measure productivity through publications in the leading academic journals in business. From our perspective, this represents the best and most objective standard of quality, as well as a widely accepted gauge of performance and academic reputation. Further notable evidence of faculty reputation is the four journals currently hosted by the College: *Journal of Accounting Literature*, *Journal of Public Policy and Marketing*, *Marketing Science Journal*, and *Southern Economics Journal*. In addition, many faculty have participated on editorial boards of the major academic journals and been tapped to head high-profile organizations (Appendix 14.2). In keeping with its mission of service to the state as a land grant institution, as well as the mission of producing seminal research, the college has established fifteen research cen-

> **RESEARCH CENTERS WITHIN THE WARRINGTON COLLEGE OF BUSINESS**
>
> Bureau of Economic and Business Research
> Business Ethics Education & Research Center
> Center for Accounting Research
> Center for Advancement of Service Management
> Center for Consumer Research
> Center for Entrepreneurship & Innovation
> Center for International Economic & Business Studies
> Center for International Business Education & Research
> Center for Real Estate Studies
> Center for Technology and Science Commercialization Studies
> David F. Miller Center for Retailing Education and Research
> Florida Insurance Research Center
> Human Resource Research Center
> Robert F. Lanzilloti Public Policy Research Center
> Public Utility Research Center

ters to support faculty in their pursuit of discovery knowledge. (The sidebar gives a complete list of centers, and Appendix 14.3 provides selected highlights about some of them.) To support such a commitment, the college uses several strategies: reward structures, research support, expense budgets, teaching loads, promotion, tenure, recruiting, and any strategies that enhance our research culture. Foremost among the reward and support strategies is the awarding of endowed chairs and distinguished professorships. Currently the college has ten eminent scholar chairs and 27 endowed professorships. Professorship endowments are funded at a minimum of $300,000, and eminent scholar chairs require a minimum of $1.5 million. (Eminent chairs are permanent appointments with academic rank. Endowed professorships can be reassigned depending on the current needs of the college.) In addition, about $2.8 million is distributed annually in research grants.

DOCTORAL PROGRAMS

Doctoral programs are the lifeblood of our faculty and crucial to creating knowledge and future research agendas. For Warrington, a growing and high-quality, research focused doctoral program is a measurable strength of the quality of our faculty. As such, doctoral programs demand the highest level of resource commitment within our graduate programs. As further resources are acquired, they will be invested in the PhD pro-

Table 14.1   New Doctoral Student Profile (2002)

Major	Degree Type	Total	GMAT	GRE	GPA
BAA	PHD—ATG.	1	680		
BAD	PHD—DIS.	2	665		3.9
BAF	PHD—FIN.	3	740	1470	
BAK	PHD—MKT.	2	695		
BAM	PHD—MGT	2	660		3.55

Note: GRE, Graduate Record Exam
     There were at this juncture 94 doctoral candidates enrolled in the college.

gram in order to attract the best doctoral candidates, enhance program operations, and continue to grow program size to better match the needs of our faculty. (See Table 14.1 for a profile of the 2002 doctoral cohort.) Program success and the ability to expand the program are performance driven and measured in placements of PhD graduates at peer (or better) business schools at the leading research universities globally. Warrington keeps extensive records concerning student placement. Table 14.2 provides a sampling of placement institutions.

A key long-term objective of the college is to have 120 doctoral students who can be adequately supported for five years (we currently have 94 doctoral students enrolled in the program). This represents an optimum ratio of 1.2 doctoral students per faculty. Such a ratio allows us to continue to maintain the intimate and close relationship between doctoral student and faculty currently experienced within the college. All candidates accepted into the program receive full support for their studies.

TRADITIONAL MBA PROGRAMS

Our traditional MBA programs have consistently focused on student quality as measured in terms of high level GMAT scores and significant postgraduate work experience at the highest level. A typical MBA student scores 660 on the GMAT, is twenty-seven years old, and has four years of work experience. Women usually make up 25 percent of a cohort, 28 percent of the students hail from other countries, and about 17 percent are students who represent U.S. minority populations. Each year Warrington accepts less than 25 percent of those who apply. One section of sixty students is admitted each year. (Table 14.3 provides student profiles of all MBA programs.)

Students participate in a conventional first-year core experience taught in four terms over two semesters. The core covers traditional business disciplines, as well as communication skills, leadership, and groups and teams. Teamwork is a significant focus of the first term. The second year incorporates electives, concentrations, or work on certificates. Each student has the opportunity to obtain a certificate in supply chain management, entrepreneurship, financial services, e-commerce, or global

Table 14.2   Examples of Doctoral Student Placements Since 1996

Accounting	Quebec, Arkansas, Central Florida, Drexel, Carnegie Mellon, Cornell, Oklahoma, California (Riverside)
Decision and Information Sciences	Purdue, Sabanci (Turkey), U. of West Indies (Jamaica), Michigan, Florida, Florida Atlantic, Arizona State
Economics	Baylor, Kobe City U. (Japan), St. Andrew's (Japan), AT&T, Asia Pacific Ltd., Federal Trade Commission, Jiatong U. (China), Florida, Duke, Ching-Yung Inst. of Tech. (Taiwan), U. of Rosario (Columbia)
Finance, Insurance, and Real Estate	Cornerstone Research, U. of Houston, Pace, DePaul, Fujen U. (Taiwan), Vermont, Kansas State, Pittsburgh, Miami, Case Western, Florida Atlantic, Miami of Ohio
Management	Auburn, Western Ontario, Florida, New Mexico, Southern Methodist University, Clemson, Delaware
Marketing	Texas A&M, California (Davis), Washington U, Penn. State, Uberlandia (Brazil), Kookmin (Korea), Thunderbird (Arizona), South Carolina, U. Chicago, Arkansas, Alberta (Canada), State University of New York (New Paltz), Notre Dame, Wharton, NYU, Miami, Baruch

management. Students can take MBA-only electives as well as choose from over one hundred electives offered within the college's other graduate programs.

Beginning summer 2003, the college offered an alternative MBA option: an accelerated, two-year MBA program (typically four semesters) that can be completed within three consecutive semesters. The program targets highly qualified top performers who can complete the rigorous program within eleven months. The design follows the European approach, a one-year program where a premium is placed on participants with significant maturity and academic ability. The program begins with a summer semester of two terms consisting of the business core, communications, leadership, and groups and teams. The fall and spring semesters consist of four terms within which students choose electives, concentrations, and certificate options, as well as participate in internship projects, study abroad, study tours, and mentorships. The program has several attractive

Table 14.3   MBA Student Profile (2001)

Traditional Two-Year Program	*Traditional One-Year Program*
Applications received: 349	Applications received: 79
Applications accepted: 74	Applications accepted: 11
Enrolled: 41	Enrolled: 5
Average GMAT: 655	Average GMAT: 664
Average GPA: 3.30	Average GPA: 3.30
Average years full-time work experience: 4.4	Average years full-time work experience: 3.3
Average age: 27.3	Average age: 28.8
Working Professionals Two-Year Program	*Working Professionals One-Year Program*
Applications received: 123	Applications received: 101
Applications accepted: 72	Applications accepted: 55
Enrolled: 60	Enrolled: 47
Average GMAT: 601	Average GMAT: 571
Average GPA: 3.20	Average GPA: 3.53
Average years full-time work experience: 6.7	Average years full-time work experience: 5.8
Average age: 29.3	Average age: 29.5
Internet Two-Year Program	*Internet One-Year Program*
Applications received: 106	Applications received: 54
Applications accepted: 57	Applications accepted: 21
Enrolled: 41	Enrolled: 17
	Average GMAT: 607
	Average GPA: 3.3
	Average years full-time work experience: 5.2
	Average age: 27.7

features. For instance, it can be completed within one year at considerable opportunity cost savings. In addition, all students admitted to the program receive tuition waivers equal to one-third their tuition costs. Students are also eligible for additional support from a $1 million scholarship and assistantship fund. Lastly, students participate in a learning experience that better fits the needs of full-time students with significant work experience, unlike most two-year programs where the summer is spent participating in an internship.

EXTERNAL MBA PROGRAMS

As part of a land grant institution, Warrington faces a considerable obligation to meet the needs of the state of Florida and the South's working population, especially those who are unable to take leave from their employment to enroll full-time in postgraduate work. Warrington College has developed four external MBA programs to address this challenge.

The Executive MBA and the Engineers and Scientists MBA use a delivery format that allows people to come to campus once a month for Friday, Saturday, and Sunday class meetings. The students take three classes per term for five terms over twenty months. The Executive MBA is designed for senior managers with ten-plus years of management experience. The Engineers and Scientists MBA attracts participants with engineering or science degrees who are assuming significant management responsibility.

The Working Professional Two-Year and One-Year programs target individuals with a minimum of two years work experience. The Working Professional programs convene once a month on Saturday and Sunday, and students take two classes each term. Individuals with nonbusiness degrees enroll in the Working Professional Two-Year, which requires seven terms of course work. The Working Professional One-Year services individuals with undergraduate degrees in business. Using the same format as the Two-Year Working Professional program, students complete the One-Year Working Professional program in four terms.

New cohorts enter the external programs each year. All the programs are in a lockstep format with a business core, skill components, extended core, and designated electives. Students receive the same MBA degree as students in the Warrington College's Traditional MBA.

SPECIALIZED MASTER'S DEGREES

Specialized Master's degrees play a significant role in the college's graduate programs. Each program caters to full-time students seeking specialized business skills. Work experience is not required for admission into these programs. The programs are primarily lockstep degrees that can be completed in ten to twelve months.

The college offers six specialized master's degrees: Master of Accounting (MACC), Master of Science in Finance (MSF), Master of Science in Decisions Sciences (MSDIS), Master of Arts in Real Estate (MARE), Master of Science in Management (MSM), and Master of Art in International Business (MAIB) (which is discussed in the International section). Except for the MSM, the programs require a business or accounting degree. The MSF emphasizes finance, particularly fixed income products. The MARE has a focus on real estate financing and urban planning. The MSDIS has two tracks: supply chain management and information systems. The MACC affords students the opportunity to specialize in one of three areas of accounting: auditing, tax, or systems. The MSM is designed for nonbusiness students who want to acquire the business core skills. Students spend one year completing the business core at the graduate level and receive a

Master of Science degree in business, with a specialty in human resources management or entrepreneurship.

DISTANCE LEARNING

Warrington has operated an Internet MBA for five years. The Internet MBA is a two-year program designed for a global clientele. Students take two courses per term for seven terms. Courses include the core, extended core (legal environment, international business, and strategic management), and designated electives. The degree requires students to attend orientation and then participate in a weekend campus visit once each term for presentations, discussions, and grading. The instructional part of the program—lectures, cases, teamwork, and projects—is conducted using the Internet. The program is lockstep and takes in one cohort each year. Participants from over a dozen foreign countries and almost every state have attended the program. A one-year Internet version is available for participants with an undergraduate degree in business. The Internet One-Year program takes four terms to complete. Warrington College faculty teach all classes, and participants receive our MBA. The Internet MBA is the highest globally ranked distance learning program in North America (by *The Economist*).

INTERNATIONAL PROGRAMS

International Programs are a central component of the University of Florida's strategic agenda. Warrington College meets this objective in several ways. First, the college offers a Master of Arts in International Business (MAIB). The MAIB is a specialized master's program that offers students with a business degree, or a minor in business, enhanced international business training, experience, and learning. Though a second language is not a program requirement, approximately 80 percent of the MAIB students speak a second language. All MAIB students also participate in a ten-day international study tour and complete an international business project. Almost 90 percent of the students engage in a term or a semester-long exchange with one of thirty partner schools in Europe, Asia, Latin America, North America, or Australia. The college also partners with Thunderbird to offer a dual degree (MBA–Master in International Management) program. Students must be separately admitted to both programs.

In addition, the college participates in a Master of Science in International Finance with Groningen University (Netherlands) and Uppsala University (Sweden). Students spend one semester at each university and complete their degree in the fourth semester at one or the other institution. The college also offers a joint Executive MBA and Master of Science in retailing with St. Gallen University in Switzerland. This five-semester program allows executives to participate in residence at St. Gallen, Florida, and Oxford University (Templeton College). The program targets high-level global retailing executives. The college is currently exploring the option of offering its Executive MBA degree in China and Portugal with university partners in those locations.

The college participates in graduate student exchanges with over fifty graduate international business programs. (Table 14.4 details the overseas graduate and undergraduate opportunities.) Warrington is the only U.S. graduate business school accredited by European Quality Improvement System (EQUIS), the leading global accreditation body in Europe. In an increasingly small world, especially in the age of global business, international connections are vital to the growth and success of any business education institution, and the Warrington College recognized this early on. EQUIS is the accrediting arm of the European Foundation of Management Development (EFMD), of which the university has been a member for a decade. The EFMD is Europe's largest network association devoted to management development, with some four hundred members from academia, business, public service, and consultancy in forty countries, in Europe and around the world. EQUIS was established as an initiative for benchmarking and accreditation of business schools operating in widely differing national contexts.

Table 14.4   Exchange Opportunities (revised 11/14/02)

• Australia: Queensland Univeristy of Technology, Brisbane	G; U
• Austria: Fachhochschulen Wiener, Neustadt	U
• Belgium: University of Antwerp, Antwerp	G; U
• Brazil: Pontifica Universidad Catolica (PUC), Rio de Janeiro (special selection process)	G; U
• Canada: Ecole Des Hautes Etudes Commerciales, Montreal	G; U
• China: Hong Kong University of Science and Technology	U
• Denmark: University of Southern Denmark, Odense	G; U
• Denmark: The Aarhus School of Business, Aarhus	G; U
• England: Aston University, Birmingham	G; U
• England: Manchester Business School, Manchester (fall term only)	G
• England: University of Manchester Institute of Science and Tech. (UMIST), Manchester	U
• Finland: Helsinki School of Economics and Business Administration, Helsinki	G; U
• France: IAE, Aix-en-Provence	G
• France: Ecole de Management (EM), Lyon	G; U
• France: EAI Tech, Nice	G; U
• France: Ecole Superieure de Commerce (ESC), Rouen	G; U
• France: Ecole Superieure de Commerce (ESC), Toulouse	G
• France: Ecole Superieure de Commerce (ESC), Grenoble	G; U
• France: MBAI, Paris	U
• France: Sciences Po, Paris	U

Table 14.4   (continued)

• Germany: International University of Germany, Bruchsal	G; U
• Germany: WHU, Koblenz	G
• Germany: University of Leipzig, Leipzig	G
• Germany: European Business School	G
• Greece: The American College of Thessaloniki, Thessaloniki	U
• Italy: SDA Bocconi, Milan (fall term only)	G; U
• Japan: International University of Japan, Urasa	G
• Korea: Ajou University, Seoul	G; U
• Liechtenstein: University of Applied Sciences: Liechtenstein (internship only)	G; U
• Mexico: Instituta Tecnologico y de Estudios Superiores de Monterrey*	U
• The Netherlands: Hogeschool van Haarlem, Haarlem	U
• The Netherlands: University of Groningen, Groningen	G; U
• The Netherlands: University of Maastricht, Maastricht	G; U
• The Netherlands: Universitaat Utrecht, Utrecht	U
• Norway: Norwegian School of Management, Oslo (Sandvika)	G; U
• Singapore: Singapore Management University	U
• Spain: ESADE, Barcelona	G
• Spain: Juan Carlos III, Madrid	U
• Sweden: Uppsala University, Uppsala	G; U
• Venezuela: IESA, Caracas	G
• Wales: University of Glamorgan, Pontypridd	U

G, graduate; U, undergraduate
Note: Agreement currently in the works: Pontifica Universidad Catolica (PUC) in Santiago, Chile.
*Not an even exchange: Student must pay ITESM tuition.

AS WE GROW

In the long run, Warrington plans to expand its programs, improve quality, and increase enrollment to about 1,500 graduate students. While it is difficult to predict new programs, key quality opportunities lie in three areas: enlarging the One-Year Traditional MBA, building more Executive MBA opportunities globally with partner universities, and increasing doctoral education. In addition, a key objective is to expand the faculty from ninety to one hundred. As part of the university, the college is beginning a period of transition, at once expanding (in faculty and graduate students) and contracting (reducing the number of undergraduates), as well as focusing on specializations, such as international programs. With the support of the university, and in step with its overall goals, the college is poised to achieve these objectives and advance in standing among its peer schools.

APPENDIX 14.1: NATIONAL NUMERICAL RANKINGS

2003

22 Best Undergraduate Business Programs, *U.S. News & World Report*, 2003

11 Undergraduate Business Specialties: Accounting, *U.S. News & World Report*, 2003

11 Undergraduate Business Specialties: Marketing, *U.S. News & World Report*, 2003

13 Undergraduate Business Specialties: Finance, *U.S. News & World Report*, 2003

20 Undergraduate Business Specialties: Management, *U.S. News & World Report*, 2003

43 Best Graduate Business Program, *U.S. News & World Report*, 2003

14 Graduate Business Specialties: Marketing, *U.S. News & World Report*, 2003

13 Graduate Business Specialties: Accounting, *U.S. News & World Report*, 2003

27 Graduate Business Specialties: General Management, *U.S. News & World Report*, 2003

2002

Best Distance Learning MBA Programs: #1 in North America, *The Economist*, 2002 (sole U.S. program selected)

Top 25 Part-Time MBA Programs in North America, *The Economist*, 2002

Top 45 MBA Programs in North America, *The Economist*, 2002

23* Best Undergraduate Business Programs, *U.S. News & World Report*, 2002

10 Undergraduate Business Specialties: Accounting, *U.S. News & World Report*, 2002

16 Undergraduate Business Specialties: Finance, *U.S. News & World Report*, 2002

19 Undergraduate Business Specialties: Management, *U.S. News & World Report*, 2002

8 Undergraduate Business Specialties: Marketing, *U.S. News & World Report*, 2002

50 Best Graduate Business Program, *U.S. News & World Report*, 2002

25 Part-Time MBA Program, *U.S. News & World Report*, 2002

Top 25 Online MBA Program, *U.S. News & World Report*, 2002

14 Graduate Business Specialties: Marketing, *U.S. News & World Report*, 2002

15 Graduate Business Specialties: Accounting, *U.S. News & World Report*, 2002

25 Graduate Business Specialties: Finance, *U.S. News & World Report*, 2002

2001

15 Best Undergraduate Accounting Programs, *Public Accounting Report*, 2001

5 Best Graduate Accounting Programs, *Public Accounting Report*, 2001

21 Best Undergraduate Business Programs, *U.S. News & World Report*, 2001

8 Undergraduate Business Specialties: Accounting, *U.S. News & World Report*, 2001

13 Undergraduate Business Specialties: Marketing, *U.S. News & World Report*, 2001

22 Undergraduate Business Specialties: General Management, *U.S. News & World Report*, 2001

14 Graduate Business Specialties: Accounting *U.S. News & World Report*, 2001

16 Graduate Business Specialties: Marketing, *U.S. News & World Report*, 2001

19 Graduate Business Specialties: Quantitative Analysis, *U.S. News & World Report*, 2001

2000

Top 50 MBA Programs, *BusinessWeek*, 2000

20 Value-Added MBA Program, *Forbes*, 2000

5 Undergraduate Business Specialties: Taxation, *U.S. News & World Report*, 2000

7 Undergraduate Business Specialties: Accounting, *U.S. News & World Report*, 2000

19 Undergraduate Business Specialties: General Management, *U.S. News & World Report*, 2000

21 Best Undergraduate Business Programs, *U.S. News & World Report*, 2000

5 Highest Number of Authors in Top Three Marketing Journals, University of Washington Study, 2000

5 Highest Number of Authors in Six Marketing Journals, *Journal of Marketing Education*, 2000

8 Highest Number of Authors 1989–1999, *Journal of Finance*, 2000

27 Overall Research Productivity, "Business School Research Productivity," *Academy of Management Journal*, 2000*

2 Marketing Faculty Productivity, "Business School Research Productivity," *Academy of Management Journal*, 2000

17 Accounting Faculty Productivity, "Business School Research Productivity," *Academy of Management Journal*, 2000

29 Finance Faculty Productivity, "Business School Research Productivity," *Academy of Management Journal*, 2000

24 Insurance, International Business, and Real Estate Faculty Productivity, "Business School Research Productivity," *Academy of Management Journal*, 2000

32 Production Operations Management Faculty Productivity, "Business School Research Productivity," *Academy of Management Journal*, 2000

39 Management Science Faculty Productivity, "Business School Research Productivity," *Academy of Management Journal*, 2000

*1997–2000 Research Productivity Adjusted per Faculty

APPENDIX 14.2: SERVICE—EDITORIAL BOARDS AND ORGANIZATIONS

Organization Leadership Positions

Chair, AACSB International–Association to Advance Collegiate Schools of Business

Chair, American Marketing Association

Director, Graduate Management Admission Council

President, Academy of Legal Studies in Business

President, American Accounting Association

President, American Real Estate and Urban Economics Association

President, American Taxation Association (2)

President, Association for Consumer Research (2)

President, Association of Directors of Doctoral Programs in Business

President, Financial Management Association

Editorial Service

Editors

American Business Law Journal, Editor-in-Chief

Decision Support Systems and Electronic Commerce, Area Editor

Economics and Politics, Associate Editor

Federal Reserve Bank of New York Economic Review, Associate Editor

INFORMs On-line, Associate Editor

International Journal of Business, Associate Editor

International Journal of Flexible Manufacturing Systems, Associate Editor

International Tax Journal, Contributing Editor

Journal of Accounting Literature, Associate Editor

Journal of Banking and Finance, Associate Editor

Journal of Business, Coeditor

Journal of Consumer Research, Editor

Journal of Environmental Economics and Management, Associate Editor

Journal of Environmental Economics and Organization, Coeditor

Journal of Evolutionary Economics, Associate Editor

Journal of Finance, Associate Editor (2)

Journal of Financial Economics, Associate Editor

Journal of Financial Intermediation, Coeditor, Associate Editor

Journal of Financial Markets, Associate Editor

Journal of Financial Services Research, Associate Editor

Journal of Information Technology and Management, Associate Editor

Journal of International Economics, Associate Editor

Journal of Marketing Research, Editor

Journal of Money, Credit and Banking, Associate Editor

Journal of the American Taxation Association, Editor (2)

Management Science, Associate Editor

Marketing Letters, Coeditor

Marketing Science, Editor

Pacific-Basin Finance Journal, Associate Editor

Regional Science and Urban Economics, Associate Editor

Review of Quantitative Finance and Accounting, Associate Editor

Southern Economic Journal, Editor

The Financial Review, Associate Editor

Editorial Boards

Academy of Management Journal

American Business Law Journal

American Economic Review (2)

Bulletin of Economic Research

Computers and Operations Research

Global Finance Journal

IEEE Transactions on Engineering Management

Industrial Organizational Review

International Journal of Business

International Journal of Computational Intelligence and Organizations

International Journal of Research in Marketing

Journal of Accounting Research

Journal of Accounting, Auditing and Finance

Journal of Advertising Research

Journal of Applied Psychology

Journal of Business Research

Journal of Consumer Psychology

Journal of Consumer Research (3)

Journal of Corporate Finance (2)

Journal of Direct Marketing

Journal of Economics and Finance

Journal of European Finance

Journal of Financial Intermediation

Journal of Financial Research

Journal of Information Technology and Management

Journal of Interactive Marketing

Journal of International Money and Finance

Journal of Managerial and Decision Economics

Journal of Marketing (3)

Journal of Marketing Research (4)

Journal of Operations Management (2)

Journal of Personal Selling and Sales Force Management

Journal of Property Research

Journal of Retailing

Journal of Services Research

Land Economics

Leadership Quarterly

Managerial and Decision Economics

Marketing and the Law: Journal of the Academy of Marketing Science

Marketing Letters (3)

Marketing Science

Multinational Finance Journal

NACADA Journal of the National Academic Advising Association

Naval Research Logistics

Organizational Behavior and Human Decision Processes

Personnel Psychology

Production and Operations Management

Review of Accounting Studies

Southern Economic Journal

Strategic Management

The Academy of Legal Studies in Business

APPENDIX 14.3: SELECTED CENTER HIGHLIGHTS

Bureau of Economic and Business Research (BEBR)

Founded in 1929, BEBR is unique within the Warrington College, as an applied research center. Its mission is to collect data and conduct research on economic, demographic, and business trends in Florida and to provide information to public and private decision makers in Florida and throughout the nation. BEBR produces Florida's official state and local population estimates and projections; collects survey data from Florida households and businesses; conducts studies of Florida's educational, health-care, transportation, and regional economic systems; publishes the Florida Statistical Abstract; and performs a number of other research, training, and service functions.

Center for Entrepreneurship and Innovation (CEI)

A *Wall Street Journal* article stated that at any given time in this country, more than seven million Americans are considering launching an entrepreneurial venture. Ideas for these ventures come most often from employees who, in their existing jobs, recognize niche markets, or opportunities to expand into markets not served well by their existing company. The CEI provides academic and practical entrepreneurial education to business students, assists in the creation and development of new ventures, and supports research in new venture creation and economic development in Florida. The CEI is also involved in developing classes, course sequences, and certificate programs in entrepreneurship.

Education

Providing forums for the discussion of entrepreneurial ventures is a mainstay of the CEI mission, and its Distinguished Speakers Series and Florida Mentors Program are ways in which this objective is accomplished. Practical experience is also critically important to students considering future entrepreneurial activity. Through its affiliates, the CEI helps students find opportunities to gain meaningful experience in entrepreneurial ventures.

- The Gainesville Technology Innovation Center, Sid Martin Biotechnology Development Institute, and Enterprise North Florida Corporation provide outlets for students to work with client companies in Gainesville, Ocala, and Jacksonville.
- Cenetec, a technology accelerator, presents opportunities to do market research and work with client companies in Gainesville and Boca Raton.
- The University of Florida Office of Technology Licensing gives students the chance to undertake market research and feasibility analysis for intellectual property developed at UF.

Service

- GatorNest is a CEI program that provides anyone with a venture idea the opportunity to brainstorm the concept with our staff and with business students. Additionally, GatorNest will assist in the development of a market plan (and perhaps even a business plan) for high potential ventures that have the prospect of providing practical experience for our students. To promote, support, and recognize successful commercial ventures, the CEI sponsors a number of programs, including the H.J. Leonhardt Business Plan Competition. Participants are eligible to receive counsel and present their plans to professional investors who offer constructive advice. Prizes totaling at least $15,000 are available to students, faculty, and staff in any college or division of the university.
- Florida100 Competition. This competition annually identifies the one hundred fastest-growing companies in Florida. A banquet is held to honor these companies and provide a forum for networking and seminar sessions on keeping their businesses on track.

Center for International Business Education and Research (CIBER)

University of Florida is one of twenty-eight prestigious universities selected by the United States Department of Education to house a CIBER. As part of this national network, UF's CIBER is a resource for businesses, students, and educators. Its goals are to promote international business (IB) through education, research, and outreach and to improve the competitiveness of American firms in global markets.

Research

CIBER supports many research initiatives across the UF campus, in particular through its International Business Competitive Research Grant Program, which provides funding to business and nonbusiness faculty and students for research in IB, including travel. This program is open to all university faculty and graduate students. CIBER's International Business Competitive Curriculum Grant Program also provides funding (including travel) to faculty for new or enhanced courses in IB.

Service

CIBER is a great source of information for Florida citizens seeking information on international business. It provides research support and outreach to assist businesses in finding export opportunities and developing international business relationships.

Education

CIBER supports and hosts many outreach programs for students, business owners, and the public, including:

- International Agricultural Trade & Policy Conference—Cosponsored with UF's Institute of Food and Agricultural Science (IFAS), the conference disseminates information about the policy process for developing new legislation and international trade agreements for policy makers and their constituents.
- Global Wireless Internet Forum—Cosponsored with Warrington's Public Utility Research Center (PURC) and the North Texas Global Telecommunications Society, the forum examines strategy, demand, and technology issues.
- Workshop on Establishing and Maintaining a Foreign Language Across the Curriculum (FLAC) Program—UF's unique approach to instituting a FLAC program has generated numerous requests from other universities for a UF training workshop on its approach. The workshop was presented at the annual CIBER Spring 2003 Language Conference "International Business Language & Technology: New Synergies, New Times."

- Study Business in Rio de Janeiro, Brazil—For MBA students and others with career interests in Latin American business, CIBER joined forces with IAG- Escola de Negócios at the Catholic University of Rio (PUC-Rio) to create this six-week, six-credit program integrating a professional-level business course with applied Portuguese language training. PUC-Rio is the oldest and best-known private university in Brazil, and IAG is one of the top business schools in Latin America.
- International Financial Markets Study Tour—provides students with practical exposure to international financial markets and international business practices.

Center for Real Estate Studies

The Center for Real Estate Studies at the University of Florida is dedicated to fostering the greatest possible expertise and the greatest possible market information for all those involved with Florida real estate. It facilitates research, industry meetings and courses, and a host of activities that bring these spheres of real estate together. An enabling foundation for these efforts is the CRES Real Estate Advisory Board (REAB). This group of some seventy industry leaders provides critical counsel and support to CRES and its programs.

Education

- Masters of Arts in Real Estate (MARE)
  The full-time Master of Arts in Real Estate Program (MARE) is a one-year program designed to ensure that students acquire advanced knowledge of the various functional areas in real estate: finance, investment, appraisal, and law. Unlike students in the traditional MBA program, MARE students are allowed and encouraged to focus their studies on real estate and directly related disciplines, such as finance, building construction, and urban planning. A minor in building construction is available to MARE students.

- The Alfred A. Ring Distinguished Speaker Series
  The series brings prominent industry professionals to campus to speak to and interact with UF real estate students and faculty.

Service

- Annual Real Estate Outlook Conference
  Each year, the Center sponsors a conference that features industry leaders in real estate information and technology who offer their insights, personal experiences, and case studies involving new and

innovative ways that information is affecting commercial real estate transactions.

- UF-FARE
  UF-Friends and Alumni of Real Estate (UF-FARE) is comprised of friends and alumni working in the real estate industry. Its purpose is to provide a network for professional growth, to actively increase the visibility and prestige of UF's real estate programs, and to provide a forum for alumni and friends to participate in the activities of UF's real estate programs and students.

Miller Center for Retailing Education and Research

The major objectives of the Miller Center are to: stimulate student interest in pursuing careers in retailing and prepare them for entry-level positions; provide continuing education opportunities for retailing professionals; improve communications between retailers and academics so that academics are more familiar with problems facing retailers, and so that retailers can take advantage of new perspectives and insights arising in the academic community; and undertake research on retailing issues, opportunities, and problems. The objectives are directed toward finding ways to increase retailing productivity and uncover effective strategies for dealing with heightened competition and rapidly changing conditions in retail markets.

The Center's activities include developing courses and other educational programs for undergraduates, hosting conferences, sponsoring workshops and seminars, serving as an international resource center for retailing, and conducting research on issues of importance to the industry. Each year, the Miller Center offers "Retailing Smarter," an executive continuing education symposium specifically designed for retailers. A group of senior retail executives from leading firms are assembled to focus on topics of strategic importance to retailers.

Retailing firms that provide support for the center are represented on an Executive Advisory Board that reviews the center's activities and determines the strategic direction for future programs.

Public Utility Research Center (PURC)

As one of the most active research centers on campus, PURC's outreach efforts illustrate how academia and public policy can interact on a local and global level. The researchers of PURC continue to engage members of the public and private sector in meaningful dialogue on the regulatory issues faced by companies and governments. In 2001, some of these initiatives included the following.

Service

- Public Utilities director Professor Sanford Berg completed his appointment as a member of the Governor's Florida Energy 2020 Study Commission, which presented its final report in December 2001.
- Berg led a two-day training program for the Florida Public Service Commission with Mark Jamison, PURC Director of Telecommunications Studies.
- Jamison, as principal investigator for the Communications Competitiveness Research Initiative, addressed the Florida House of Representatives Committee on Utilities and Telecommunications and the Florida Senate Committee on Regulated Industries.
- PURC's Director of Energy Studies Paul Sotkiewicz spoke at forums sponsored by EUCG/Nuclear Energy Institute, Gulf Power, and Calpine Eastern. Sotkiewicz also attended the GridFlorida Advisory Committee Meeting in Tampa and met with representatives of NARUC and the International Resource Group, Ltd., in Washington, D.C.

Education

Recent examples of PURC educational activities include its annual conference; the semi-annual PURC/World Bank International Training Programs on Utility Regulation and Strategy; a one-week training program in Bolivia for SIRESE; participation in a seminar on Brazil's electricity crisis sponsored by the National Federation of Engineers (Brasilia); and speaking engagements and workshops at the University of Buenos Aires' Centro de Estudios de la Actividad Regulatoria Energetica, the University of Capetown, South Africa, Panama, and Hong Kong.

Research

PURC received a $25,000 contract from the World Bank to develop and implement a pilot certification exam for regulators. Researchers connected to the Center worked with the London Business School to develop an international conference, "Corporate Control and Industry Structure in Global Communications," participated in roundtable discussions for the Florida House of Representatives' Information Technology Committee regarding IT economic development, and provided research and advice to the Governor's Information Service Technology Development Task Force (itFlorida.com). In 2001 alone, PURC researchers presented seminars or research in Antigua, Argentina, Bolivia, Brazil, China, Ireland, Moldova, Panama, Tanzania, Uganda, and the United Kingdom.

15

A Phoenix on the Rise: Arizona State University's W. P. Carey School of Business

Elizabeth O. Farquhar and Larry Edward Penley

On a rainy day in February 2003, William Polk Carey, an eminent New York City real estate investment banker, stood before a large crowd under a dripping canopy to announce his gift of $50 million to the College of Business at Arizona State University. Carey's support was both substantial and symbolic. Coming on the heels of the university's successful capital campaign, Carey's $50 million gift formed a sturdy platform for future improvement. But the gift was also a monument to the rapid rise and promising future of the W. P. Carey School of Business. The backing of a businessman like Carey—a leader in the select circle of New York City's financial executives—represented the ASU business school's arrival as a program of national and international relevance, a peer with elite programs. An ad that ran in the *Wall Street Journal* that day captured the moment. "East Meets West" was the headline— saguaro cacti filled the foreground of a photo of the New York City skyline.

THE BEGINNING

A seventeen-day train journey in 1879 brought John Samuel Armstrong to the Arizona territory to teach school on a reservation in the desert south of the Salt River. Three years later, he moved his family into the budding town of Tempe, where he began to develop business interests and a reputation among his neighbors for getting things done. In 1884 Armstrong was elected to the Arizona Territorial Legislature, and a year later he filed legislation creating a teachers college in his district. Tempe Normal School was off to an immediate strong start, providing teachers for the mining camps and settlements that were springing up around the territory.

From the beginning, business was a factor in the creation and development of ASU. The institution that eventually developed into the W. P. Carey School of Business grew out of a response to economic need. At every stage of its evolution, this has remained the case.

FROM BUSINESS EDUCATORS
TO EDUCATED BUSINESSMEN

Consistent with the mission of a teachers college, the first business curriculum was designed to prepare high school teachers. By the time World War II came to a close, however, the focus changed. Discharged service people were ready to start over, and many who saw the southwest for the first time during military training returned there to live. Because the GI Bill offered veterans money to pay for education, Arizona State Teachers College braced for an influx. Not everyone, however, wanted to become a teacher. This was a turning point. Soon the program designed to turn out business educators evolved into a program that produced business practitioners.

The Arizona Board of Regents authorized the teachers college to grant a business administration degree in 1946, and approved a business research center—the Bureau of Business and Economic Research—five years later. In 1954, the regents established the College of Business Administration. Over the next twenty-five years, Glenn Overman, dean of the college, engineered the creation of large AACSB-accredited graduate and undergraduate business programs with a strong teaching faculty and buildings of its own.

The burgeoning student populations brought challenges, though. The strain of serving continually increasing numbers of undergraduate students with a tuition mandated to be "as close to free as possible" began to threaten quality. Although the college offered the MBA, it was a degree program that attempted to meet the needs of full- and part-time MBA students within the same classroom. The doctoral programs in business and economics were already reasonably large.

A NEW FUNDING MODEL

In 1982, the college came under new leadership. L. William Seidman brought experience in the White House and a lifelong interest in higher education when he became dean in 1982. "When I arrived the college was one of the largest business schools in the country—academically sound, but with a very small research-centered faculty and no real involvement with the business community," Seidman said recently. "And, there was practically no funding except from the state."

Seidman's tenure proved pivotal for the college. Under his leadership a new concept of public business education began to take shape. Seidman set out to make the college an indispensable part of the corporate community, expand academic research, and improve teaching productivity. He set up numerous research centers for which external funding would be necessary.

To do so, he created a tiered business community advisory support system. The Economic Club of Phoenix, now a fixture on the local business calendar, presents nationally prominent speakers monthly to lunch crowds of two hundred to three hundred. Membership supports summer faculty research and the Bank One Economic Outlook Center. The Dean's Council of 100, comprised of high-level local business executives, provides continuous fiscal support to some of the college's best scholar teachers. It also gives advisory input to the dean. In effect, Seidman set the stage for the school's reduced dependence on state funds and tuition. John Kraft, Seidman's successor, continued his emphasis on research and began to address the issues of overcrowding and graduate business programs that were dwarfed by the very large undergraduate programs. By the time Larry Penley became dean in 1991, the stage was set, but it was still unclear what direction the college would take.

NOT THE BIGGEST—THE BEST

The scene was a lunch meeting at ASU's University Club between Penley and a core group of advisors from the Dean's Council of 100. The issue that day was, What kind of business school did the corporate community need? The conversation soon developed an edge. At last, Jack Henry, a local business executive, made the defining statement: "It's not important to be the biggest business school you can be, but the best; don't focus on giving us the most graduates possible, but the best graduates possible." Thus, the dynamic for Penley's tenure as dean was established. Somehow, Arizona State University would find balance in a paradox: to fulfill the state constitution by providing business education to the public, yet focus on turning out better students—not more.

The means to resolving this paradox was a strategic planning process, launched in 1991, called Business Partners. Its name recalled the origins of the university in the nineteenth century, but it was also intended to capture the destiny of the business school as one in which the business community and College of Business were linked. It was also to be the vehicle for change. Dean Penley appointed a businessman—former Dean's Council chairman Richard C. Kraemer—as its leader. Kraemer marshaled a team of twelve top corporate leaders, three faculty, two students, and a consultant who made a comprehensive study of the college's mission and programs.

While there were discussions among Business Partners members to the effect that the ASU business college should run like any well-managed company, the group recognized that academic institutions are not companies. It was Craig Barrett, CEO of Intel and a former Stanford engineering professor, who helped the group to focus on the business school—not as a business—but as an academic entity. Yes, academic entities can have a clear vision—to be among the top twenty-five—and they can retain their focus on vision and mission. But they must capitalize on core capabilities and build the resources needed to hire the best faculty, offer scholarships to the best students, and provide ample facilities for learning.

The next step of the Business Partners process was an internal focus. Task forces were established with substantial faculty representation, but they also included students, staff, and businesspeople. The task forces took the data developed by the Business Partners steering committee and developed strategic plans for the undergraduate, MBA, and doctoral programs; the Seidman Research Institute; and faculty development. Key themes emerged in those plans that guided the school throughout the 1990s and into the twenty-first century: the need for continuous program improvement, an emphasis on building strengths, responsiveness to advances in technology, openness to diversity, a focus on *skills* as well as *knowledge* in professional programs, and globalization.

Among the first action steps was the establishment of an optimal number for enrollment in the undergraduate program. When Kraft was dean, measures had been implemented to pull undergraduate enrollments back from the highs they had reached under Overman. Penley had seen the effects of trying to serve too many students during his first week on the job in the summer of 1985 as chair of the management department. A line of unhappy students stretched down the hall outside his office door. They were in danger of missing their graduation date because the classes they needed were full. As dean, Penley wanted to solve the problem of matching students to teaching resources. Reducing admissions was his answer.

ASU's provost worried that capping the program would create a problem for students who were closed out. Penley, however, already foresaw the declining demand for undergraduate business education in the early to mid-

1990s. Moreover, providing for an opportunity to develop a greater focus on graduate business education meant shifting resources. Demographic trends were pointing to declining demand at the undergraduate level, Penley thought, but demand for graduate programs—especially the MBA—was burgeoning. Penley also proposed a business minor for those undergraduates closed out of the business major by the 2,600 cap. It was a risk.

With the support of influential Dean's Council members, President Lattie Coor and Provost Milton Glick, the cap was set: 2,600 upper-division students. By any standard it was still a very large program—necessarily so, for the Phoenix area was growing. But it also meant that resource needs for the undergraduate program could be readily forecast, and MBA programs could be supported with a shift of teaching resources to the nascent full-time MBA that Kraft had initiated in his last year.

Among the many advantages to a smaller undergraduate program was the creation of a mystique surrounding the business degree. Penley sought to develop an admissions process that would evaluate students' career goals and communication skills along with grade point average. Over time, the high standards set during the Business Partners process transformed business into one of the most competitive degrees on the ASU campus.

Once enrollments were brought under control, the college began formulating a plan to give the business community the "best" graduates. The seeds of the now prestigious Business Honors Program had been sown in the last years of John Kraft's tenure as dean, and the new venture was taking root. But setting aggressive goals for growth, providing staff support, and conceiving of the Business Honors Program as the foundation and focus for undergraduate business education meant a very different direction for ASU's College of Business. The thirty-year old MBA program began to emerge from its relatively unstructured and general beginnings. Students in the very small full-time program were no longer free to take courses days or evenings at their leisure. Still, the part-time program remained unchanged, at least for a short time.

It was a good beginning, but ASU's business programs had little visibility nationally. In fact, the 1991 *U.S. News & World Report* ranking placed the full-time MBA 197th out of the 273 AACSB-accredited programs. The Business Partners concluded their work, but the process itself became a prototype for academic/practitioner collaborations that addressed other major changes in coming years. Individual Business Partners remained influential advisors long after the ad hoc group had reported its recommendations.

FUELING CHANGE

The changes growing out of Business Partners required a rich stream of funding, one more generous than the college could expect from tuition and state funding. Penley and Kraemer began to discuss the need for a capital campaign. The urgency was clear. The college's endowment stood at $1 million in the early 1990s, and tuition was among the lowest in the United States. Only one program, the Executive MBA, charged an additional fee, a typical situation among U.S. business schools. At that time ASU was not yet prepared to launch the capital campaign that would be so successful for the university and the business school at the close of the twentieth century. And so, the college turned to two new and more immediate funding options in the mid-1990s—its annual fund and, significantly, graduate program fees.

As a part of the Business Partners process, the college had established a goal of having MBA programs of equal high quality. This strategic goal was important for a public business school with local responsibilities, and it was also uncommon as growing national pressure fell on the leading business schools to focus only on their full-time programs that were nationally ranked. In fact, rankings were already driving many business schools to emphasize their full-time MBA programs at the expense of part-time MBAs, doctoral programs, and undergraduate programs. But Penley and Associate Dean Lee McPheters felt a strong responsibility to the Greater Phoenix community and Arizona. McPheters had insisted that the Business Partners strategic goal include a commitment to high-quality programs. That public university commitment along with a "private university" need for resources set the stage for a significant change in direction.

Part of that change was seeking regents' approval for fees in addition to tuition. Few inside the university thought approval likely, but with Penley's support, Associate Dean Stephen Happel prepared the proposal that ultimately was approved. One administrator claimed: "Of everything that has been done, the creation of fees for the MBA program was perhaps the most significant. Program fees allowed the college to blossom."

But the change was not merely one of pricing the part-time MBA higher. Penley believed it included taking important, groundbreaking steps to redesign the part-time MBA with the Business Partners' strategic goal of "equal high quality" as the focus. McPheters and Happel worked with Penley in two critical directions. The program was renamed the Evening MBA. Students were admitted in cohorts, and they took courses in lockstep, mirroring the full-time program. Shorter, ten-week "trimesters" were established, with longer classes that inhibited lecturing. With the commitment to building skills, teams were used in and out of class and collaborative learning was encouraged. Electives were taught in intensive formats—in a few weeks in the summer, on multiple weekends, and during traditional academic holidays. Some faculty had forecast the demise of the part-time program with these changes. They believed that working adults would not and could not tolerate the demands of the schedule and the lack of flexibility. The results stood in stark contrast to those forecasts. Student satisfaction grew, program size and graduation size, especially, increased. And along with those changes came substantially higher revenue and, perhaps most important, the organizational knowledge about working adult programs that would enable the college to launch new MBA offerings, such as a technology-focused MBA, a China-based program, and on-line curriculum delivery.

With a commitment to technology in its mission, with quality programs as the goal and enhanced resources as a means, the college began to build its technology infrastructure. The college first made its classrooms more technologically sophisticated; it added hardware and software as information management technology advanced and faculty needs for research and teaching became more varied. Most important, the school added an in-house computer support staff to operate its increasingly complex system. Significantly as well, it augmented the staff with e-learning specialists, beginning with its first hire in 1993. With more than forty employees, the W. P. Carey School's business information technology staff today remains a standout at ASU and business schools in general. The college has been able to stay ahead because of innovative change that differentiated it from other business schools and a focus on continuous investment in its selected strategic direction.

THE MODERN W. P. CAREY MBA

In the mid-1990s, Penley felt some frustration with the speed at which ASU's business program was gaining recognition. Its reputation was still very much dependent on the full-time MBA. Faced with the need to move ahead more rapidly, Penley called for an external review of the program by two deans and two faculty members, all from better-ranked programs. Like the Business Partners members, these four outsiders urged the college leadership to focus on its strengths as it improved programs and raised the quality of its MBA.

Already ASU's MBA emphasized diversity with its PepsiCo Scholars program. In the late 1980s, PepsiCo had made what was then the largest gift ever to ASU of $1 million to support minority (particularly Hispanic) MBAs. But the MBA lacked other distinctive characteristics. The four outside reviewers had reminded ASU faculty that it could not easily compete with Stanford and University of California at Berkeley if it continued to offer a generic MBA. ASU did have particular strengths. They were not, however, integrated into the MBA.

Parlaying Strengths into Peer Recognition

ASU had long been known for purchasing and logistics, and its faculty included scholars who helped develop the concept of supply chain management. The college's supply chain research center—CAPS Research—is cosponsored by the Institute for Supply Management, the leading industry think tank in that field. Developing a curriculum focus around supply chain management seemed a natural to some and a deviation from the mainstream to many others.

ASU's business faculty also pioneered a new field in marketing that took a fresh look at services. Dr. Stephen Brown was one of the original voices in a debate over the value of services to business. Their new concept, that services are a product that can lead to bottom line profitability, has been explored and applied through the research and executive education of the Center for Services Leadership. Internationally known scholars such as Drs. Mary Jo Bitner and Beth Walker ground this MBA specialization.

Other high-profile fields began to shine at the college. It was about this time that the college reorganized Accountancy and Decisions Information Science into a single unit that gave it momentum in information systems under the leadership of Dr. Phil Reckers. With additional faculty, the school was able to launch the Center for the Advancement of Business through Information Technology (CABIT), which is designed to help industry explore the ramifications of knowledge management.

The W. P. Carey School also has unique strength in health with its School of Health Administration and Policy. With a change in direction from hospital management to the health industry as a business, the school was able to integrate this focus into the MBA as well. Another MBA specialization grew out of ASU's prominence in athletics, along with growth of the sports industry locally and nationwide. As well, ASU saw an opportunity to compete in corporate finance, given regional business needs.

Out of those strengths, ASU faculty created a powerful second year of specialized courses that students can tailor to meet their career objectives. The options include supply chain management, services marketing and management, financial markets and management, information management, health administration and policy, and sports business.

In addition, from the first semester, community service and ethics are woven into the fiber of the program. MBA students take a course in business ethics and participate in a mandatory case competition that poses the traditional strategic issues while adding challenges associated with ethics and globalization. An award and prize money go to the team that best solves the ethical dilemma presented in the case. Students give time to community organizations, and the W. P. Carey MBA Volunteer Council sponsors a successful road race for charity every spring.

The horsepower that results from these changes formed the basis for a new national reputation. By 1994, the flagship full-time MBA at ASU had climbed into the top fifty programs in the nation. Today, it sits at number seventeen among MBA programs housed at public universities, and is poised to move into the top tier.

Outside of the W. P. Carey MBA Program, the school grants five other highly respected master's degrees: Master of Accountancy and Information Systems, Master of Health Services Administration, Master of Public Health, Master of Science in Information Management, and Master of Taxation.

CORPORATE PARTNERSHIPS AND THE MBA

In 1996 attention turned to a phenomenon occurring at many tech companies. The most common path to the top in the booming sector was engineering, but companies had realized that they needed managers with business acumen as well. Associate Dean Lee McPheters noticed that 30 to 40 percent of the students in the evening program were engineers. "We saw an opportunity to respond to the growth in the technology industry and shape a new partnership with business," Penley said. Moreover, the school had already made a commitment to technology via Business Partners. At the same time, Motorola University's new training facility at the ASU Research Park was nearing completion. Talks had been underway for years with ASU's College of Engineering and Applied Sciences about programs that could bridge the gap between engineers and managers. In discussions with local technology leaders, including Tommy George and Gary Tooker (Motorola) and Craig Barrett (Intel), the Technology Program was born. The College of Business took the symbolic step of partnering with Motorola to teach the program in its training facilities at the ASU Research Park. It was only a short while before the collaboration with the College of Engineering became a reality.

Testament to the urgency of the need: Despite the lengthy university review process involved in starting a new program, the first students were admitted within a year. Although it is part of the W. P. Carey MBA Evening Program, the program has a technology focus that sets it apart. Class discussions, cases, and projects are drawn from the tech industry where the students work during the day. Courses are team-taught by professors from engineering and business. An applied integrated project is the common thread during the second year. In it, teams of students use what they learn in class to create business plans for new products. For the first time, in 2002–2003, they worked on ASU patented research ready for commercialization.

The successful collaboration with Motorola soon led to the development of another W. P. Carey MBA, the China program. As a part of the original Business Partners process, a global strategic initiative was established, designed to engage faculty first and then students in international business education. Its faculty development focus was coupled with the intent to have a limited number of regional relationships (e.g., Motorola) with global implications (e.g., China).

In August 1995, leaders recognized that the college had not yet achieved the desired geographic diversity. A small group met to discuss alternatives. The meeting concluded with the decision to propose an MBA in collaboration with a Chinese school and a U.S. company that had a need to develop indigenous talent. Professor Buck Pei was identified as the faculty member to pursue this collaboration. Motorola had already been considering how it could lower the high cost of ex-patriot management in its business in China, and at the same time develop talented Chinese nationals. In essence, Motorola wanted to offer an American-style MBA, but the company did not want to send its employees to the United States to study.

The W. P. Carey MBA China Program was launched in fall 1998 with about thirty students, all of them high-potential Chinese middle managers working in Motorola's Beijing offices. Students take one course at a time, taught in person by W. P. Carey professors who rotate into Beijing for the three-week sessions. A partnership with Tsinghua University, the premier engineering and business school in Beijing, resulted in a technology transfer of sorts: American professors demonstrating Western curriculum and pedagogy to Chinese professors.

With the launch of the China program, the W. P. Carey School of Business significantly deepened its international capabilities. Faculty returning from classes in Beijing began to enrich classes with examples from the Asian markets almost immediately; thus, the global strategy with its focus on faculty was being implemented.

Because of innovations in the ten-week trimester format of the MBA, the business school had already enabled itself to deploy its faculty more effectively in ways that support scholarship and short-term teaching opportunities like those in Beijing. The China Program added several new dimensions to the school's experience and organizational knowledge about running cross-disciplinary, global programs. From the China program, the college learned how to conduct very intensive classes at a distance. It learned how to work in China and with the Chinese government, and it learned how to work with a corporate partner. Thus, the stage was set for both ASU's Corporate Online MBA and the next major endeavor in Shanghai in collaboration with China's Ministry of Finance.

CORPORATE ONLINE MBA PROGRAM

Mototola's need to educate managers without removing them from their assignments is shared by many corporations, including Deere and Co., the Moline, Illinois manufacturer of farm equipment. Deere was already involved with the W. P. Carey supply chain management faculty through research, internships, and recruiting. Like Motorola, Deere represented a trusted partner. When the college began to consider its corporate online MBA as a means of competing via e-Learning, it needed a partner who had confidence in ASU to build and deliver an entirely new MBA, who could pay the price of a more expensive new program, and who could provide the initial working capital for its development.

Deere, like many firms, had identified a group of managers posted in facilities around the country and abroad who had demonstrated leadership potential. The company wanted to develop these managers without losing their services for two years to a campus-based MBA program. A high-quality, mixed-media program with intense executive education seemed to be the answer. The W. P. Carey School was also interested in growing into the distance learning market, but only if the resulting product matched the standards of the other W. P. Carey MBA programs.

Under the leadership of Professor Andy Philippakis, the W. P. Carey School built an innovative approach that blends traditional teaching methods with technology while managers remain at their desks. The W. P. Carey MBA–Corporate Online Program builds on the cohort concept with classes of thirty or more taking courses and graduating together. Like the China program, the students tackle one course at a time in intensive formats. The first class session brings students and professor together face-to-face for a day patterned after executive education. Then the managers scatter to their posts and work on the material using CDs, textbooks, and Web-based applications. Team projects—a key component of all W. P. Carey MBA programs—take on a new importance in this program. Because the students are part of the same company, real-time business problems can be assigned to groups of managers, under the supervision of the school's high-profile faculty, with real benefits in innovation and cost savings to the company.

The first Deere class graduated in 2002. Since then, cohorts from corporations, such as Intel, Lucent Technologies, United Technologies, and ChevronTexaco have participated in the program. More recent cohorts have brought together managers from every part of the world into a single collaborating class and onto very diverse teams. What the corporate online program did was build on the initial steps taken in the early 1990s with the first staff member involved in e-Learning. The program allowed the college to develop its e-Learning capability for a programmatic endeavor rather than enriched stand-alone classes. It also enhanced the college's ability to work with corporate partners in an executive educational format, and substantially improved the ability to develop excellent digital learning materials.

DOCTORAL PROGRAMS

Throughout its history with graduate education, ASU has included doctoral education as a critical element. Early on it offered the doctor of business administration degree, which became the more research-intensive PhD in 1984. As a part of Business Partners, the W. P. Carey School had committed itself to raising the quality of its doctoral program. It established a review process that evaluated each field's program against the goal of placement of its students in more competitive institutions and Carnegie-Classified Research I Institutions. The strategic intent was twofold: to raise the quality of the doctoral students as a means to attract and retain excellent faculty and to position ASU among faculty as a source of excellence in scholarship and faculty development.

UNDERGRADUATE PROGRAMMING: DOING IT THE HONORS WAY

To most observers of ASU prior to the 1990s, its primary focus had been its undergraduate program. In 2003, it was a very different program, consistent with the strategic direction presented by Business Partners and the transformation of the MBA. The average GPA of students admitted to the upper-division professional program majors was over 3.4. Just eight years ago students were admitted to some business majors with a 2.9. The profile of the class of spring 2003 was similar to those graduating from other top undergraduate programs.

The program that struggled to fit students into the classes they needed in the mid-1980s has become a highly selective major on the Arizona State University campus. Undergraduate studies at the W. P. Carey School of Business were ranked twenty-fifth among accredited business programs in the 2002 *U.S. News & World Report* survey.

The school attracts great students in part because of the honors program. The program that began with a handful of students during John Kraft's deanship grew to more than three hundred upper-division students and four hundred lower-division students. Although affiliated with ASU's Barrett Honors College, it has always been a complete unit within the business school, making it one of the few freestanding business honors programs in the country. Business accounts for only 19 percent of the baccalaureate degrees awarded at ASU, but nearly 40 percent of the honors graduates are business majors.

Business Honors is a key strategy in satisfying the paradox that faces the W. P. Carey School. By creating challenge and opportunity for hardworking, talented students, the school has succeeded in focusing on the few and the many at the same time. Business Honors offers students an enriched experience in classes through small breakout sections, additional projects, and the honors thesis.

The Rodel Community Scholars Program is an opportunity for Business Honors students to apply their skills in a community service setting.

Founded to promote civic leadership in undergraduate students, the program embodies the W. P. Carey School's commitment to community via helping solve the high school dropout problem. Business Honors students work in teams and approach the retention issue in their assigned high school as a business problem. Teams have drafted business plans and started implementation in four schools. Over time, they hope that high school students touched by their interaction with business honors students and affected by their business plans will finish high school and enroll at ASU.

In 2003 a new initiative called Honors Consulting was launched for undergraduate students. Modeled after the successful Masters Consulting Group in the W. P. Carey MBA, Honors Consulting offers the talent of W. P. Carey's best undergraduates to area businesses on a consulting basis. The group's first project focused on the businesses along the path of a light rail line to be constructed in Central Phoenix. Students conducted well-business evaluations for participating firms and offered strategies for mitigating or capitalizing upon the mass transit project. Business Honors is the highlight in a program that offers quality to all.

CORE VALUES ACROSS PROGRAMS

After more than a decade of significant change, the culture of the W. P. Carey School of Business evidences several core values: managing with technology, real-world applications, ethics in action, building global awareness, and community citizenship. Those values grew, not just from the recent history of the school nor from the fifty-year history of a business program, but from the founding forces that created the university as a response to the needs of the European-origin pioneers of the nineteenth century.

Technology Infusion

By 1998 the college had already made a major commitment to technology—as a means to support learning and as an essential field of study in the increasingly complex IT setting of American business. Once again Penley brought out the Business Partners template to address a major question. The e-Business Task Force was a corporate/faculty partnership that studied the fundamentals of ASU's business program in the light of a rapidly evolving technology environment. The task force, which included representatives of technology companies, such as Cisco Systems and Honeywell, began by defining the landscape. Every functional area of the business world had been at least touched if not transformed by technology. Technology and information management was a distinct industry sector, and no businessperson—or business school—could afford to ignore its overarching influence. The task force recommended programmatic changes that reflected these new conditions.

Beginning in 2002, students in every undergraduate business major were being exposed to technology, starting with their first core business course in supply chain management. Weaving technology throughout the MBA requires easy access to the tools. The school was one of the first in the country to install wireless capability throughout its classrooms and common areas. Thin client server technology allows wireless access to large databases and the complex software programs that run them. Any place where a wireless access node was available became a W. P. Carey computer lab, and any classroom became a computer classroom.

Real-World Application

Some 60 percent of W. P. Carey undergraduates work twenty hours per week or more while they are attending school. This bank of experience enriches the classroom, and gives W. P. Carey graduates competitive advantage in the job market. The Certificate in Dealership Management program is an excellent example of the school's commitment to real-world experience in its undergraduate program. Ford Motor Company partners with the school to provide students with opportunities to obtain industry-specific expertise while pursuing a business major. The program consists of a dealership management course, seminars, and an internship in a dealership business. Minority graduates of the program qualify for Ford's postgraduate dealership program, also delivered at the W. P. Carey School.

Ethics in Action

Carey's rich MBA and undergraduate curriculum unfolds in a context that demands high ethical values. The Lincoln Center for Applied Ethics, now a university-wide initiative based in the College of Liberal Arts and Sciences, was founded in the business school because of its longtime emphasis on ethics. The Lincoln Professor of Ethics, economist Lin Zhou, is a business faculty member. It is no surprise, then, that all graduates and undergraduates must take a course in law, ethics, and regulation, nor is it a surprise that students consider the case competition with its focus on ethics and globalization as central to the learning experience of the Full-time MBA. Every graduate understands the school's newly proposed slogan, adopted from benefactor Wm. Polk Carey: "Doing good while doing well."

Global Awareness

The W. P. Carey School has had a long history of international connections, but its strategic focus from the Business Partners planning period gave special impetus in the last decade. And even though the initial strategic intent was faculty development, the changing character of the school's students over more than a decade has had its effect. MBAs, especially from the Evening and Executive programs, have extensive opportunities to learn about the global business environment. The growth in excellent students at the undergraduate level via Business Honors has meant that demand for international learning opportunities has increased substantially as well. Although business undergraduates are only 7 percent of ASU's total enrollment, they account for close to 30 percent of the students who go abroad.

Following a model the school has often used, it began its globalization with one program—in this case the Executive MBA—and then extended what it had learned to other programs. The school introduced a course in global economics and a European experience in the early 1990s. It expanded its commitment to building global awareness with a number of steps as non-U.S. partnerships were established. Intensive summer classes in Europe and Asia were added for evening MBAs. The global economics class was extended to all MBA programs, and undergraduates were required to select from among a set of international classes.

Now the school is expanding its MBA in Beijing to Shanghai in an agreement with the Chinese Ministry of Finance with a focus on the most senior managers in the financial sector. A second degree program targeting the computer manufacturing sector in Taiwan is under consideration. Additional MBAs in Europe and Latin America are planned for 2004.

Community Citizenship

The W. P. Carey School houses the Center for the Advancement of Small Business, a vital link to the enterprises that make up the bulk of the Arizona economy. The center's first project was the creation of a small business minor, open to students from across the university. The center is now involved in developing its Family Business Forum, a community outreach program that links the resources of the W. P. Carey School to family-owned businesses.

The W. P. Carey School is also a major source of the business data used by companies to make financial and planning decisions. The Bank One Economic Outlook Center is the source of key indices—including the Bank One Index of Leading Economic Indicators, the Arizona Business Conditions Index, the Tourism Barometer, and the Job Growth Forecast—concerning the local and regional economy. The Arizona Real Estate Center tracks activity and trends in the Arizona market. Through the Center for Business Research, the W. P. Carey School monitors population, income, and other demographic data. The Blue Chip publications produced by the L. William Seidman Research Institute are quoted nationally.

Involvement with the community is taken seriously at the W. P. Carey School of Business. After all, business graduates will have far more wealth than the average citizen; they can use that wealth to have an impact on the quality of community and the quality of life of citizens in it. As business graduates they also leave with a perspective and cognitive approach that is problem-solution–oriented. Their ability to make a difference is supported by the leadership perspective engendered by a quality business education. This is why the Rodel Community Scholars Program at the undergraduate level is so important to the school. It is why the charity challenge at the MBA level and the Undergraduate Business College Council's charity events are seen as integral to business education.

PROMOTING THE AGENDA

The rapid advances made by the W. P. Carey School could not have been achieved without incentives and support. The school encourages excellence in its faculty by structuring rewards on teaching *and* research accomplishments. Student evaluations conducted at the end of every semester are weighted similar to published research productivity in faculty performance reviews. This inner drive toward improvement is complemented by support flowing from the community.

During ASU's Campaign for Leadership in the late 1990s, the business college reaped its reward for all of the lunch conversations and advisory board meetings. Individuals and businesses responded to the tune of more than $50 million. By the time the books closed, the W.P. Carey School had added almost thirty endowed chairs and professorships. These positions, and the accompanying financial support, help to build strength in the institution by attracting the best faculty.

The $50 million gift from the W. P. Carey Foundation established a stable financial base for the school, but further fundraising is on the horizon. The school launched a $50–$60 million capital campaign shortly after receiving the Carey gift. The new campaign will secure funding for a new building, to be located at the northwest corner of campus, overlooking downtown Tempe.

The school has long needed facilities that are designed for a technology-rich business program. During its last AACSB accreditation review, the school was told what it already knew, that its cramped quarters would soon threaten its quality. A $6.9 million renovation campaign carved out new offices for the undergraduate and MBA programs, allowed for closer working space for PhD students and faculty, and implemented technology infrastructure upgrades. Still, the school is some 105,000 square feet short of the space considered necessary to operate a top business program.

STRENGTH IN DYNAMICS

The W. P. Carey School at Arizona State University draws strength by finding connections in opposites. Consider the image of saguaro cactus combined with the New York skyline. Located far from the nexus of the financial world, the school nevertheless attracted the attention of one of the century's most successful New York bankers. The W. P. Carey School has learned to extract energy from paradoxes: Deliver excellence to the many while cultivating the few.

Going forward, the W. P. Carey School will have to maintain steady balance between the poles while increasing acceleration toward improvement. Grounded by Mr. Carey's generosity, the school will aggressively pursue academic stars to lead the way. Great students will be lured by the excitement they create. A new culture that pulls faculty, staff, and students into closer relationships will nurture the growth.

As the ad says, "East meets West" at the W. P. Carey School of Business.

Part III

Strategies for Moving into the Future

16

Being Strategic about Innovation: Lessons for Business Schools, Future Graduate Students, and Potential Employers

Mimi Wolverton and Larry Edward Penley

We began this book by suggesting that in an individualistic society, such as the United States, business schools housed at public universities continually strive to be measurably better than their peers. In fact, this trait is clearly evident in each of the case studies. But although each school mentions rankings of various types, there is definitely more to each story. These institutions clearly understand and demonstrate in concrete detail how to establish a competitive advantage and use it to determine and build necessary bridges to sustainable futures. Taken as a whole, their stories reveal the answer to the question: What really makes them tick? They illustrate how innovative schools can and do reinvent business education. Figure 16.1 illustrates commonalities found across the twelve business schools and brings into focus the critical elements of excellence that surfaced. In sharing their experiences, critical incidences in their histories, and elements they deem essential to their success, they provide blueprints to thinking about and embracing innovation strategically.

Figure 16.1
Elements of Excellence

The crucial distinction between these schools and hundreds of others, however, lies in their realization that while strategies are plans for the future, they also reflect patterns of the past, which sometimes need to be altered (Mintzberg, 1989). A wise person once said, "If you always do what you've always done, then you'll always get what you've already got" (Urbanski, 1991, p. 34). In essence, to set themselves apart from other business schools, these twelve institutions built an inner capacity for "getting different" (Hamel and Prahalad, 1994).

Focus, whether derived from institutional uniqueness or not, does not guarantee continued success. Buggy whip manufacturers were very focused and made excellent buggy whips—a strategy that proved lucrative until there were no more buggies. In failing to anticipate the future of transportation, they ensured their eventual demise. Business schools in this book chose not to go down the same path. Instead, they engaged in behaviors deemed necessary for successful change: innovative strategizing, coalition and community building and communication, seeking long-term gains predicated on short-term wins, continual refocusing for the future, and anchoring new behaviors in their organizational cultures (Kotter, 1996). They each possessed leaders that helped shape direction and kept them on task. And in the end, their penchant for excellence demanded that, as organizations, these schools remain forward thinking and change tolerant.

In *Competing for the Future*, Hamel and Prahalad (1994) suggest six broad organizing principles, which, when paid attention to, lead to sustained industry leadership. These themes provide an organizing framework within which business schools that want to raise their academic profiles can begin to apply lessons learned from the twelve case study business schools. In brief, Hamel and Prahalad contend that organizations intent on being at the top of their industries do so, in part, by "creating the markets of tomorrow." They suggest that premier organizations engage in variants of the same six strategies:

- Establish a competitive advantage.
- Find the future.
- Mobilize for the future.
- Get to the future first.
- Build gateways to the future.
- Secure the future.

ESTABLISH A COMPETITIVE ADVANTAGE

Establishing a competitive advantage involves knowing your institutional self. Each of our study schools understood what made it unique—whether ethics at TAMU or engineering at Georgia Tech—and all established foci in international business, technology, or entrepreneurialism. Early on, they determined where their competition lay. Smith at Maryland sensed that it could not compete in the geopolitical arena of Washington, D.C., as successfully as could business schools that were located in the country's capitol. Instead, it concentrated its efforts in an area (technology) where its competition placed relatively little emphasis. UW set out to determine whom it served and quickly delineated the markets in which it wanted to participate and had an edge, namely, Seattle and the Pacific Rim countries. Several schools initiated their international efforts in one or a small number of countries (ASU in China and Mexico, Purdue in Germany, Pittsburgh in the former Soviet bloc), instinctively understanding that they should not overextend their resources.

These schools added unique elements to their programs that helped them establish distinct niches. Pittsburgh developed an executive coaching program for its two-year MBA. As a result of finding a niche, Georgia State has a finance program that is described as one of the most intriguing in the country. ASU developed strands for individuals who want to specialize in the sports industry or the health industry. Georgia trains prospective corporate board members and teaches about servant leadership. TAMU's ethical heritage permeates its newly developed program as does an extremely strong emphasis on building communication skills. Each of these efforts separates study institution programs from those of their competitors.

In general, these schools developed competitive advantages by

- comprehensively examining their strengths, weaknesses, opportunities, and threats in relation to the environments in which they exist.
- determining a niche.
- exploiting specific strengths in building program offerings.

FIND THE FUTURE

Here is where planning, strategy, innovation, leadership, and change come together. Thinking and planning strategically requires that we question customary practice, perhaps not entirely forgetting the past, but certainly moving beyond it. That indeed, we sense a need for change. It demands foresight: How do we anticipate the shape and direction of programs and business schools early enough to take advantage of such knowledge? In fact, Indiana specifically mentions a need for foresight, and many others spoke of transforming themselves and reinventing what they do. More importantly, once they discovered their niches, these schools used them as rallying points in setting direction. Several made reference to synchronizing vision, as defined by focus, with mission as established by institutional purpose.

Such strategic intent helps maintain focus. But focus must be just that, focused. Those institutions that described institutional planning and new program creation delineated five or six priorities and aligned one to three measurable targets under each priority. Purdue's plan revolves around six strategies and twelve milestones to be accomplished over the next five to ten years. UW set five priorities; Maryland has six key areas of emphasis, each with three clearly specified outcomes attached to it. Such moves constitute embracing innovation strategically. In effect, these business schools became architects of their own destinies. They built blueprints for future, purposefully directed change.

Two elements—leadership and evidence of change—are crucial to this approach to future building. Leadership might start with specific direction-setting by a dean, as in the case of Maryland; it can manifest itself at multiple organizational levels almost simultaneously, as with UW; or it can fall somewhere between these two extremes. Many, like Georgia Tech, Georgia, and Arizona State, incorporated corporate advisory boards into their planning processes to take advantage of a different type of leadership as well as the impact those advisory boards can have—within the business school, at senior levels of the university, and with the community. The important issue is that leadership must emerge.

Similarly, all the planning for change in the world is useless unless conspicuous evidence of change materializes. Florida is very clear about how it measures results: in terms of research productivity. UW produces corporate and school report cards. Purdue's milestones are extremely specific, as are Maryland's goals.

Themes that cut across these planning initiatives suggest six common-sense strategies that have produced extraordinary results:

- Use active leadership at multiple levels of the organization, with the dean playing an essential role in setting the stage and moving the college or school toward its future.
- Create a vision based on a clear focus that sets direction and moves the college or school out of its comfort zone.
- Possess a disposition toward action.
- Develop a plan with strategic intent.
- Limit priorities to five or six imperatives.
- Select a few specific, measurable targets that are tied to each priority.

MOBILIZING FOR THE FUTURE

For business schools, mobilizing for the future, in effect, means aligning resources so that they can realize their goals. It involves taking inventory of what counts as resources, redirecting existing resources, and building and finding new ones. Whether intentionally or not, many of these schools sensed that their students are a resource. Instinctively, they understood that if, at a minimum, the demographic makeup of the students in their programs mimics those of the global community, then their graduates will emerge better trained and equipped for the workplace of tomorrow. Indiana, Purdue, Pittsburgh, Georgia State, Arizona State, and TAMU spoke of broadening their student demographic mix to better reflect the realities of today's workplace. Likewise, Georgia Tech, Florida, South Carolina, Washington, and others serve sizable international populations. These schools view this type of institution-environment fit as crucial to their success.

Resources are always a sticky issue, whose lack provides organizations with easy excuses for not mobilizing for the future. We argue that although resources are important, resourcefulness probably bears more consequence. In fact, a lack of resources may not be as much of a problem as failing to think creatively about how to leverage existing resources to promote precise goals and objectives.

Mobilizing for the future requires that you judiciously put available resources to work. Maryland did just that by differentiating faculty positions and workloads across faculty types to better meet its unifying goal of providing educational excellence for students who will work in technology-driven companies. Several schools, including South Carolina, Arizona State, Maryland, and Georgia Tech, entered into full-fledged marketing campaigns to advertise their programs. Others (Purdue, Washington, Arizona State, and Maryland) sought tuition or fee increases and negotiated joint funding strategies with their universities (Indiana and Maryland).

To mobilize for the future also requires that institutions stretch themselves, creating new programs, new coalitions, and new avenues of research and study. TAMU redesigned its signature program—the full-time MBA. UW entered into a coalition with a Korean university to provide MBA programming. ASU (in China and Mexico), Purdue (in Germany), and Georgia (at Oxford Univesity) did the same. Florida interacts with more than thirty partner institutions to provide programs worldwide. Arizona State invested heavily in information technology and e-Learning in order to create new programs (e.g., its Corporate Online program) and reduce faculty demands in others (e.g., the China MBA with Motorola). And Maryland, Florida, Georgia, Georgia Tech, and Arizona State, to name a few, continually reinforce research agendas that further their strategic agendas.

In effect, mobilizing for the future requires that schools

- use available resources wisely.
- leverage programmatic position through strategic coalition building.
- find alternative funding approaches.
- market what they do best.
- change the student mix to better mirror the global nature of the nation and the world.

GET TO THE FUTURE FIRST

The schools described in this volume set their sights on being leaders in what they consider their core competencies. This requires not only striving to be the best, but also getting to the market first with innovative ideas and programs. Their records include a litany of firsts. Pitt was the first to establish joint teaching and research centers in former Soviet Bloc countries; first to offer a one-year, full-time MBA program; first to offer a dual techno-MBA degree; and one of a very few to offer a PhD in business environments, ethics, and public policy. Florida became the first U.S. graduate business school accredited in Europe. Georgia Tech built one of the first college campus buildings to be certified as environmentally friendly by the U.S. Green Building Council. Purdue's MBA in agribusiness was the first of its kind, and their traditional MBA program was the first in the nation to focus on communication skills. Arizona State was one of the first to transform its evening program to include advantages from lockstep, full-time programs, and it was also the first MBA to offer a specialization in services marketing. Georgia is the only business college in the nation with a student residential facility located on a foreign campus. Among Indiana's firsts is the distinction of housing one of five MBA programs tracked by the Educational Benchmarking Corporation as a standard for curricular innovation. In addition, each school can point to either master and doctoral programs or research faculty that rank first among their peers.

Those institutions with the opportunity to hire new faculty did so in ways that aligned the school's areas of expertise with its strategic intent. The University of Maryland and Georgia Tech both hired faculty who could strengthen their programmatic emphases on technology through research and teaching. The ability to move quickly in recognizing their strategic goals because of new hires sped their moving to the future first. In similar ways, primarily through faculty and doctoral student research productivity, all case study institutions continually compete for intellectual leadership in their areas of emphasis. Strategies that helped these institutions get to the future first include

- striving to be first.
- hiring faculty that help build reputation and programs through research and teaching.
- recruiting the best master and doctoral students.

BUILD GATEWAYS TO THE FUTURE

Although building gateways to the future demands an understanding of what their core strengths are and a striving for excellence based on these strengths, it also requires a realigning of reward systems to reinforce and guarantee continued preeminence in key areas. Maryland, Washington, Florida, and ASU provide excellent examples of business schools that emphasize preferred behaviors by tying resources to them. They also build infrastructure by aligning research centers with their strategic agendas and providing faculty with the technological support they need to do their jobs. They upgraded facilities. Georgia Tech, in fact, was quite politically astute when it invited central administration for a tour of its building. Only then did the university realize the importance of DuPree's ability to create the proper image and include the business school in its Technology Square. Others entered into agreements with their universities to develop viable funding strategies to fill capital building needs. In essence, study schools:

- Reward desired behaviors in faculty, staff, and students.
- Build the infrastructure to support desired activities.
- Pay attention to physical image and value buildings, whether new or old.

SECURE THE FUTURE

To secure the future, these business schools created new competitive spaces, drew on the collective wisdom of multiple constituents, and planned for action. First and foremost, these schools excel at what they do, in part because they revisit the process of change to determine whether what they offer has benefit to those constituents who invest their time, energy, and money in their programs. Such efforts help them ensure program vitality and sustainability in the long run and keep them at the forefront of graduate business education programming.

All of the study schools mentioned the importance of building internal, local, and global partnerships. Georgia State's spokesman suggested that "the classroom, boardroom, and community converge to shape the future of business." The dean at UW spoke of drawing on alumni time, expertise, advice, resources, and political clout. Others attested to cross-discipline collaborative efforts that helped them anticipate future workplace needs. Georgia Tech encourages such endeavors through its Shared Idea Laboratory and by rotating space for interdisciplinary centers on a competitive basis. Such efforts enhance their ability to deliver viable programs. Moreover, they enrich the learning environment not only for students, but for faculty as well.

Every school was explicit about the advantages of building partnerships with the business community, not only in terms of curricular viability, but also as primary mechanisms for raising needed funds. Community involvement, in general, often lent voice to their arguments for greater state funding as well. Although most of these institutions did receive large infusions of funding, such supplemental resources tell only a portion of the story and usually came on the heels of massive faculty and leadership involvement, not as a precursor to it. Each school works diligently to ensure that a quid pro quo relationship exists between their partners and them. Reciprocity and partnership are key. These study schools work at securing their futures by

- exhibiting a penchant for excellence.
- possessing a willingness to revisit change.
- being creative about tapping into and attracting resources.
- being involved in the community and having the community involved in them.

STRATEGIES IN ACTION: LESSONS FOR RISING BUSINESS SCHOOLS

These six deceptively simple sounding strategies—establishing competitive advantage, finding and mobilizing for the future, getting there first, building gateways, and ensuring that the future is sustainable—take time, effort, energy, and concerted dedication on the part of deans, faculty, alumni, and the communities with which the study institutions interface and serve. They can, however, be emulated.

In effect, they provide a beginning, a guide for plateaued business schools ("stuck at good but wanting to be great," as the dean at UW put it). They require enthusiasm, determination, and a willingness and the capacity to think strategically about innovation, not necessarily to create anew, but to think in different ways about what gets done to what purpose. We hope that in sharing our stories, other business schools can develop their competitive advantages and secure prosperous futures predicated on a commitment to excellence.

IMPLICATIONS FOR FUTURE STUDENTS

This book also provides a handbook of sorts for potential business college graduate students. Obviously, the case studies highlight the strengths and emphases of study-schools. But also, and more importantly, together they suggest a set of overarching characteristics that can direct the selection of programs and business schools as potential education homes for students.

Students intent on maximizing their educational experiences take more than program costs into consideration (although that is important, and clearly a benefit attached to publicly supported institutions). The experiences of these case study schools offer potential students a rubric of institutional selection criteria. Such criteria can be used in examining the strengths and weaknesses of graduate business schools prior to any decision to apply for admission. The following questions, garnered from the practices of the case study business schools, capture the basic criteria of an assessment rubric:

- What is the focus of the school?
- What makes the school unique?
- Does it demonstrate a compelling commitment to education excellence?
- Does diversity play a role in enhancing the education experience?
- How does it view programmatic and institutional change?
- Does it strategically embrace innovation?

By *strategically embrace innovation*, we mean:

- Does the school's leadership provide a catalyst for change?
- What evidence of change exists?
- What is the school's plan for the future?
- How does it involve the business community, alumni, and other local and regional constituents in the ongoing business of the school?
- How well does the school anticipate its future?

A SCREENING MECHANISM
FOR POTENTIAL EMPLOYERS

The same set of questions can provide a matrix through which potential employers can examine business schools to determine where to recruit future employees. The investment a firm makes in a new hire demands that such decisions be made judiciously. "Haste makes waste" clearly applies here. Yet recruiting becomes habit, and firms habitually return to the same institutions year after year. Understanding the basic premises that guide a school's educational philosophy can help potential employers broaden or realign the way they target institutions where they engage in recruiting activities. Excellent education environments breed education excellence in program graduates. Capitalizing on these forms of excellence gives employers a leg up in their own pursuits of excellence.

CLOSING COMMENTS

Public business schools that house elite MBA programs are indeed more than their signature programs. In fact, a zealous pursuit of excellence underscores everything they do. Inspired leadership, determination, an uncanny acceptance of change as reality, and targeted planning initiatives that thrust them into the trenches of the communities they serve propel them along a continual journey in search of continued excellence.

References

Berry, L. L., & Parasuraman, A. (1990). *Marketing services: Competing through quality.* New York: Free Press.

Birnbaum, R. (1994). The quality cube: How college presidents assess excellence. *Journal for Higher Education Management 9*(2), 71–82.

Bowditch, J. L., & Buono, A. E. (2001). *A primer on organizational behavior.* New York: Wiley.

Carr, D., Hard, K., & Trahant, W. (1996). *Managing the change process: A field guide for change agents, consultants, team leaders and reengineering managers.* New York: McGraw-Hill.

Cole, J. R., Barber, E. G., & Graubard, S. R. (Ed.). (1994). *The research university in a time of discontent.* Baltimore: Johns Hopkins University Press.

Conger, J. A. (1998, May). The necessary art of persuasion. *Harvard Business Review,* 84–95.

Cook, C. E., & Sorcinelli, M. D. (1999). Building multiculturalism into teaching-development programs. *AAHE Bulletin 51*(7), 3–6.

Cox, T., Jr. (1994). *Cultural diversity in organizations: Theory, research and practice.* San Francisco: Berrett-Koehler.

Drucker, P. F. (2002, August). The discipline of innovation. *Harvard Business Review,* 95–104. (Original article published in 1985.)

Galbraith, J. R., Lawler, E. E., & Associates. (1993). *Organizing for the future.* San Francisco: Jossey-Bass.

Gibson, J. L., Ivancevich, J. M., & Donnelly, J. H. (2000). *Organizations: Behaviors, structures, processes.* Boston: Irvin-McGraw-Hill.

Glaser, B., & Strauss, A. (1967*). The discovery of grounded theory: Strategies for qualitative research.* New York: Aldine de Gruyter.

Goldenberg, J., Horowitz, R., Levav, A., & Mazursky, D. (2003, March). Finding your innovation sweet spot. *Harvard Business Review,* 120–129.

Guskin, A. (1996, July). Facing the future: The change process in restructuring universities. *Change,* 26–37.

Hamel, G., & Prahalad, C. K. (1994). *Competing for the future: Breakthrough strategies for seizing control of your industry and creating the markets of tomorrow.* Boston: Harvard Business School Press.

Hilosky, A., & Watswood, B. (1997). *Transformational leadership in a changing world: A survival guide for new chairs and deans.* (Eric Dcoument Reproduction Service No. ED 407027)

Kanter, R. M. (1985). *The change masters.* New York: Simon & Schuster.

Keller, G. (1983). *Academic strategy: The management revolution in American higher education.* Baltimore: Johns Hopkins University Press.

Kotter, J. (1990a). *A force for change: How leadership differs from management.* New York: Free Press.

Kotter, J. (1990b, May–June). What leaders really do. *Harvard Business Review,* 103–111.

Kotter, J. (1996). *Leading change.* Boston: Harvard Business School Press.

Manning, P. K., & Cullum-Swan, B. (1994). Narrative, content, and semiotic analysis. In N. K. Denizen & Y. S. Lincoln (Eds.), *Handbook of qualitative research* (pp. 463–477). Thousand Oaks, CA: Sage.

Miles, M. B., & Huberman, A. M. (1984). *Qualitative data analysis.* Beverly Hills, CA: Sage.

Mintzberg, H. (1989*). Mintzberg on management: Inside our strange world of organizations.* New York: Free Press.

O'Toole, J. (1995). *Leading change.* San Francisco: Jossey-Bass.

Pearson, A. E. (2002, August). Tough-minded ways to get innovative. *Harvard Business Review,* 117–126.

Pinchot, G. (1985). *Intrapreneuring.* New York: HarperCollins.

Porter, M. (1985). *Competitive advantage: Creating and sustaining superior performance.* New York: Free Press.

Quinn, J. B. (1980). *Strategies for change: Logical incrementalism.* Homewood, IL: Business One Irwin.

Richardson, R. C., Jr., & Skinner, E. F. (1991). *Achieving quality and diversity: Universities in a multicultural society.* New York: ACE/Macmillan.

Rowley, D. J., Lujan, H. D., & Dolence, M. G. (1997). *Strategic change in colleges and universities.* San Francisco: Jossey-Bass.

Tierney, W. G. (1998). *The responsive university.* Baltimore: Johns Hopkins University Press.

Urbanski, A. (1991). An education reformer's New Year's resolution. *American Educator 15*(3), 34–35.

Wolpert, J. D. (2002, August). Breaking out of the innovation box. *Harvard Business Review,* 76–94.

Wolverton, M. (1998). Champions of change, change agents, and collaborators in change: Leadership keys to successful systemic change. *Journal of Higher Education Policy and Management 20*(1), 19–30.

Wolverton, M., & Gmelch, W. H. (2002). *College deans: Leading from within.* Westport CT: ACE/Oryx.

Wolverton, M., Gmelch, W. H., Montez, J., & Nies, C. T. (2001). *The changing nature of the academic deanship.* San Francisco: Jossey-Bass.

Yin, R. K. (1994). *Case study research: Design and methods.* Thousand Oaks, CA: Sage.

Index

International Master's in Management
    (IMM), 151
International Resource Group, Ltd.,
    192
International students, 30–31, 74, 125,
    153
  costs for, 75
  enrollment of, 55
Internet, 85, 86, 164, 168, 179
Internet MBA, 179
Internships, 42, 81, 112, 124, 139, 151,
    160, 161
  international, 110–11
  participation in, 176, 177
  Affairs, 98, 99, 100

Jamison, Mark, 192
JD, 54, 124
Jefferson, Thomas, 76
Jerry S. Rawls Hall, 152, 155
Jeuland, Abel, 148
J. Mack Robinson College of Business,
    105–18
J. M. Tull School of Accounting, 79
Job Growth Forecast, 207
Joint Law Degree programs, 137
Joseph M. Katz Graduate School of
    Business, 18, 28, 119–34
  building, 133–34
  change at, 30
  classrooms at, 133–34
  faculty at, 126–27
  funding for, 121
  history of, 123–24
  innovation at, 124
  intellectual stimulation at, 24
  international flavor of, 125
  minority students at, 31
  naming of, 123
  PhD program at, 128–33
  Pittsburgh and, 119–20, 121, 133
  renovation of, 121
  students at, 127–28
Journal of Accounting Literature,
    173
Journal of Applied Psychology, 66
Journal of Consumer Research, 127
Journal of Corporate Finance, 127

Journal of Current Issues and Research
    in Advertising, 66
Journal of Hospitality and Tourism
    Education, 116
Journal of Information Systems, 66
Journal of International Business Eco-
    nomics, 127
Journal of International Business Stud-
    ies, 136
Journal of Management, 66, 117
Journal of Management Accounting,
    127
Journal of Management Account
    Research, 127
Journal of Marketing, 66, 127
Journal of Marketing Research, 127
Journal of Organizational Behavior, 66,
    127
Journal of Public Policy and Market-
    ing, 173
Journal of the Academy of Marketing
    Science, 66

Kamien, Morton, 148
Kane, James F., 135, 141
Katz, Joseph M., 123
Katz Volunteers, 126
Kelley, E. W., 158
Kelley Direct Program, 163
Kelley Executive Partners (KEP), 163,
    165
Kelley Scholars, 158
Kelley School of Business, 157–70
  graduate programs at, 158–65
  history of, 157–58
Killinger, Kerry, 41
Kiplinger's Personal Finance Maga-
    zine, 172
Koestenbaum, Peter, 165
Kraemer, Richard C., 196, 198
Kraft, John, 195, 196, 197, 204
Krannert, Ellnora, 145
Krannert, Herman, 145
Krannert Center for Executive Educa-
    tion and Research, 146
Krannert Executive Education Pro-
    grams (KEEP), 151, 153
Krannert Executive Forum, 149

About the Editors and Contributors

NATHAN BENNETT is the senior associate dean and a professor in the College of Management at Georgia Tech. His current research interests include multilevel modeling of organizational phenomena. Previous research has appeared in the *Academy of Management Journal*, the *Academy of Management Review*, the *Journal of Applied Psychology*, and the *Journal of Management*. He is also actively involved in executive education programs both in the United States and abroad.

TERRY C. BLUM has been the dean of the College of Management since summer 1999. She was named to the Tedd Munchak Chair in Entrepreneurship in 1996, making her the first woman at Georgia Tech to be awarded an endowed chair. She has researched and published extensively on topics related to innovation and technology transfer in behavioral health care. She serves on a National Institutes of Health study section, and is a co-investigator for research grants related to the study of organizational and entrepreneurial factors that mediate the transfer, adoption, and diffusion of innovation to for-profit and not-for-profit health treatment organizations.

JAN COLLINS is an editor at the Moore School of Business, University of South Carolina. She is also a freelance writer and coauthor of two nationally syndicated newspaper columns, "NextSteps" (on the legal, financial, and practical issues of aging and retirement) and "Flying Solo" (on divorce and separation issues). A former newspaper journalist in Michigan, North Carolina, and South Carolina, Jan was a Nieman Fellow at Harvard University and a Congressional Fellow of the American Political Science Association.

ELIZABETH O. FARQUHAR coordinates media relations for the W. P. Carey School of Business at Arizona State University. Before joining Arizona State, Farquhar was a newspaper reporter and columnist in Boston.

HOWARD FRANK is dean of the Robert H. Smith School of Business of the University of Maryland. Previously he was director of the Defense Advanced Research Project Agency's information technology office, where he managed a $300 million annual budget aimed at advancing the frontiers of information technology. He was founder, chairman, and CEO of Network Management Inc.; president and CEO of Contel Information Systems (a subsidiary of Contel); president, CEO, and founder of the Network Analysis Corporation; a visiting consultant within the Executive Office of the President of the United States, in charge of its network analysis activities; and an associate professor at the University of California, Berkeley. He is widely recognized as a world-class information technology expert whose accomplishments include fundamental contributions to the development of the Internet. He is also a seasoned information industry executive with more than twenty years of senior line management experience as well as experience in the venture capital and mergers and acquisitions fields. He is a member of the National Academy of Engineering, a Fellow of Informs and a Fellow of the Institute of Electrical and Electronic Engineers (IEEE), and a recipient of the IEEE's 1999 Eric Sumner Award. He was awarded the Distinguished Service Medal by the secretary of defense (the Defense Department's highest civilian honor) for his contributions during his four years at the Defense Advanced Research Projects Agency.

YASH GUPTA served as dean of the University of Washington Business School between 1999 and 2004, and prior to that was dean of the University of Colorado–Denver College of Business Administration for seven years. In 2004, he became dean of the Marshall School of Business, University of Southern California. At these schools he spearheaded the development of new programs, marshalled increased support from alumni and the business community, and improved the reputation of the institution. In 1994 and 1996 he was ranked as the most prolific scholar in the United States in the area of operations management.

PAUL KARR is a prize-winning writer, editor, and writing consultant for the University of Georgia's Terry College of Business, the University of Chicago, and the Center for International Trade and Security, among other clients. He specializes in writing the histories of corporations, educational institutions, and institutional programs; he also specializes in benefactor– and competitive grant–oriented publications and research publications of all kinds.

JOHN KRAFT was business dean at Arizona State University before taking a similar post at the University of Florida in 1990. He has been a consultant to *Fortune* 500 Companies, has directed nonprofit organizations, and has held executive positions at federal agencies and tenured positions at Florida and at Arizona State. He has authored more than one hundred articles, books, and monographs. Kraft served as chair of AACSB–The International Association for Management Education in 2001–2002, and is a member of its board of directors. He also served on the Graduate Management Admission Council (GMAC) board and as governor of the Beta Gamma Sigma board of directors.

GARY W. McKILLIPS is director of communications and external affairs for Georgia State University's Robinson College of Business in Atlanta. He joined the college in 2000 after three years as assistant vice president for university relations at the University of Tennessee. Prior to that, he was vice president-corporate and sports PR for Turner Broadcasting. In 2002, McKillips was elected to the College of Fellows of the Public Relations Society of America (PRSA). He is also cochair of Public Relations in Management Education (PRIME), a committee of AACSB, the association of business schools.

RHONDA MULLEN is a freelance writer in Atlanta and Georgia State PhD alumna. She has written on a wide range of topics, including business, the health sciences, and the arts, for nonprofit and university audiences.

TIM NEWTON is director of external relations and communications for Purdue University's Krannert School of Management. Prior to joining the Krannert School in 2000, he was director of communications for the Purdue Alumni Association and editor of the *Purdue Alumnus* magazine (1992–19w99). He was an editor with the Purdue News Service from 1989 to 1992.

LARRY EDWARD PENLEY is president of Colorado State University and Chancellor of the Colorado State University System. Previously he was professor of management and dean of the W. P. Carey School of Business at Arizona State University for more than a decade.

DAN H. ROBERTSON is a Regents' Professor of Marketing and assistant dean of graduate studies at Texas A&M University. He has held a variety of administrative positions there including director of the Mays MBA program and chair of the Graduate Management Admission Council (GMAC). He is the author of numerous journal articles and business publications.

CATHERINE HINES WILLS is director of marketing at the Moore School of Business, University of South Carolina. Her responsibilities include advertising, branding, and public relations for the Moore School. Prior to returning to her alma mater, she was senior vice president of marketing for Maybelline Inc., a division of L'Oreal, in New York City.

JAMES C. WIMBUSH is the chair of the Department of Management, associate dean of the faculties, and professor of business administration. He joined Indiana University in 1991 and has served as chair of doctoral programs in business and, most recently, chair of the Kelley MBA Program. In addition to his administrative duties, he has been recognized for both teaching and research. His current research interests include measurement issues for the collection of sensitive data, integrity testing, and ethical issues in human resources management.

FREDERICK W. WINTER has been the dean of the University of Pittsburgh's Joseph M. Katz Graduate School of Business since 1997. Before that, he was dean of the School of Management at the State Univesity of New York at Buffalo. For twenty-three years he was with the University of Illinois, where he served in a number of capacities, including professor of marketing and head of the Department of Business Administration. A specialist in marketing strategy, market research, and market segmentation, Winter serves on several corporate boards and is an active business consultant.

MIMI WOLVERTON is an associate professor and the higher education leadership program coordinator at the University of Nevada, Las Vegas. She has more than twenty years of executive experience in private sector organizations; writes extensively in the areas of leadership, organizational change, educational policy, curriculum and instructional improvement, and innovation; and develops and provides professional development opportunities for propsective and sitting academic deans and department chairs.